THE ELECTRONIC SILK ROAD

THE ELECTRONIC SILK ROAD

HOW THE WEB BINDS THE WORLD IN COMMERCE

ANUPAM CHANDER

Yale
UNIVERSITY PRESS
New Haven & London

FOUNDATION®
BOOKS

FOUNDATION®
BOOKS

Foundation Books is an imprint of Cambridge University Press India Pvt. Ltd.

Cambridge House, 4381/4 Ansari Road, Daryaganj, New Delhi 110 002

www.cambridgeindia.org

This edition was published by arrangement with Yale University Press.

First South Asia edition 2014

Printed in India at Bhavish Graphics, Chennai

ISBN 978-93-82993-22-3 Hardback

For

Madhavi Sunder, sine qua non,

and

Harish Chander and Yash Garg,
who sacrificed so much to embrace the opportunities of globalization

I think of the ancient Silk Road as the Internet of antiquity.

—Yo-Yo Ma

CONTENTS

ACKNOWLEDGMENTS

Before there was trade in services via cyberspace, people moved. My parents migrated to the United States right before the celebrations marking the Bicentennial, my dad arriving in 1974 and then my mother, with my brother and me in tow, the following year. We flew from New Delhi via Beirut and London to New York, a route that would soon become impossible because of war. A legal change in 1965 made this flight possible. Before immigration law revisions that year, US law had set a quota of merely a hundred Indian immigrants per year. My parents' move made possible the extraordinary education I received in the United States and, such are the ironies of globalization, allowed me to study under the great Indian Nobel laureate Amartya Sen.

In 2003, two disparate media sources I read, the crowd-sourced technology site Slashdot and the Indian-American paper *India Abroad*, converged on the phenomenon of "outsourcing." The phenomenon bridged my two different scholarly areas of expertise—in international economic law and cyberlaw. By examining the issue from a legal perspective, I began to see that "outsourcing" was part of a larger phenomenon—trade in services via electronic networks. This insight helped me see the crucial link that binds together both Bangalore and Silicon Valley. Invited to a cyberlaw retreat on Cape Cod by Harvard University's innovative Berkman Center for Internet and Society, I presented my initial thoughts on the subject in August 2003 in a paper then titled "NetWork." There, Tim Wu pressed me on the implications of the General Agreement on Trade in Services for this new kind of trade.

Over the past decade, I have learned much about the subject from my colleagues at various institutions. I remain indebted to Deans Kevin Johnson and Rex Perschbacher at the University of California, Davis, for remaining unfailingly supportive at every turn. I am grateful to my colleagues Afra Afsharipour, Diane Amann, Vik Amar, Mario Biagioli, Chris Elmendorf, Tom Joo, and Peter Lee for very helpful comments on drafts. I am grateful to colleagues at other institutions, including Susan Crawford, Tino Cuéllar, Mark Lemley, Adam Muchmore, and Michael Reisman.

During the writing I had the privilege of being a visiting professor at Chicago, Cornell, Stanford, and Yale law schools. I am also grateful to Harold Koh, then dean at Yale Law School and currently the legal adviser of the United States Department of State, who challenged me to think more about "Trade 1.0" when I was discussing "Trade 2.0." At lunch with Jack Balkin and me, Bruce Ackerman inquired whether global law was the natural outcome of the developments I describe herein. Daniel Markovits and Alec Stone Sweet led a brilliant dissection of my argument in a workshop that I regret not recording. I am grateful to Jed Rubenfeld for an important dialogue on tensions between democracy and globalization.

I thank Dean Saul Levmore of the University of Chicago Law School for welcoming me into the fervent intellectual environment of his law school for a year. In a faculty workshop at the University of Chicago, Martha Nussbaum, philosopher and thinker nonpareil, urged me to make my normative vision explicit.

Professor Dr. Rolf Weber of the University of Zurich offered incisive commentary when I lectured on the subject at the World Trade Institute's annual World Trade Forum, hosted by Thomas Cottier and Mira Burri. Mira Burri and Ted Jaenger read the entire manuscript and provided superb suggestions. I thank Harvard's Mark Wu for his thoughtful commentary in an online symposium on my paper, "Trade 2.0," for the *Yale Journal of International Law*. I learned a great deal from law faculty workshops at Chicago, Connecticut, Emory, Florida State, Illinois, Oregon, Northwestern, UC Davis, UCLA, and Washington University (Saint Louis) as well as technology law and international law workshops at Stanford and Georgetown, respectively, and the Harvard-MIT-Yale Cyberscholar Workshop.

Over the years, I have learned so much from my students. I acknowledge in particular students Kuang-Cheng Chen and Taejin Kim for educating me on cyberlaw in Taiwan and South Korea, respectively. Students such as Jessica Karbowski and Janice Ta of Yale Law School and Sarah Anker, Rubina Chuang, Audrey Goodwater, Angela Ho, Jordy Hur, Uyen Le, Kathryn Lee, Johann Morri, Dimple Patel, and Louis Wai of UC Davis performed invaluable research. Librarians extraordinaire Aaron Dailey, Margaret "Peg" Durkin, Susan Llano, Elisabeth McKechnie, Erin Murphy, and Rachael Smith helped locate all manner of legal materials.

Special thanks to Connie Chan, James Lawrence, Stratos Pahis, for excellent editing of earlier articles.

Parts of this book are adapted from earlier published articles and book chapters and are used here with the permission of the publishers: "Trade 2.0," *Yale Journal of International Law* (2009): 281–330; "Facebookistan," *North Carolina Law Review* 90 (2012): 1807–44; "International Trade and Internet Freedom," *Proceedings of the American Society of International Law Annual Meeting* 102 (2009): 37; and "Globalization Through Digitization," in *The Impact of Globalization on the United States*, ed. Beverly Crawford, vol. 2 (New York: Praeger, 2008), 73–97.

At Yale University Press, Michael O'Malley, himself a noted author, championed the book. My editor Joseph Calamia carefully shepherded the book through production and provided thoughtful recommendations on the entire manuscript. I could not have asked for an editor more deeply committed to my project. Laura Jones Dooley provided a very careful copyedit. Another book from Yale University Press, Nayan Chanda's *Bound Together*, helped me think about the role of individuals in globalization.

In 2012, I received a Google Research Award to support related research on the Internet and free speech.

My love and thanks to my children, Anoushka and Milan, for abiding a father who might go off on a hot Saturday to work on a chapter rather than taking them to the pool. My deepest debt is to Madhavi Sunder.

FOREWORD

If China is the factory to the world, will India become its back office? Certainly, there are legions of brilliant and diligent Indians who can process the world's data, write the world's programs, and mediate relations between consumers and corporations or governments. The same is true as well of Brazilians, Filipinos, Nigerians, Vietnamese, and countless others in places that should also become services powerhouses to the world. The Internet has given these individuals a global reach never before possible in human history.

But these Indians and others in the developing world cannot hope to succeed in the new world of global competition in services based on their sheer effort alone. Their ingenuity and entrepreneurship will fail if the law proves inadequate to support their ambitions, or worse, thwarts them. I am not suggesting the absence of law, a void that will only be filled by those with few ethical constraints. Nor am I suggesting a suffocating license Raj, the legacy of an imperial government that saw private activity as a dangerous counterweight to its authority. Rather, the young hard-working Indians seeking a brighter future for themselves and India need a law that helps individuals, associations, and companies to grow.

If the reader will permit a lawyerly excursion, I will offer an example of a poorly drafted regulation. In 2011, the Indian Ministry of Communications and Technology published privacy rules implementing certain provisions of the Information Technology Act of 2000. The Ministry understandably sought to protect privacy and increase the security of sensitive personal information, such as financial and medical information. But the way the rules were drafted, they would have stifled even ordinary processing of data. The rules prohibit the transfer of sensitive personal data unless the transfer is either "necessary" or has been consented to by the individual whose data is being transferred. Because it is difficult to establish that it is "necessary" to transfer data, this would generally require that the individual consent to the transfer. The rules do not make it clear how consent for onward transfer from the information collector to the information processor is to be obtained. When it comes to collecting the personal information in the first instance, the rules require consent provided in writing, via fax, or through email—which (depending on how "writing" is interpreted) would seem to foreclose even the typical webpage with an "I agree" button. Legal commentators observed that the consent requirements were "far more restrictive" than what is required under United States or European Union law. Many concluded that the rules would threaten the outsourcing industry. Following an outcry, the Ministry clarified that the rules would not apply to the outsourcing industry or to foreign companies located outside India. While patching over one problem, the clarification discourages foreign companies from investing in India, which would bring them under the purview of the rule. It is far better to write rules that make sense for all companies, rather than making occasional exceptions to a bad rule.

Moreover, the rules make life difficult for Indian companies. Even after the clarification, the rules would appear to require an Indian company that seeks to outsource to another country to seek consent of all the individuals whose information is to be transmitted. The rules would thus make it difficult for an Indian start-up to utilize a global cloud service to store or process data. The irony is that United States opponents of outsourcing to India have long sought similar rules in the United States—requiring consent of Americans before their information could be transferred to India. New York's Senate has for many years considered a similar bill, one stating its official purpose to "stem the flow of skilled and unskilled labor out of New York state." Indian rules thus offer a precedent for others to follow—against India.

The courts, too, play a crucial role. The Delhi High Court has recently interpreted the Public Records Act to bar the transfer of government data outside India. This, of course, calls offshoring into question. Perhaps the court is unaware that Indian outsourcing companies have long worked on projects for foreign governments, and that such outsourcing often requires the transfer of government data to India. Indeed, when other governments have barred the export of government data abroad, India has previously properly denounced this as protectionist. Can India now call out other governments for protectionism when it practices the same?

India is hardly alone in bad laws pertaining to the information economy. In 2010, the United States Congress wanted more money to police the Mexican border. It found the money by raising fees on the H1-B visas that Indian companies use to send engineers to serve clients in the United States. As the New York Times wrote, Congress "would pay for more security along the Mexico border by raising fees for companies from India that operate in the United States and hire so many Indian workers." Indians are being asked to pay so that Mexicans can be barred at the border.

To add insult to injury, the United States levies pension taxes on the Indian engineers working in the United States, and then keeps their money. The United States has entered into "Totalization Agreements," which send pension contributions home with the workers, but only with countries in Europe as well as with Canada, Chile, Japan and South Korea. Under these agreements, a foreign worker's pension contributions to the United States return home with him or her. And a United States citizen's contributions to the pension systems of those countries are similarly repatriated to the United States. However, the United States refuses to enter into such an arrangement with India (or with Mexico, for that matter). Indian professionals thus contribute more than a billion dollars each year to the U.S. pension system, from which they will draw not a dime. This is in addition to the regular income taxes that they pay to the United States government. Countries such as Japan and Sweden have signed Totalization Agreements with India, even though these agreements require highly lopsided payments in favor of India.

To create better laws, one needs institutions that can be critical of the government. I want to single out three. First, a quarter century ago, the Indian information services industry presciently established its industry association, NASSCOM. NASSCOM has proved a crucial organization to seek better laws in New Delhi and even abroad. NASSCOM is responsible, for example, for the Indian Ministry clarifying and improving the privacy law described above, as well as the research cited above on Indian contributions to the United States pension system. Second, civil society organizations such as Bangalore-based Centre for Internet and Society act as a watchdog to try to prevent the broad surveillance powers offered by electronic media from being abused, an increasing threat as the Indian government expands its national security powers. A healthy democracy needs potent critics. Third, law schools such as the National Law School in Bangalore, NALSAR in Hyderabad, the National Law Universities in Delhi and Jodhpur, the National University of Juridical Sciences in Kolkata, and the Jindal Global Law School in New Delhi are essential not only to educate the next generation of lawyers and leaders, but also to subject the law to scholarly examination.

I want to highlight two other civil society organizations, both focused on how technology can improve people's lives. Bangalore-based Janaagraha seeks to improve the quality of life in India's cities and towns through brilliant initiatives such as the crowd-sourced website IPaidABribe.com, where individuals report on corruption they encounter. A second association, The Indus Entrepreneurs (TiE), brings together South Asian entrepreneurs and engineers in the United States and across the world, providing a crucial network for information.

If India needs better laws, the rest of South Asia trails even farther behind India in developing an information economy. Each country in the region should seek to incubate an entrepreneurial spirit, embracing the Information Age for its potential to leapfrog stages in development. All the countries of the region must begin by reexamining their laws.

The last decade has seen technology help transform parts of India. Better law for the information economy will be crucial if India and the rest of South Asia are to use the Electronic Silk Road to improve the lives of the quarter of the world's population that lives in the region.

Anupam Chander
Davis, California

INTRODUCTION

Tracing a Silk Road Through Cyberspace

The Silk Road linking the ancient world's civilizations wound through deserts and mountain passes, traversed by caravans laden with the world's treasures. The modern Silk Road winds its way through undersea fiber-optic cables and satellite links, ferrying electrons brimming with information. This electronic Silk Road makes possible trade in services heretofore impossible in human history. Radiologists, accountants, engineers, lawyers, musicians, filmmakers, and reporters now offer their services to the world without passing a customs checkpoint or boarding a plane. Like the ancient Silk Road, which transformed the lands that it connected, this new trade route promises to remake the world.

Today the people of the world are engaged in international trade with a greater intensity than ever before in human history. The subjects of international trade, too, are far more personal than ever before. They implicate our habits and hobbies, our travels, our communication, our friends, our politics, our health, and our finances. As our lives increasingly are reflected online, the range of activities subject to international trade grows. Services now join goods in the global marketplace, with workers in developing countries able to participate in lucrative Western markets despite immigration barriers and Western enterprises able to reach a global audience, often free of tariffs or local bureaucracies.

In 2012, Apple announced that leading carmakers from across the world, from Mercedes-Benz to Toyota, would soon install buttons in their vehicles allowing direct access to Siri, Apple's voice command system. Siri interprets natural human speech, thus allowing the driver to ask the computer assistant to send messages, select music, check stock prices or the weather, or even make restaurant reservations. These buttons will also bring Apple's music and video-retailing service, iTunes, into automobiles around the world. Siri is a cloud-based service, meaning that it performs the bulk of its processing not on the user's computer (or in the user's car) but far away in some computer farm. Apple's Siri processes the commands it receives in California. Debuted in English, Siri now understands Mandarin and a host of other major human languages. Drivers on roads from Marrakesh to Mandalay will soon be talking directly to Cupertino, California, to get directions or plan dinner.

This radical shift in the provision of services becomes possible because of advances in telecommunications technologies. This is the rapidly growing phenomenon I call *net-work*—information services delivered remotely through electronic communications systems. Net-work encompasses not just the services outsourced to Accra,

Bangalore, or Manila but also the online services supplied by Silicon Valley to the world. *Apple, eBay, and Yahoo!, too, are exporters of information services, revealing the Internet to be a global trading platform.* Silicon Valley enterprises serve as the world's retailers, librarians, advertising agencies, television producers, auctioneers, travel agents, and even romance matchmakers. Silicon Valley's ambition is no less than to become middleman to the world.

Many of the services made possible by the Electronic Silk Road are so new that they are hardly recognizable as trade. After all, many of the services appear to be free, more gifts than exchange. A computer voice assistant like Siri does not resemble any traditional service, except perhaps a butler. To add to the mystery, even the word *services* defies definition. The leading international treaty on services, the General Agreement on Trade in Services (GATS), forgoes a definition. The *Economist* magazine offers a quip, in lieu of a definition, calling services the "products of economic activity that you can't drop on your foot." Disputes brought before the World Trade Organization (WTO) now often turn on whether something is a service. In *Canada-Periodicals*, Canada argued that because magazine advertising was a service, not a good, any obligation not to impose taxes on US goods did not apply to taxes on magazine advertising.[1] In *China-Audiovisual*, China claimed that *electronic* distribution of US audio products did not constitute "sound recording distribution services."[2] Both claims proved unavailing, as we will see in chapter 6. The economist Jagdish Bhagwati observes that as late as the 1970s many in his profession did not believe that services were susceptible to international trade on the belief that they must be consumed at the point of service, an idea he ridicules as the "haircuts" view of services.[3]

Even as they defy easy characterization, such services are powering economic development across the world. India has emerged unexpectedly as a powerful global trader, with new global multinational corporations often based in Bangalore offering advanced information services to companies around the world. American firms, largely centered in Silicon Valley, use the Internet to offer old and new services to the world's consumers. Increasingly, if a company in Germany or Ghana wants to reach its own compatriots, it needs the help of a firm in Silicon Valley. In such cases, advertising is hardly the only economic activity crossing borders. Some of the activity has traditional precedents, such as travel agencies, news services, or brokerage services. Other activity lacks analogs in traditional commercial services, such as information search services, dating services, restaurant reservations, or software (or "app") clearinghouses. Having emerged as its home country's biggest music retailer in the span of merely five years from launching into the business, Apple hopes to become the world's leading audiovisual entertainment retailer as well.[4]

The existing infrastructure of trade, developed over millennia for a paradigm of goods, proves inadequate either to enable or to regulate this emerging Trade, version 2.0. The WTO and regional arrangements such as the European Union, North American Free Trade Agreement (NAFTA), and ASEAN (Association of Southeast Asian Nations) commit nations to liberalize barriers to trade in services, but these broad mandates have found little elaboration to date. Net-work companies, lacking legal precedents or authoritative guidance, must innovate not only technological methods and business models but also legal structures that span the globe. Net-work trade has yet to develop counterparts to the medieval *lex mercatoria* that helped resolve commercial disputes among European traders, the bills of lading that helped resolve shipping disputes during the last century of international trade, and other conventions on contracting that emerged over centuries of experience with trade in goods.

The risks to interests such as privacy and financial security from net-work are evident. Google's privacy officer observes that "every time you use a credit card, your details are passed through six different countries."[5] The difficulty of enforcing rights—or even demarcating them—across the World Wide Web is enormous. If an event in cyberspace occurs both "everywhere and nowhere" (in the words of a former Grateful Dead lyricist), whose law governs?[6] But there is a more fundamental risk. While there have been earlier eras of globalization, characterized by cross-border flows of people, goods, and capital, the globalization of services today poses a unique challenge to regulation.[7] When individuals migrated to provide services, they could be expected to conform to the laws of their new home. When people desired goods banned locally, they would have to make a run across a county line and smuggle them home. But cybertrade enables individuals to provide or receive services across the globe without leaving home. Will work be performed from jurisdictions without adequate protections? Is law itself at risk, now avoidable by a mere single click?

The jurisdiction-hopping implicit in cybertrade poses hurdles for the enforcement of law. Consider two famous examples from the past decade. Kazaa, long the leading peer-to-peer file trading system, was founded in the Netherlands by a Swede and a Dane, programmed from Estonia, and then run from Australia while incorporated in the South Pacific island nation of Vanuatu.[8] The online gambling site PartyGaming was founded by an American lawyer and an Indian expatriate programmer and run from headquarters in Gibraltar, using computer servers on a Mohawk Indian reserve in Canada, a London marketing office, and a workforce based mainly in Hyderabad, India.[9] Where regulation is oppressive and contrary to universal human rights, such evasion should be encouraged, not condemned (an issue we turn to in chapter 9). But for liberal democratic states, the ability to exploit the Internet to perform an end run around local law is troubling. Left unattended, cybertrade from everywhere and nowhere might imperil domestic laws, replacing local law with the regulation, if any, of the net-work provider's home state. I argue that the importing of services should not require us to import law as well.

At the same time, trumped-up fears of foreign service providers can support protectionist policies, shielding domestic industries from the bracing glare of global competition. In response to a campaign by a public sector union, the Canadian province of British Columbia now requires public entities that send personal information abroad for processing or storage to do so only with the specific permission of the data subjects. This rule makes it practically impossible for a British Columbia public university to use Gmail even if students have consented to the use of Google's services. The 2012 provincial guidelines implementing the law declare that if a student's "email contained the personal information of the friends she made during spring break, the public body would have to get their consent too." Fear of foreign service providers has been used against enterprises from Bangalore as well. In 2005, New Jersey passed a law requiring that "all services under State contracts or subcontracts be performed within the United States." Other states, including Alabama, Colorado, Illinois, Indiana, North Carolina, South Carolina, and Tennessee, have legislated a preference for local suppliers in their government procurement contracts. Ohio governor Ted Strickland instituted such a preference by executive order. A proposed federal bill, promoted by the Communications Workers of America, would deny federal loans to American companies that send call-center jobs overseas.

By recognizing the phenomena of outsourcing and the information services as being different species of net-work, it becomes possible to recognize the stake we all have in promoting trade. It unites Silicon Valley and Bangalore in a common cause for free trade. It also makes it harder to vilify one or the other, as many of the countries of the world increasingly hope to be exporters of one or both types of net-work. Countries vying to nurture the next Silicon Valley or Bangalore might be reluctant to encumber such trade.

The pressure on law from both kinds of net-work is clear. Consider some transnational flashpoints from the first decade of the twenty-first century: Antigua's WTO challenge to US rules barring online gambling; the outsourcing of radiology to India; Brazil's demands to Google to identify perpetrators of hate speech; an Alien Torts Statute suit in the United States charging Yahoo! with abetting torture in China; a WTO complaint brought by the United States against Chinese state media controls on foreign movies, financial information, and music such as iTunes. These cases reveal the unsettled legal issues at stake in cybertrade, from jurisdiction to protectionism, from consumer protection to human rights.

Services constitute an increasing bulk of human economic activity.[10] In 2011, the value of trade in commercial services in official reports was more than *$4 trillion*, nearly one-fifth of all world trade.[11] Yet for much of its history, the legal regime governing international trade neglected services in favor of liberalizing commerce in goods. But as Western economies became increasingly service-oriented, they began to recognize the opportunities for export in telecommunications, media, financial, and other services. Business leaders from three proudly "American" corporations—American Insurance Group, American Express, and Pan Am—propelled the US government in the 1970s to seek to liberalize trade in services.[12] Such efforts in the Uruguay Round of trade negotiations resulted—over developing nation opposition—in the General Agreement on Trade in Services, forming one pillar of the World Trade Organization established in

1995. GATS subjected services for the first time to the international trade regime's far-reaching disciplines.[13] Regional arrangements go further still. The European Union has ambitiously declared a Single European Market, seeking "an area without internal frontiers in which the free movement of goods, persons, services and capital is ensured."[14] Both NAFTA and the Central American Free Trade Agreement (CAFTA-DR) require national treatment and market access for service providers across their respective regions.[15] America's new bilateral free trade agreements with Australia, Bahrain, Chile, Colombia, Morocco, Oman, Peru, and Singapore all include broad obligations to liberalize services. Southeast Asian nations have promised to create a free trade zone including services by 2015.

Free trade's apostle was David Ricardo, an Englishman who in 1817 offered one of the most influential insights economists have yet brought. Contrary to the reigning mercantilism of his day, Ricardo showed that countries that traded with each other would each stand to gain from the trade. Ricardo began by hypothesizing two countries, England and Portugal, each of which produced both wine and cloth, with closed borders. A bit of simple multiplication and addition is all one needs to show that if each state produced the good for which it had a comparative advantage, there would be a greater total amount of both wine and cloth (or at least more of one of the two and an equal amount of the other), which could now be traded to mutual advantage. The same arithmetic can show the superiority of specialization and trading anything for which humans create, from accounting to engineering.[16]

Yet with the advent of trade in services such as these, a vocal minority has raised doubts about free trade in services. Some worry that liberalization will erode the wages or threaten the livelihoods of workers now forced to compete on a global stage. A few hold that Ricardo's insight about the mutual benefits of trade in goods cannot be readily extended to services. Economists Alan Blinder and Paul Samuelson, the latter a Nobel laureate, have raised questions about the benefits of cross-border outsourcing of services to rich countries like the United States. Blinder, however, does not counsel protectionism but rather advocates increased support for displaced workers.[17] It must also be kept in mind that critics of such trade do not include the benefits to American enterprise and American workers from trade in such services conducted by Silicon Valley. *Google and Facebook earned 54 and 50 percent, respectively, of their income abroad in the first half of 2012.*[18] It will be difficult for the United States to decry the entry of information service providers from Bangalore while pressing for the liberalization of information service providers from Silicon Valley. And the same is true of India. The great majority of economists believe strongly in free trade in both goods and services. As the *Wall Street Journal* has noted, the few critics represent a "minority among economists, most of whom emphasize the enormous gains from trade."[19] Ricardo's theory itself applies to all trade, whether trade in food and clothing or trade in information. Countries across the world now vie to be both the next Silicon Valley and the next Bangalore, and they must embrace the flow of trade in both directions. At the same time, governments must retrain persons dislocated by the disruptive force of technology and provide a social safety net to take care of those who are most imperiled.

The promise of Trade 2.0 is enormous. The changes wrought to commercial practices are no less revolutionary than those described by Alfred D. Chandler Jr. in his classic twentieth-century business study, *The Visible Hand: The Managerial Revolution in American Business*. Sellers of both goods and services now can have direct contact with their consumers around the world, and vice versa. Individuals and companies can find new purchasers for their services across the globe. Consumers now find their choice of providers increased manyfold. Like the globalization of manufacturing, the globalization of services promises to boost efficiency, facilitating economies of scale and spurring investments in human capital. Increasingly, the bulk of humanity will find itself involved in trade along this Electronic Silk Road.

Through the Khyber Pass or around the Cape of Good Hope, merchants have long made arduous journeys laden with the world's treasures. Trade law developed with such merchants in mind. Law accommodated trade conducted over the high seas, the Silk Road, and the Grand Trunk Road, not through undersea fiber or via satellite links. Trade depends on the legal environment in two crucial ways: first, the law must *dismantle protectionist legal barriers* erected through history (this is the standard focus of teaching and writing in international trade law); second, the law can facilitate cross-border trade by *erecting a legal infrastructure to reduce uncertainty* in international transactions (this is the standard focus of teaching and writing on international business transactions).[20] Let us label both features of the legal environment, taken together, the *Trade Plus* regime. A Trade Plus regime crafted for goods is unlikely to serve well the demands of the burgeoning trade in services delivered through the ether.

This book proceeds as follows. The first part reviews controversies in cybertrade, which demonstrate both the need to remove legal obstacles to cybertrade and the need to protect the capacity of states to regulate themselves. The second part offers principles that seek to achieve this balance. Freeing cybertrade requires a commitment to two principles: (1) a *technological neutrality* principle that rejects attempts to bar net-work because of its electronic nature; and (2) a *dematerialization* principle by which states undertake to dematerialize the services infrastructure—that is, to make physical presence unnecessary for authentication, notification, certification, inspection, and even dispute resolution.

The footloose nature of cybertrade raises the specter of two races to the bottom: a deregulated world in which service providers decamp to minimally regulated jurisdictions from which they supply the world; and an overly regulated world in which some service providers eager to maximize revenues become complicit in state repression. To curtail the race to the deregulated bottom, I suggest the occasional necessity of legal *glocalization*—requiring a global service to conform to local rules, where both the rules and their assertion to a particular transaction are consistent with international legal norms. Glocalization rejects protectionism yet maintains local safeguards over culture and security; it resolves the dilemma of net-work, navigating between the Scylla of protectionism and the Charybdis of laissez-faire.

But will this assertion of local law tear apart the global web into local fiefdoms? The key to avoid this tearing apart of the web is to limit local demands on global e-commerce to important issues. International and domestic US law constrains excessive extraterritoriality while international trade law counsels us to work toward global standards. In order to promote a flourishing cybertrade beneficial to both the world's service providers and its consumers, states will have to work toward legal *harmonization* wherever agreement may be found. Thus I suggest this rule: harmonization where possible, glocalization where necessary.

To disrupt the race to the oppressive bottom, I argue that cybertraders should establish ground rules to, at a minimum, *do no evil*. Here, I flesh out the maxim that Google officially embraces. Given that authoritarian regimes function by repressing information, information service providers will always be the locus of such repression—and the potential route for subversion.

The book is divided into two parts. In the first chapters I illustrate the challenges of Trade 2.0 through case studies. In the second part I offer a framework for breaking down barriers to free trade while protecting public policy objectives. To help readers interested in different sections of the book, I sketch below the arguments in each chapter of the book.

Chapter 1. The New Global Division of Labor

Where the industrial age led to a global division of labor in manufacturing, the information age expands that global division into services. Once theorized as nontradable, services now join goods in the global marketplace, allowing workers in developing countries to participate in lucrative Western markets despite immigration barriers and Western enterprises to reach a global audience, often free of tariffs and even absent a local distribution network. This marks a major shift in the organization of production, as technology shifts the calculus determining the boundaries of the firm and spurs firms to buy services cross-border. At the same time, however, the emergence of trade in services creates insecurity among people worldwide who must now face global competition. The efficiencies of net-work counsel liberalization of trade in services, as well as the creation of a robust and widely accessible infrastructure for making and enforcing contracts across borders.

Chapter 2. Western Entrepôt: Silicon Valley

The information technology revolution has not only enabled a global division of labor, it has also spawned entirely new kinds of services, often with global ambitions. Information search services such as Google and Yahoo! and social networking services such as Facebook and MySpace have become popular far outside their home jurisdiction. Such services have often acted with indifference to borders until forced to reckon with them by local authorities. Yahoo! and Google, for example, have run afoul of laws that criminalize speech that is legal in their home jurisdictions. In this chapter I survey the kinds of legal difficulties that global cyberspace companies are beginning to encounter. To better understand the challenges, the chapter describes three legal conflicts in particular. Yahoo!'s encounter with French laws barring Nazi paraphernalia generated lawsuits on both sides of the Atlantic, with Yahoo!'s lawyer decrying the "French imperialism" of a Parisian court order against Yahoo!'s California-based enterprise. A Brazilian judge reproached Google for evincing a "profound disrespect for national sovereignty" when its Brazilian subsidiary professed an inability to produce information identifying perpetrators of hate speech and other crimes using Google's first social network, Orkut. Both Yahoo! and Google have stumbled in China, where they have been accused of aiding state political repression, most directly in an Alien Torts Statute claim against Yahoo! accusing it of acting as an auxiliary to torture. Faced with compromising its role as a global information provider, Google ultimately retreated from China.

Chapter 3. Eastern Entrepôt: Bangalore

Where China has become the factory to the world, India and other developing countries may become the world's back office. In the span of a decade, Indian companies have integrated themselves into the global supply chain, providing services from accounting to information technology. While electronic networks have been necessary to Trade 2.0, a kind of network as old as human migration has helped power this trade. Diaspora networks that connect Silicon Valley to the Deccan Plateau have reduced information costs across continents, enabling Indian companies to find Western buyers, and Western buyers to find Indian suppliers. Indian outsourcing giants have grown into multibillion-dollar, multinational companies. Indian outsourcing companies now scour the world for talent, establishing or acquiring operations in

Latin America, eastern Europe, China, and even the United States. Developing nations from Africa to Latin America seek to replicate India's success, at times establishing the services counterpart to the export-processing zone popular for manufacturing. But a review of the political and legal issues raised with respect to the outsourcing of radiology from Massachusetts General Hospital to Bangalore shows that these enterprises face important legal challenges.

Chapter 4. Pirates of Cyberspace

Offshore havens now offer not only freedom from taxes or bank regulations but also potentially freedom from law itself. Because of the global reach of the Internet, an entrepreneur can take advantage of the seeming safety of an offshore haven to offer services that might violate local law where the services are consumed. Two cases help make this point plain. In the 1990s, Antigua set out to become the Las Vegas of cyberspace. American entrepreneurs set up companies on that Caribbean island to offer gambling principally to American consumers. When the United States began prosecuting these entrepreneurs, Antigua turned to a perhaps unexpected venue: the World Trade Organization. Antigua charged the United States with violating its free trade commitments by barring online gambling. If Antigua is the Las Vegas of cyberspace, Russia may well be the Wild West. Taking advantage of Russian rules that allow only minimal royalty payments for music, a website called AllofMP3.com permits users worldwide to download entire albums for the price of a single iTune. The United States declared AllofMP3.com "the world's largest server-based pirate website" and even threatened to block Russian entry into the WTO because of it before the site was shut down. Cross-border trade in services also raises special legal problems, including risks to information privacy and the difficulty of enforcing rights abroad.

Chapter 5. Facebookistan

Who rules how Facebook connects more than a billion monthly users, some 80 percent outside the United States? In this chapter I review why countries might want to regulate Facebook and describe how countries have actually sought to do so. National efforts to assert control have been stymied by confusion about who has jurisdiction over Internet enterprises such as Facebook. I conclude that the world of Facebook is currently governed by a complex of nation-states, users, and Facebook's corporate officers.

Chapter 6. Freeing Trade in Cyberspace

In this chapter I return to Antigua's claim against the United States before the WTO. Given the United States' further strengthening of prohibitions against online gambling since the debut of the complaint, is international trade law powerless against barriers to net-work trade? I suggest that the decision in the case carries the seeds of a net-work revolution, with world trade rules deployed to break down legal barriers to net-work. Indeed, the United States successfully filed its own WTO complaint against China to dismantle some regulatory impediments to the distribution in China of American audiovisual products, including downloads from Apple's iTunes store.

Chapter 7. Handshakes Across the World

The architecture of real-world transactions promotes security, privacy, monitoring, trust, and enforceability between parties, which in turn fosters marketplace contracts with strangers. In order to foster trade in services, governments, corporations, and state and industry associations will need to re-create security and trust in cyberspace. They will need to establish the electronic counterparts to handshakes, ink signatures, demeanor evidence, word of mouth, and the ready ability to seek legal redress. I argue for a *dematerialized architecture* for cyberspace trade and describe incipient efforts toward that goal.

Chapter 8. Glocalization and Harmonization

Like liquor stores across the county line, computer servers permit individuals to evade local regulations by a simple exercise, here a few keystrokes. The nature of net-work increases the likelihood that a service provider might relocate to take advantage of regulatory environments that it finds favorable. The strategy of legal *glocalization*—requiring a global service to conform to local rules—removes one principal mechanism for regulatory competition by short-circuiting the attempt of a company to choose its governing law simply through its choice of situs. Flags of convenience and the regulatory arbitrage they entail lose force if they are met by states unwilling to cede regulatory authority to foreign jurisdictions. At the same time, international law limits state exercises of extraterritorial jurisdiction. Excessive assertions of local law may unduly Balkanize the Internet; I suggest limits to glocalization to maintain the worldwide nature of the web. Specifically, states should seek to harmonize their rules where possible, maintaining heterogeneous rules only after due consideration.

Chapter 9. Last Stop: Middle Kingdom

The ancient Silk Road helped transmit the culture and technology of China to the world. Today, however, Chinese authorities stand as guardians along the new Silk Road, censoring knowledge flowing within, into, and out of China. History's most efficient platform for information dissemination faces its greatest test at the gates to the Middle Kingdom. In the wrong hands, the Internet can bring the specter of a pernicious Big Brother closer than ever possible in George Orwell's time. When allied with willing Internet service providers, websites, software providers, and financial intermediaries, a government can gain an omniscience heretofore unknown. Eager to supply the world's most populous Internet market, service providers have bent to official Chinese demands, censoring themselves and even passing along information that uncovers dissenters. In this chapter I consider the challenge of totalitarian states to the global Internet. At a minimum, service providers should seek to "do no evil" if they engage with totalitarian states. I explore what this might mean by contrasting Yahoo!'s and Google's strategies for China, asking whether liberal home states should impose any extraterritorial regulation on their new media services abroad to compel behavior consistent with human rights. I also suggest that liberal governments can seek to use the tools of international trade law to bolster political freedom around the world. Unexpectedly, the General Agreement on Trade in Services might emerge as a human rights document.

This is a book about how law can both foster and regulate trade in services. We must protect local control of global Internet trade without jeopardizing either human rights or the worldwide nature of the web. Globalization with a human face will require us to manage cybertrade to allow us to engage with the world yet at the same time feel that we are not at the world's mercy.

1

THE NEW GLOBAL DIVISION OF LABOR

What an extraordinary episode in the economic progress of man that age was which came to an end in August, 1914! . . . The inhabitant of London could order by telephone, sipping his morning tea in bed, the various products of the whole earth, in such quantity as he might see fit, and reasonably expect their early delivery upon his doorstep.

—John Maynard Keynes, *The Economic Consequences of the Peace*

Adam Smith could never have dreamed of the global division of labor that is quickly coming to pass. It would take two centuries after *The Wealth of Nations* for the global manufacturing process to be perfected. Where the twentieth century saw the rise of the global supply chain in manufacturing, in the twenty-first century technology now permits the rise of a global supply chain in services. Relying on suppliers around the world, a garage entrepreneur can coordinate the production and delivery of a service from anywhere. Firms can transfer processes to foreign third-party vendors, relying on the discipline of the market rather than the discipline of supervisory management. The search for talent has gone global, hurdling the barriers to labor factor mobility posed by restrictive immigration laws.

Not only can firms find inputs anywhere, but they can find buyers everywhere. Firms can offer their services directly to consumers across the world without investing in extensive local distribution networks. They can leverage this worldwide consumer base to achieve economies of scale. Firms can locate their headquarters where they might have most ready access to capital, especially venture capital, and their servers where they can find cheap and plentiful energy. They might locate their operations in a jurisdiction that provides tax incentives to encourage job creation. Because technology now allows firms and consumers to turn to service providers far from home, suddenly the local information broker—from the reporter to the auctioneer to the yenta—must now compete with suppliers across the world.

This organizational revolution puts pressure on law. The movement from make to buy, from status to contract, will require a robust transnational legal framework to facilitate cross-border contracts and information flows. The risks to security and privacy as information crisscrosses the world between consumers and service providers will require a legal response. Rather than the Silk Road's disputes among merchants or modern goods traders' disputes regarding bills of lading and shipping documents, disputes in this new international market for services will grow among household buyers and sellers located across the globe, between ordinary citizens and global websites.

In this chapter, I describe this evolution in the organization of production, arguing that we will likely see increasing cross-border contracting between unaffiliated parties as firms move internal processes to third-party vendors. Where there are contracts, there are eventually contractual disputes, requiring a legal infrastructure of dispute resolution. The open-source programming that drives much of this trade itself relies on the enforceability of contract and property rights across borders—supplemented by reputation and reward systems. In the final section of this chapter, I describe the close and mutually beneficial connection between outsourcing and open-source production methods.

Butcher, Baker, Information Broker

"In the lone houses and very small villages which are scattered about in so desert a country as the Highlands of Scotland, every farmer must be butcher, baker, and brewer for his family."[1] Adam Smith began his 1776 study of the wealth of nations by examining the division of labor. The division of labor, he observed, depended in large part on the size of the market, which in turn depended largely on geography and technology. In remote locations, the absence of extensive markets limited the division of labor. But those with better access to means of transportation could reach larger markets, and thereby improve efficiency: "by means of water carriage a more extensive market is opened . . . and industry of every kind naturally begins to subdivide and improve itself."[2] Specialization would improve productivity by reducing the time wasted in transferring among multiple tasks, increasing the dexterity of the individual worker at a specific task, and spur the invention of machines that perform specified functions.[3] Smith critiqued the reigning mercantile political economy of his day, which sought to encourage exports but discourage imports. While Smith spoke in terms of absolute advantage and not comparative advantage, he argued that liberal rules for both export and import would deepen the division of labor and enrich nations.

Smith wrote at a time when the medieval age's dusty silk roads and wooden ships were soon to give way to the railroads and steamships of the industrial age. Industrial revolutions in mechanization, transportation, and communications technology deepened the national and international division of labor. Technology eroded the decisive role of geography in the organization of production. Mass-production techniques and the modern management systems they spawned swelled the international trade in goods.

The economic benefits of this globalization have been distributed widely—but many have also borne the pain and dislocation that follow from global competition.[4] Merchandise producers reduced their costs by shifting manufacturing to advantageous locations, often in maquiladoras or other export-processing zones in the developing world.[5] This shift led to the loss of blue-collar jobs in the industrialized nations, the rise of sweatshops in the developing world in some cases, and the dazzling array of affordable merchandise available at the local superstore.

As economic historian Alfred Chandler describes, technological innovation shifted not just the location of production but also its organization. By enlarging both output and markets, the nineteenth century's industrial revolution required the creation of the managerial hierarchies (managers who manage managers) characteristic of the modern business enterprise.[6] These colossus corporations, increasingly capitalized through the public markets, brought inside the corporate walls functions that had historically been provided by third parties. These corporations integrated mass production and mass distribution within the firm and its subsidiaries, replacing the invisible hand of the market with the visible hand of management.

The multidivision corporation (dubbed the "M-Form" corporation) would rapidly extend itself internationally to become the multinational corporation that came to dominate the twentieth century.[7] Even at the dawn of the twentieth century, some Europeans labeled this the "American invasion" and fretted about the "Americanisation of the world."[8] The multinational corporation would become a principal vehicle for cross-border trade in services. Hollywood began to recognize the global audience available for its media products. Software enterprises, too, sought global markets. Microsoft has subsidiaries in more than 110 countries, from Albania to Zimbabwe.[9] Financial institutions extended themselves around the world; Citigroup today has offices in nearly a hundred countries worldwide.[10] Western telecommunications companies similarly found opportunities for growth in the developing world. The global wave of privatizations of government services beginning in the 1980s increased the local presence of multinational corporations in a variety of fields from banking to telecommunications to water services.

But with the exception of finance, this cross-border trade in services did not generally require the real-time transmission of large volumes of data across borders.[11] Microsoft and Disney developed their products in one country—typically the United States—and then disseminated that product globally. Local subsidiaries were simply translators and distributors. Thus, while service providers in certain industries in the developing world faced competition from Western corporations with local distribution channels, service providers in advanced, industrialized nations did not face a reciprocal competition from service providers in the developing world.

Unlike merchandise, which typically can tolerate the lag between product design and product production imposed by international shipping, many services require a real-time exchange of information between the service provider and its consumer. Accordingly, for the bulk of human history, services had to be performed on-site or near-site. The digital revolution disrupted this requirement through two related innovations: the creation of global digital networks and the digitization of information itself. First, the introduction of the Internet and other high capacity transcontinental electronic data networks made possible remote collaboration on a real-time basis, with parties separated by continents able to share data almost as readily as if they had adjoining cubicles.[12] Second, the digitization of information spurred its wide dissemination. The adoption of computers as a tool for work meant that information was often created originally in digital form. The World Wide Web established one common information-sharing platform, taking advantage of both digital networks and digitized information. Information that had been held locally now found wide distribution. Take, for example, the US Securities and Exchange Commission's EDGAR database, with its immense storehouse of information about publicly traded companies, and the Patent and Trademark Office's databases, which make every patent and registered trademark searchable. It was not long ago when accessing SEC or PTO public records required hiring a runner to photocopy files in a Washington area basement, delivering a copy by either Federal Express or fax. With the rise of the World Wide Web, these databases became available for free to people across the world.[13] The global information platform allowed the creation of new services, such as search engines, video and other information-sharing depositories, and personal social networks.

Today, cross-border outsourcing includes "typists, researchers, librarians, claims processors, proofreaders, accountants and graphic designers."[14] Cross-border trade in services also includes engineering,[15] architectural services,[16] legal services,[17] animation, and movie special effects.[18] The jobs are both "big—100-page investment reports requiring weeks of work—and small."[19] Chennai-based "Iayaraja Marimuthu, for instance, is designing a program for [the] wedding of Ann and John, a Texas couple proclaiming their joy in being 'together for life.'"[20] (The flower arranging, alas, cannot be outsourced cross-border, even if the flowers themselves come from the tropics.) Today, telecommuting can occur across hemispheres. A

Wall Street Journal article offers a vivid example of what it calls "extreme telecommuting": although Paolo Conconi's "work is in Europe and China, his office is a table by the pool of his villa in Bali, Indonesia. As he goes through his mail, he sips his favorite Italian coffee. An attendant lights his cigarette."[21]

Manufacturing, too, has been transformed by electronic networks. Even a trade as ancient as Persian carpet weaving "is guided, these days, in part by e-mail missives on the tastes of rich customers in the West."[22] This is an example of the design services that are a key input into the manufacturing process.

The Organisation for Economic Co-operation and Development (OECD) estimates that one-fifth of all service jobs in the developed economies will be affected by cross-border trade in services.[23] This does not mean that such a large fraction of jobs will soon be outsourced but, rather, that the terms of these positions will change as a result of international competition. The deepening division of labor represented by cross-border outsourcing of services increases efficiency, just as the international division of labor in manufacturing increased efficiency. An inefficient service sector functions as "a prohibitive tax on the national economy."[24] By removing this unproductive tax, trade in services should improve growth across the world. Of course, even while many more will gain, many will lose. The personal misfortunes that will result will be enormous. Retraining and adjustment programs are necessary measures, but not all countries can afford them.

Vendor or Captive? Reinterpreting "Make or Buy"

The first claim to fame of the economist Ronald Coase was his 1937 inquiry into why firms existed at all, rather than individuals who contracted with one another in the marketplace. The question has been translated into the query: Make (inside a firm) or buy (through a market)? Often overlooked is that Coase placed technology at the heart of his explanation of the determinants of the boundaries of the firm, recognizing that technology would influence both the transactions costs of marketplace contracting and the organization costs of internal hierarchy.[25] In 2000, the *New York Times* linked the organizational shift to a prediction of Coase's theory: "Sixty years [after Coase's paper], transaction costs have plunged, thanks to the Internet. . . . As a result, companies can get complete information about potential suppliers and business partners within a few clicks, and can therefore set up supplier agreements or form alliances with other companies for a fraction of what it would have cost even a decade ago."[26] Electronic data networks reduced not only the costs of marketplace transactions but also the costs of managerial hierarchies. The first effect—the reduction of transaction costs—tends to reduce the size of the firm by increasing the use of the marketplace for purchasing inputs into the production process. However, the second effect—the reduction of hierarchy costs—tends to increase the size of the firm as the costs of internalizing production inputs fall. In his original paper, Coase was uncertain whether improvements in communications technology (he offered the example of the telephone) would put greater downward pressure on market transaction costs or internal organization costs.[27] Today, the standing view seems to be that the greater effect has been on market transaction costs, implying an increase in third-party outsourcing.[28]

Yet the choice of employing a service provider abroad does not necessitate a turn to the market. Many Western corporations outsource by establishing local subsidiaries rather than by employing independent vendors. In the parlance of international businesspeople, nonchalant about the evocation of colonial rule, these are "captives." Restated in the language of organizational economics, the

Western corporations that outsource through captives choose "make" over "buy." (Economists consider obtaining an input from a foreign subsidiary "making," not "buying," the input because it is produced in-house by a corporate arm.) The General Electric Company pioneered this type of outsourcing in India, in large part by accident. In 1997, as GE was establishing an Indian office to process credit applications from Indians for a credit card joint venture with an Indian bank, the "light went on." "We started to think, we can do this for the rest of the world," says Pramod Bhasin, a former GE Capital executive who helped create GE Capital International Services ("Gecis") and serves as its chief executive. Now Gecis reviews credit card applications from New Delhi to New York. "By the late 1990s," the *Wall Street Journal* reports, "GE began turning its attention from simply buying software from India to using the country as a base for data entry, processing credit-card applications and other clerical tasks." GE realized "savings on backroom operations alone" of about $300 million a year. By 2000 the outsourcing had deepened further, as GE established the John F. Welch Technology Centre in Bangalore, named after its storied CEO, employing "thousands of researchers working on everything from new refrigerators to jet engines."[29]

New institutional economists have refined Coase's insights into the determinants of the organization of the firm. Today economists explain the decision to make rather than buy as turning in part on the existence of *asset specificity*. Certain types of marketplace contracts might be subject to post-contractual opportunistic behavior, leading companies to bring those functions within the corporate hierarchy. When either party invests in assets specialized to that particular contract, the counterparty can exploit that investment by renegotiating the terms of the contract, recognizing that the party making a specialized investment cannot readily divert its resources to alternative productive uses.[30] In cross-border outsourcing, either the vendor or the procurer of services may face the risk of exploitation: the vendor might be required to engage in extensive information gathering about its client or create processes and systems narrowly tailored to the client's needs; the client, meanwhile, might come to rely on proprietary systems owned and supported by a particular vendor. The vendor's investment in knowledge may leave the client vulnerable, at least in the short run, if such knowledge will be difficult for another vendor to replicate readily in the future. At the same time, the vendor may be vulnerable because of its extensive asset-specific human and other capital investment in the project of the procurer, an investment that will be amortized only over a long term.

Firms faced with asset-specific inputs might avoid the possibility of exploitative behavior by entering into long-term contracts that provide remedies for exploitative behavior. However, such contracts might be quite expensive, both to write and to enforce.[31] This problem is compounded by the difficulty of pricing idiosyncratic inputs. Because neither the buyer nor the seller will find it easy to predict exactly how many resources the input will ultimately require, the contractual price may be subject to adjustment under the contract terms. The price escalation clause makes it difficult to distinguish legitimate pricing adjustments due to unexpected cost increases from behavior exploiting the counterparty's asset-specific investments. At times, one party will accept the risk of exploitation by the other side, a risk that it will presumably price. Reputational sanctions and the withdrawal of expected future business often prove a means to discipline exploitative behavior.

The principal alternative to contracting as a response to the difficulties posed by asset specificity is vertical integration—that is, buying or building the supplier instead of buying the supply. Rather than rely on contracts with third-party vendors, corporations might choose to bring the function in-house. They can do so even with inputs to be delivered across borders, typically through establishing a local subsidiary in the foreign country. General Electric did exactly this when it expanded its financial services operations in India.

But vertical integration increases hierarchy costs and fails to take full advantage of the market. Managing subsidiaries cross-border is an especially expensive proposition. More important, keeping a function in-house reduces the opportunities for benefiting from economies of scale. Of course, a firm could create a subsidiary that serves not just that firm but also other companies. But third-party vendors can more readily serve multiple clients. This represents a division of labor across firms rather than within them. The approach is the opposite of the twentieth-century firm described by Alfred Chandler, either the conglomerate that makes everything from tires to rolls of bathroom tissue (similar only to the extent that both are circular) or the vertically integrated multidivisional firm. Contemporary organization theorists see investments through public and private markets, rather than managerial hierarchy, as the superior mechanism in most cases for diversifying risk and investing in opportunities in diverse markets. A stand-alone enterprise not confined to one buyer finds it easier to scale up by offering its service to multiple demanders. A diversity of demanders also increases the efficiency with which that service is used, as slackened demand by a customer here (say, as a result of regional or sectoral recession) can be compensated by increased demand elsewhere. By providing services to multiple companies, third-party vendors also develop specialized expertise not readily available to a supplier for a single entity. As one expert notes, captive centers must "derive one's own learning, unlike in a third-party scenario where they would have picked up best practices from other clients and processes."[32] The efficiencies of third-party vendors hold a financial payoff: the *Economist* magazine reports that captives may tend to be more expensive than independent vendors, with costs up to 50 percent higher.[33]

Indeed, the pioneer in outsourcing to India, GE, has spun off its Gecis subsidiary, selling a majority stake to US-based private equity firms.[34] The sale "allowed Gecis to begin working for companies other than GE, including Japan's Nissan Motor Co."[35] One of the many India-based outsourcing companies to list on the New York Stock Exchange, WNS (Holdings) Limited, followed a similar path, beginning life as the in-house services provider for British Airways, until the American private equity group Warburg Pincus purchased a majority stake. Today the company, which is incorporated in Jersey, Channel Islands, continues to serve British Airways but also serves Air Canada, Virgin Atlantic Airways, and numerous financial institutions.[36] The trend seems to be continuing. Citigroup, for example, sold its Indian subsidiary Citigroup Global Services to Tata Consultancy Services at the end of 2008 for half a billion dollars. Tata took on the twelve thousand employees of the subsidiary and agreed to provide services to Citigroup for the next decade. Citigroup then sold another Indian services subsidiary to Wipro, simultaneously agreeing to a five-year contract to outsource certain services to Wipro. The Swiss bank UBS sold its Indian business-process outsourcing unit to outsourcing firm Cognizant.

The decision to outsource a function through a foreign subsidiary rather than a third-party vendor often turns on yet other factors beyond asset specificity or efficiency. Companies are especially wary of turning "strategic" or "core" functions over to third-party entities. The concern is especially evident when such functions involve proprietary and secret information, given the fear that the foreign vendor might appropriate such information and use it to enhance a competitor. But some management consultants argue in a *Harvard*

Business Review article that even "critical functions like engineering, R&D, manufacturing, and marketing can—and often should—be moved outside."[37] Even the definition of what is "strategic" and "core" is susceptible to change over time. The history of the integrated circuit chip industry reflects this dynamic:

> In the 1980s, large U.S. integrated circuit chip ("chip") design companies began moving manufacturing of their chips to offshore fabrication facilities (or "fabs") that also leveraged economies of scale to produce large volumes of chips for many chip companies. . . . The benefit for these companies included reducing their costs to produce their chips, while freeing up capital and time to develop newer and better chips. Today, almost every new U.S. chip company is "fabless"; they design their semiconductor products and turn to offshore fabrication facilities to produce them.[38]

Intel remains an important exception to this rule, maintaining plants across the world. Outsourcing production of even a company's most valued products is commonplace: Apple outsources its star products—iPhone, iPod, and laptop production—to Taiwanese vendors. In 2012, Apple's CEO Tim Cook visited the Chinese plant where 120,000 workers employed by the Taiwanese company Foxconn build Apple's products.[39] Apple also announced plans to renew limited manufacturing in the United States. Over time, the pressure to minimize costs may increase demand for third-party vendors with respect to services, but only as long as issues of intellectual property, privacy, security, and contract enforcement are adequately resolved. As outsourcing to third-party entities deepens, we may see a reversal of the trend famously noted by Alfred Chandler: a move from the visible hand of management to the invisible hand of the market.

From Open Source to Outsource

Outsourcing shares much in common with open-source production processes, an increasingly important mode of organizing production. Harvard theorist Yochai Benkler describes what he calls "commons-based peer production," whereby individuals, usually working as volunteers, contribute to a communal project in a "self-selected and decentralized, rather than hierarchically assigned" manner, rewarded principally only in reputation or in the use of the final product. Benkler suggests that these volunteers can "beat the largest and best-financed business enterprises in the world at their own game."[40] Both outsourcing and open sourcing require that a larger task be divisible across numerous persons who are geographically dispersed, a division made immeasurably easier by the emergence of the Internet. Both thus embody the increasing *deconstruction* of the firm, with the functions of the firm disaggregated via piecemeal work performed remotely.[41] In this section, I explore the relation between the two, suggesting that outsourcing can benefit from the adoption of open source and open standards.

Open-source production can be understood as a species of network: in commons-based peer production, the person originating the project outsources development to others around the world, though without the command directive or purchasing conditions typically present in a traditional outsourcing transaction. Consider Linux, the exemplar of the peer production and open-source movement. The kernel to this operating system was developed by Linus Torvalds from his home in Finland, built atop code developed by Richard Stallman. Since 1991, when he released his source code to an Internet newsgroup, Torvalds has coordinated a global production process, now from the West Coast of the United States.[42] The Linux kernel today contains more than fifteen million lines of code and powers the great bulk of the world's top supercomputers.[43]

In computer software, languages evolved to promote modular programming, which facilitates collaboration.[44] Programming now often involves extending a "library" of functions, each performing a well-defined operation upon the receipt of specified parameters. The rationalization of business processes, too, has increasingly standardized some corporate functions.

In peer production, the ability to collaborate depends on a related fundamental characteristic: the decision to publish the necessary standards (and often the underlying code) for modifying or extending the given project. Opening up the source and the interfaces enables a largely spontaneous division of labor across unaffiliated parties. The web itself has been called "the apotheosis of open standards."[45] The web's principal designer, Tim Berners-Lee, sought to ensure that the programming underlying a webpage would be publicly available (thus the feature of most desktop web browsers that allows one to look at the page's programming).[46] The decision of some companies to open their application programming interfaces (even without necessarily revealing the underlying code) to the world enables others to access the application's functionality and extend the application in unforeseen ways. Today a website can mash up the mapping service offered by Google with the photography service offered by Flickr mixed in with Amazon's sales services.

One of the principal attractions of the open-source process is that it reduces opportunistic behavior exploiting asset specificity.[47] Proprietary standards for any given system limit the potential market for suppliers who might manage or extend that system. At least in the absence of reverse engineering (which is both costly and potentially imperfect), only the original supplier of the proprietary system or its licensees will have the information required to modify that system. Where a system is open source, in contrast, many suppliers can potentially modify that system. Consider the journey of IBM, which practically invented proprietary computing systems, to its current embrace of open source. Its CEO, Samuel Palmisano, now evangelizes open standards: "Everywhere, economic activity is turning outward by embracing shared business and technology standards that let businesses plug into truly global systems of production."[48]

Open-source projects have gone viral across borders without paying much attention to the legal niceties usually accompanying cross-border licensing. Yet given their global scope, open-source projects rely on the global enforceability of licenses. They do not limit themselves either to contributions from coders from jurisdictions likely to enforce the license or to users from such jurisdictions. Eben Moglen and Richard Stallman, the authors of one of the most popular open-source licenses, the GNU public license (GPL), acknowledge that version 2 of the GPL was "a license constructed by one US layman and his lawyers, largely concerned with US law."[49] Even its current third version neither chooses governing law or forum nor offers variations based on jurisdiction. The Creative Commons licenses, by contrast, have been "ported" to more than fifty jurisdictions. Version 3 of the GPL was, however, written with the substantive harmonization requirements of international intellectual property treaties in mind. The GNU license disclaims warrantees and asserts claims over the distribution of derivative works without reference to any particular jurisdiction's laws.[50] Thus far, this failure to consider choice of law and local property and contracting problems does not appear to have proven detrimental, perhaps because of the disciplinary force of informal reputation sanctions in the programming community. In drafting the third version of the GPL, which they characterize as a "Worldwide Copyright License," Moglen and Stallman observed that, despite the lack of international foundations, the "GPL version 2 performed the task of globalization relatively well."[51]

The economic logic of net-work—specifically, the increase in productivity arising from a deepening division of labor—supports the lowering of protectionist barriers against trade in services.[52] But more is required. International trade flourishes in a legal infrastructure of enforceable contracts. This is ever more urgent as firms turn increasingly to buying over making, as they outsource production processes to third-party vendors in alien jurisdictions. The increased legal risks of the market mechanism operating cross-border might be reduced through better transnational dispute resolution frameworks. I turn to these issues in chapter 7.

Despite the efficiencies of global commerce, national borders remain crucial. Law, after all, is defined largely at the national level. States will be loath to abandon their law in the face of offerings mediated by the Internet. In the coming chapters I show how the nations of the world are reconfiguring themselves for global e-commerce and how the law can both facilitate and regulate such commerce. Adam Smith deplored the mercantilism of his day, which would erect barriers to imports so that no specie left the homeland. In this book, I argue that we must dismantle the logistical and regulatory barriers to net-work trade while at the same time ensuring that public policy objectives cannot easily be evaded through a simple jurisdictional sleight of hand or keystroke.

2

WESTERN ENTREPÔT

Silicon Valley

We can glimpse Silicon Valley's global ambitions on the tiny screen of the iPhone. Each icon on the display is a portal to a service offered by a distant provider. With a few taps of her finger, a Londoner might purchase Persian rugs via eBay, download an e-book by the latest Booker Prize winner from Amazon, write her work reports using Microsoft's online enterprise software, manage customer relationships via Salesforce, find business clients via LinkedIn, and manage her London stocks investments via Fidelity.

Pulling out his phone in Japan, a resident of Tokyo might search for information on local history on Google, organize a party via Evite, make a restaurant reservation via OpenTable, keep in touch with friends via Facebook, purchase tickets for a local concert via Tickets.com, find a date via Match.com, read the news on CNN's Japan service, play word games with friends via Zynga, store his emails and photos on Google's servers and his health records on Microsoft's HealthVault, all the while humming along to the latest iTune by a US pop star. The iPhones of both the Londoner and the Tokyoite might be populated by services headquartered mostly along the West Coast of the United States.

This montage reflects the increasingly international penetration of American companies on the wings of the Internet. Apple offers its iTunes download store in some 50 countries in the industrialized world (even charging different prices for the same iTune, with British and Japanese music aficionados paying twice the usual price).[1] Ticketmaster offers its ticket-brokerage services in 18 countries.[2] eBay's financial intermediary PayPal is available in more than 190 countries and regions, and in twenty-five currencies.[3] PayPal wants you to use its service "whether you're buying soccer shoes from Chile, a cell phone from China, or selling surfboards in Costa Rica."[4] MySpace hosts garage bands from Mexico City to New York, all seeking a global audience.[5] From its Dallas headquarters and its Beijing, Rio, and Tokyo offices, Match.com offers dating services in 57 countries, in more than a dozen languages. A handful of years ago, when Google was already "available in 160 different local country domains and 117 languages," its founders lamented that it had physical "business operations in just 20 countries."[6] Today, Google has business operations in more than 50 countries, regions, and territories.[7] Via the Internet, Silicon Valley firms seek to become the intermediaries for the world.

Despite common perception to the contrary, the globalization of services does not entail a one-way drive toward developing country suppliers. *Silicon Valley has emerged as the world's leading net-work provider*. While some companies, especially in the developing world, use the Internet to provide traditional services like radiology, accounting, or gambling across borders, Silicon Valley enterprises such as Facebook, Yahoo!, and Google offer a newer breed of information services to the world. Yahoo! and Google in particular help organize the world's information, and they earn a handsome living in the process. In 2011, Google drew 54 percent of its total revenues from its operations outside the United States. Google attributes these revenues in part to "increased acceptance of our advertising programs" and "our continued progress in developing localized versions of our products for these international markets." More than half of Google's traffic came from users outside the United States. Yahoo! meanwhile provides services "in more than 45 languages and in 60 countries" and earns more than half of its revenues outside the Americas.[8]

These companies' operations outside the United States contribute to their enormous market value. Google boasts a market capitalization of $200 billion, Yahoo! $18 billion, and Microsoft $275 billion, which we might compare to the $45 billion, $34 billion, and $27 billion market values of Indian net-work providers TCS, Infosys, and Wipro, respectively. Indeed, I calculated these figures while in Shanghai on March 15, 2012, using Yahoo! Finance and Yahoo! Currency Converter. Apple, which earns income through both hardware and software, is currently valued at $550 billion and has far surpassed ExxonMobil as the biggest company in the world (which has a market capitalization of $405 billion). Microsoft continues to dominate sales of "office" software around the world, while Google and others vie to create virtual offices in the sky. Silicon Valley's ambitions to encompass the wide range of human services are clear: "Hundreds of companies in Silicon Valley are offering every imaginable service, from writing tools to elaborate dating and social networking systems, all of which require only a Web browser."[9]

Despite public perception to the contrary, the United States actually exports far more services (counting both electronically mediated and other services) than it imports. The United States had a net surplus in commercial services trade of $187 billion in 2011, increasing from $157 billion in 2010 and $139 billion in 2009.[10] India imported ($130 billion) almost as much as it exported ($148 billion) in 2011, a net export surplus of $18 billion, representing a turnaround from 2010's net *deficit* of $7 billion. At the moment, at least, the United States has a stronger claim to being the world's back office than India—and strong reason therefore to disfavor services protectionism. For that matter, even the United Kingdom might be more likely to merit the services silver medal title than India, with a net services surplus of $103 billion in 2011 (compared to $71 billion in 2010 and $80 billion in 2009).

If Indians staff the world's back office, Americans are supplying personal services directly to the world's masses—America as financial intermediary, matchmaker, librarian, newspaper editor, investment adviser, advertising agency, and record keeper. When aggregated across millions of consumers worldwide, these personal services can be even more lucrative than the silk and spices ferried across the ancient Silk Road.

A century ago, American companies might have conquered the local market before seeking customers abroad. Today the global rollout is central to the business plan at the get-go. IBM unveils a recent initiative to the world in Shanghai and names an initial customer: the government of Vietnam, in a project with a "non-US automaker."[11]

So far, I have described what appears to be a process of globalization driven largely by the twin forces of technology and economics. The rise of Silicon Valley is typically attributed to this techno-economic good fortune. However, while the global forces leading to trade from Silicon Valley might seem to be indifferent to law, law is in fact very much in the picture.

Governments have adopted industrial policies to promote information services. In 1997, President Bill Clinton and Vice President Al Gore released their *Framework for Global Electronic Commerce*, setting out the government's approach to regulating the Internet. The title demonstrates a global ambition early on. Announcing the initiative, Clinton observed, "If we establish an environment in which electronic commerce can grow and flourish, then every computer can be a window open to every business, large and small, everywhere in the world." Clinton made it clear that he hoped that this would open up global markets to American enterprise: "This vision contemplates an America in which every American—consumers, small business people, corporate CEOs—will be able to extend our trade to the farthest reaches of the planet." In his remarks, Clinton described himself as a "technophobe" and joked that for people like him a "floppy disk" meant a Frisbee. Despite his professed ignorance, his administration adopted a set of policies that favored Silicon Valley innovation.[12]

President Clinton declared that the Internet should be a "global free-trade zone."[13] Thus, the United States has been pressing its trading partners to commit to the liberalization of e-commerce. Since the United States–Jordan Free Trade Agreement, signed in 2000, every free trade agreement entered into by the United States has included provisions for e-commerce. I turn to the content of those free trade agreements in chapter 6, but one provision—a moratorium on customs duties—deserves early mention.

A central goal of US trade policy over the past two decades has been to eliminate tariffs on products delivered electronically. At the urging of the United States, the World Trade Organization in 1998 adopted a moratorium on "customs duties on electronic transmissions."[14] That moratorium has been renewed repeatedly over the past fifteen years, though some countries remain uneasy about the potential loss of customs revenues owing to the increasing delivery of entertainment and other information via the Internet. The United States has made this a key pillar of its bilateral and regional trade agreements as well. As mentioned, since the US agreement with Jordan in 2000, every subsequent US free trade agreement has contained an e-commerce chapter banning customs duties on digital products, delivered either online or on a carrier medium (such as a CD or DVD). Thus, if a Chilean downloads an album by the Black Eyed Peas or streams a Disney film from the United States, Chile cannot collect any customs duties on that action. The same would apply to the purchase of Chilean music or movies by Americans, of course, but countries with large entertainment or software industries stand to be the principal beneficiaries of this policy.

Many countries across the world have worried that they have failed to develop indigenous Internet industries that could rival Silicon Valley. In 2006, President Jacques Chirac of France called on Europeans to develop an indigenous information search capacity to respond to "the global challenge posed by Google and Yahoo."[15] Japan, too, has established public-private partnerships to promote next-generation search technologies.[16] No strong government-funded alternative has yet emerged to challenge the dominance of West Coast firms. However, locally operated companies such as Naver and Yandex hold a significant share of the local language search market in countries such as Korea and Russia.

My goal in this chapter is to show the crucial role of the law both in enabling Silicon Valley's global success and in complicating its global ambitions. Law figures in at least three important ways. First, a framework of laws permits Silicon Valley enterprises to raise enormous sums of capital for highly risky ventures. Second, the law largely insulates Internet intermediaries hailing from the United States from liability, at least in their home jurisdiction. Third, the laws of foreign jurisdictions can threaten the global reach of Silicon Valley enterprises by erecting significant barriers to trade or imposing special responsibilities on information service providers.

Three cases involving Internet giants Yahoo! and Google demonstrate the legal conflicts that occasionally arise as Silicon Valley enterprises extend themselves across the world. Yahoo!, Google, and their peers provide platforms for people to communicate, whether for discussing politics or sports, selling goods or services, or, on occasion, facilitating crime. Because speech regulations vary across countries, both Yahoo! and Google sometimes find themselves in the difficult position of juggling inconsistent demands. Because both companies are based in the United States, where freedom of speech is especially broad, their global reach has on occasion tested the limits of speech in other jurisdictions. The first case, the Yahoo! conflict in France, may be familiar, but it represents the most fully elaborated international cyberlaw conflict and thus merits careful review.

Yahoo! in France

The most famous international dispute involving cyberspace centers on a clash between two different legal cultures—one cherishing free speech and the other criminalizing hate speech.

Yahoo!'s encounter with French laws barring Nazi paraphernalia produced the most elaborate judicial consideration to date of the potential conflicts of law arising from net-work. Yahoo!'s efforts to provide information services to France from the United States produced a titanic clash between two liberal approaches. The conflict drew a sharp response from both sides of the Atlantic. The French judge in the case hyperbolically declared Yahoo! "the largest vehicle in existence for the promotion [of] Nazism."[17] Yahoo!'s lawyer for his part decried what he perceived to be the "French imperialism" implicit in a Parisian court order against Yahoo!'s California-based enterprise.[18] Across the ocean, some federal judges in the United States would declare efforts to enforce that order as unwarranted extraterritorial intrusions of French law into the United States.[19]

Yahoo! is founded and run from a country with broad constitutional protections against state infringement of speech. The terrifying histories of other lands, however, have led them to bar certain types of speech.[20] Like many countries across Europe, French laws bar speech invoking or glorifying Nazism.[21] More specifically, the French penal code declares it a crime to display or exchange Nazi memorabilia. Yahoo! provides a number of services that potentially run afoul of this law: its search engine services allow people to locate the websites of Holocaust deniers; its (now defunct) Geocities webpage service allowed someone to post *Mein Kampf* and *The Protocols of the Elders of Zion;* and its auction services, which match buyers and sellers around the world, permitted the traffic of material glorifying Nazism. In April 2000, the French Jewish Students Union (UEJF) and the International League Against Racism and Anti-Semitism (LICRA) filed a complaint in Paris seeking to enjoin Yahoo! from hosting auctions featuring Nazi material.

In May 2000, Judge Jean-Jacques Gomez of the Paris Tribunal de Grande Instance offered his first interim ruling, ordering Yahoo! to "take all measures necessary to block access by Internet users in France through yahoo.com to the disputed sites and services. "Yahoo! insisted that this was technically impossible because the nature of the Internet made it impossible for it to deny access to French citizens without simultaneously denying access to Americans.

Yahoo! sought, undoubtedly, to place itself within an earlier precedent, a case in which a French superior court judge had ruled that "since it was technically impossible to block or filter foreign-based Internet sites, . . . ISPs could not be held criminally or civilly liable for objectionable United States–based content accessed by French citizens."[22] Responding to Yahoo!'s claim of technical incapacity, Judge Gomez appointed an international expert panel to determine whether Yahoo! could identify French web users, in order to deny them certain content. The panel consisted of American Internet pioneer (and currently Google's chief Internet evangelist) Vint Cerf, Ben Laurie of the United Kingdom, and François Wallon of France. The panelists concluded that technological means known as "geolocation" allowed "over 70% of the IP addresses of surfers residing in French territory to be identified as being French," and two of the three panelists (not Cerf) suggested that asking surfers to declare their nationality would raise the success rate of identifying French residents to approximately 90 percent (though this latter opinion seems more appropriate for sociologists than computer experts).[23] Geolocation relies largely on the Internet Protocol (IP) address of the user to determine that user's physical location, associating physical location with the particular Internet service provider to whom that IP address is allocated.

This was sufficient for Judge Gomez, who ruled that "effective filtering methods" were available to Yahoo!. A crucial aspect of Judge Gomez's approach deserves special notice. Judge Gomez did not rule that French law required Yahoo! to desist from making Nazi material available to French persons regardless of the effect on US users. He first established (at least to his own satisfaction) that Yahoo! could specifically deny French residents access to the material without removing it more generally. Of course, Judge Gomez believed that a "moral imperative" should motivate Yahoo! to remove this material universally, but he did not order this. Rather, his order was drawn to deny access only to those within France, though whether this is in fact possible is highly questionable. Judge Gomez's approach thus reflects the international law principle of comity, that is, respect for the laws of other nations exercised within their own territory. While Judge Gomez himself believed that banning Nazi materials would satisfy "an ethical and moral imperative shared by all democratic societies," he cabined his order to effects felt within France. Nonetheless, as we will see in chapter 8, the practicalities of implementing the order might well compromise speech in the United States.[24]

Not only did Yahoo! face an injunction and a penalty of, at first, 100,000 euros (later reduced to 100,000 francs) per day, but both the company and its American CEO faced criminal charges. In 2001, prosecutors, acting on a complaint by groups concerned about racism and anti-Semitism, brought charges against Yahoo! and its CEO, Tim Koogle, for "justifying a crime against humanity" and "exhibiting a uniform, insignia or emblem of a person guilty of crimes against humanity," crimes punishable by up to five years in jail for Koogle and fines of 45,735 euros.[25] The charges arose from the same facts underlying the earlier civil action. In 2002, the Paris criminal court held that it had jurisdiction in this criminal case but acquitted the defendants based on a lack of evidence that the defendants had praised Nazi atrocities.[26] Koogle's acquittal was upheld on appeal in 2005 on the ground that "the simple act of hosting auctions of Nazi memorabilia from a Web site based in the United States did not meet the tight standards French courts have previously used when ruling in Holocaust negation cases."[27]

After losing in the French civil court, Yahoo! sought protection from the French judgment in its home jurisdiction, seeking a declaration that the French order was unenforceable in the United States.

Yahoo! had, in the interim, slightly modified its policies (of its own accord, and not in response to the French ruling, Yahoo! insisted) to bar the sale of items promoting hate, but the policies made an exception for books and films and did not affect Yahoo!'s search engine services, which still allowed users to search for Holocaust denier material.[28] Yahoo! said that possible enforcement of the French orders hung over it like a "Damocles sword."[29] Finding a genuine case or controversy, District Judge Jeremy Fogel ruled on the merits that the French orders were unenforceable by a US court because they violated public policy embedded in the First Amendment.[30] LICRA and UEJF appealed, and a divided Ninth Circuit panel dismissed the case for lack of personal jurisdiction over the French defendants.[31]

Emphasizing the critical issues at stake, the Ninth Circuit reheard the case en banc. In a set of six heavily divided opinions, the court dismissed the case, but without a rationale that drew majority support. Three judges voted to dismiss for lack of ripeness (that is, the conflict is not ready for adjudication as it turns on future events that may or may not occur as anticipated). They argued that it was not yet clear that Yahoo! faced any risk from the French judgment because Yahoo! had voluntarily amended its policy and it was not clear that the French court would penalize it further. Three other judges voted to dismiss for lack of personal jurisdiction, arguing that the defendant French groups had not taken sufficient affirmative steps targeting Yahoo! in California to justify having to defend themselves in California (that is, the court lacks the power over these particular defendants in such a case). These votes sufficed on an eleven-person en banc panel to dismiss the case.[32] The dissenting judges would have reached the merits. Judge Raymond Fisher, writing for himself and four other judges, would have held that enforcing the French order would impose a prior restraint on Yahoo! and would do so in an overly vague and broad manner—and thus would be repugnant under the First Amendment.[33] However, Judge William Fletcher, writing for himself and two other judges, was not so certain. He distinguished between two forms in which the First Amendment repugnancy claim could arise: (1) the French court might require Yahoo! to take additional steps that did not restrict access to users in the United States; or (2) the French court might require Yahoo! to take additional steps that had the necessary consequence of restricting access by users in the United States. In suggesting that "the answers [to the questions of whether each of the two forms is constitutional] are likely to be different," Judge Fletcher seemed to suggest that the first form might not be repugnant under the First Amendment, while the second form might well be. Yahoo!, for its part, would have declared even the first fact scenario to present an unconstitutional intrusion, asking rhetorically "whether foreign nations can enlist our citizens and courts as reluctant policemen to insure that their own citizens are not exposed to ideas the foreign governments consider offensive."[34] Judge Fisher agreed and would have declared the order constitutionally repugnant because it required Yahoo! "to guess what has to be censored on its Internet services here in the United States . . . even if limited to France-based users."[35]

This momentous case thus ended with a whimper, leaving the fundamental issues about international conflicts in cyberspace unresolved. In chapter 8, I argue in favor of Judge Fisher's view, that the First Amendment forbids a US court from enforcing a foreign censorship order. In practical terms, the case demonstrates that network companies will, at least at times, change their offerings in concert with the demands of a foreign jurisdiction. Rather than change its site for one country and leave it unchanged everywhere else, Yahoo! changed its offerings globally.

Google in Brazil

In their introduction to their company's 2006 annual report, Google's founders proudly declared that "Orkut,™ our experiment with social networking, is now part of the social fabric for the majority of online users in such countries as Brazil and[,] more recently, India." The annual filing also revealed uncertainty as to Google's "ability to generate revenue from services in which we have invested considerable time and resources, such as YouTube, Gmail and orkut." Legal risks were also on the company's mind: "Our business is subject to a variety of U.S. and foreign laws that could subject us to claims or other remedies based on the nature and content of the information searched or displayed by our products and services."[36]

Indeed, Google faced a significant legal challenge in 2006. Orkut's embedding into the Brazilian social fabric meant that it was being used there to create online communities on all manner of human activities, dismayingly including child pornography, incitements to commit crime, neo-Nazism, cruelty to animals, racism, religious intolerance, homophobia, and xenophobia.[37] Brazilian law declares such activities illegal. When the Brazilian prosecutors sought Google's Brazilian subsidiary's assistance in identifying the participants in Orkut groups devoted to such banned activities, that subsidiary professed a lack of control over the information demanded. The information, the subsidiary reported, resided on the parent company's servers in the United States. Unhappy with this answer, a Brazilian judge reproached Google for evincing a "profound disrespect for national sovereignty."[38] Brazilian authorities readdressed the subpoena to Google's Silicon Valley headquarters, and Google promptly complied.

Why might Brazilian data be stored on computer servers in the United States rather than in Brazil? Google reportedly maintains a "policy of keeping data about its users in the US to protect it from disclosure to foreign governments."[39] Call this the *Safe Server Strategy*—locating a server in a jurisdiction where constitutional guarantees of free speech will prevent that jurisdiction's courts from enforcing an order supporting state suppression of information. In this case, Google decided that the Brazilian request to root out hate speech and child pornography did not justify trying to forestall turning over the information through the possible shield of American free speech law. I return to this issue in chapter 9, when considering the responsibilities of social media services in repressive countries. The Safe Server Strategy is hardly foolproof. Witness Yahoo!'s decision to change what its US-based servers provided, perhaps as a result of French pressure. Yet it does complicate a government's efforts to enforce law, which might be especially useful to avoid the Balkanization of the Internet resulting from excessive national regulatory efforts, a point I return to in chapter 8.

Yahoo! in China

Yahoo! was one of the early American Internet pioneers in China. Its CEO and cofounder, Jerry Yang, had been born in Taiwan. In 2000, Yahoo! webcast a fashion show featuring Swatch watches from atop the Great Wall of China. Swatch offered that it "chose Yahoo! to broadcast this event online because of Yahoo!'s global reach and scale and its ability to help us target Swatch wearers in Asia and throughout the world."[40] Before the end of the first decade in the twenty-first century, Yang would find himself in the US Capitol, bowing deeply in apology to the mother of the imprisoned Chinese dissident journalist Shi Tao. Yahoo! would also be accused of abetting the torture of Chinese dissident Wang Xiaoning in a California federal court. Fast-forward a few years still, and Yahoo!'s investments in China (and Japan) would prove to be its crown jewels, providing the bulk of its market value.

The risks of net-work providers operating in China is perhaps made clearest in the Yahoo! case involving Shi Tao. After receiving a complaint alleging that Yahoo! had improperly disclosed email subscriber's Shi Tao's personal information to the Chinese authorities, Hong Kong's privacy commissioner investigated. The commissioner found that Yahoo! supplied information on Shi Tao to Chinese authorities pursuant to an order from that country's State Security Bureau.[41] He observed that the Chinese court (the Changsha Intermediate People's Court) had cited information supplied by Yahoo! in reaching its verdict against Shi Tao, with the court reporting:

> Account holder information furnished by Yahoo! Holdings (Hong Kong) Ltd., which confirms that for IP address 218.76.8.201 at 11:32:17 p.m. on April 20, 2004, the corresponding user information was as follows: user telephone number: 0731–4376362 located at the Contemporary Business News office in Hunan; address: 2F, Building 88, Jianxiang New Village, Kaifu District, Changsha.[42]

Despite this, the privacy commissioner absolved Yahoo!'s local Hong Kong subsidiary of complicity. The commissioner concluded that connecting an IP address to a physical location did not constitute a revelation of "personal data" under the ordinance because the IP address might not "relat[e] directly or indirectly to a living individual" as required by the ordinance.[43] In any case, the commissioner concluded, the supply of information was in fact made by Yahoo!'s Chinese operations without the direction or control of Yahoo!'s Hong Kong subsidiary.[44] This suggests that the servers that held the relevant data were located in mainland China, which then turned the data over to the authorities. The commissioner concluded that the California parent company did indeed exercise control over the Chinese operations but determined that the California parent was outside the jurisdiction of the Hong Kong privacy commissioner.[45]

Shi Tao's was not the only case that implicated Yahoo!. In August 2007, Yu Ling filed suit in federal court in Oakland under the Alien Torts Statute and the Torture Victims Protection Act, alleging that Yahoo! and its subsidiaries had violated international law by helping the Chinese government uncover the identity of her husband, Wang Xiaoning, a political dissident. Using a Yahoo! email account (bxoguh@yahoo.cm.cn) and a Yahoo! Group (aaabbbccc), Wang Xiaoning had for years distributed political writings anonymously from his home in Beijing. When the authorities discovered Wang's identity, they detained and, according to the lawsuit, tortured him. The suit alleged that the authorities beat and kicked him, forcing him to confess to engaging in "anti-state" activities. The Beijing Higher People's Court held him guilty of sedition. It determined that "Wang had edited, published and contributed articles to 42 issues of two political e-journals, advocating for open elections, a multi-party system and separation of powers in the government."[46] Wang was imprisoned in Beijing Prison No. 2, sentenced to a ten-year term for "incitement to subvert state power."[47]

"Yahoo betrayed my husband," Yu charged, arguing that Yahoo! facilitated her husband's arrest and conviction. Yahoo! disputed her claims, but the Chinese judgment demonstrates at least some level of Yahoo!'s involvement in the case. A review of the Chinese judgment by the group Human Rights in China reveals the following:

> The evidence against him included information provided by Yahoo Holdings (Hong Kong) Ltd. stating that Wang's "aaabbbccc" Yahoo! Group was set up through the mainland

> China–based email address bxoguh@yahoo.com.cn. Yahoo Holdings (Hong Kong) Ltd. also confirmed that the email address ahgq@yahoo.com.cn, through which Wang sent messages to the Group, was a mainland China–based account.[48]

Yahoo! argued that its Chinese operations had to comply with lawful official requests for information and that it cannot know how authorities will use information that it shares with them: "Yahoo China will not know whether the demand for information is for a legitimate criminal investigation or is going to be used to prosecute political dissidents."[49] Despite the Chinese court's judgment, which cited Yahoo!'s Hong Kong subsidiary's cooperation in the case, Yahoo! insists that there was "no exchange of information" between its Hong Kong subsidiary and "mainland security forces."[50]

Yahoo! reached a settlement with the Shi and Wang families in 2007. It also set up a human rights fund to provide "humanitarian relief" to families of dissidents imprisoned for expressing their views online. Noting that he had not been CEO during the period of the disclosure, Yang declared, "Yahoo! was founded on the idea that the free exchange of information can fundamentally change how people lead their lives, conduct their business and interact with their governments." He continued, "We are committed to making sure our actions match our values around the world."[51]

Yahoo! had already reconsidered its strategy in China. In 2005, it transferred its Chinese operations to the leading Chinese e-commerce company, Alibaba. But that did not mean that it was quitting the market entirely: it simultaneously invested $1 billion into Alibaba, gaining a 40 percent stake in the company.[52] In 2012, it sold half of that stake to Alibaba for $7 billion. The year 2012 also marked Wang's release from prison. Shi Tao, however, remains imprisoned.

Yahoo!'s foray into China raises a central issue for net-work: How can a company supplying services around the globe comport itself to the laws of repressive regimes without fouling human rights? The issue is especially salient for net-work providers as they traffic in information—precisely the target of repressive regimes. Human Rights Watch identifies a "race to the bottom" in which Western corporations seek to outdo each other in assisting Chinese political repression.[53] Yahoo! has chosen to withdraw, at least behind a minority shareholding, which it has recently reduced. Yahoo! has also joined the Global Network Initiative, which commits it to protecting freedom and expression and privacy around the world, subject to external audits. I discuss this initiative further in chapter 9.

The various difficulties faced by Google and Yahoo! in their global offerings preview some of the difficulties that will attend the rise of the current wave of computing. I now turn to the emergence of cloud computing.

Trade from the Clouds

"Cloud computing"—the use of enormous computers to store and process data at a distance—has risen to prominence in recent years. In one sense it represents a return to the era when terminals simply provided connections to a big computer, an era before personal computers like the IBM PC and the Apple IIe reinvented computing. The terminals of the 1960s and 1970s simply served as input-output devices for a large brain in some well-cooled backroom. I can recall the enormous Hewlett Packard 3000 "minicomputer" to which I connected as a child through a line of terminals in the 1970s at my local Midwestern university. But now rather than residing in a backroom to which the wires run, the large brain today is pulsing far from the user, often in a different state or even a different country.

Even in the 1960s and 1970s, one could use telephone modems to log in remotely to one's account on a big computer in the main office. The widespread deployment of the shared communication protocols of the Internet, however, make it possible for all of the world's Internet-enabled computers to connect with the remote computer virtually instantaneously. With cloud computing, your computer—whether your desktop, laptop, or smartphone—becomes simply an on-ramp onto this electronic highway of information.

By its very nature, cloud computing typically involves crossing borders. Cloud computing can represent a paradigmatic instance of offshore outsourcing: moving a computer service to remote computers, typically with the user both largely unaware of the jurisdiction or jurisdictions from which the service is actually supplied. Also like offshore outsourcing, cloud computing offers the advantage of allowing a business employing the service to quickly scale up or down, depending on demand.

Cloud computing entails remote computers performing the entire range of computer-assisted functions from "analyzing risk in financial portfolios, delivering personalized medical information, even powering immersive computer games."[54] Cloud computing is already a daily reality. Google's search services offer a model for the architecture for cloud computing—with endless arrays of computer servers holding enormous quantities of data (measured in terabytes) and supercomputers searching those arrays to supply us almost instantaneously with the information we seek. Google has ambitious plans to expand that model, as summed up by one reporter: "If there is one common theme to Google's latest moves, it's that the company wants all Internet users to do everything online, and store everything they do online, from sharing digital pictures to creating spreadsheets."[55] Google is hardly alone. IBM, Microsoft, and Amazon, too, have deployed enormous cloud services.

Mobile computing will likely accelerate this shift. The limits of storage and processing on handheld units, the convenience of databases that are automatically shared across multiple devices, and the risks of losing data stored on a broken or misplaced tablet or smartphone are spurring users to turn to cloud computing.

Cloud computing seems to defy law. Like most cloud providers, Google tells users that it "processes personal information on our servers in many countries around the world."[56] Thus, users often cannot know in what country their data are being stored and processed. Google will not want to use jurisdictions that place its users' data at risk, but given that it has a global client base, it wants the flexibility to employ different jurisdictions as techno-legal-economic conditions warrant.

The move to place computing metaphorically in the clouds would seem to offer an escape from the earthly shackles of burdensome regulation. When one's attention is turned toward the heavens, law would seem a distant afterthought. But the reality, of course, is that the computer servers holding the data, the computers performing functions on that data, the people whom the data processing affects, and the users of those computers reside very much on terra firma.

Declaring the cloud to be law-free seems appealing, but only at first glance. Consider the following examples, all ripped from existing controversies: What if the cloud holds details of the names and addresses of doctors who perform abortions, with those who have been murdered crossed out?[57] What if the cloud holds a video showing the brutal treatment of an autistic child because of the child's autism, when targeting people on the basis of their disability is considered a hate crime? What if a website collects links to fast downloads of illegal copies of Hollywood or Bollywood movies? What if the cloud holds the complete health dossiers of individuals? These examples demonstrate that anyone concerned about the ability of countries to govern themselves—to protect their people or to protect property interests—cannot allow the cloud to become a legal black hole.

Contrary to the effort to deny the importance of physical location, it is notable that the leading cloud computing enterprises with global ambitions are based largely in the United States. Cloud computing exemplifies Silicon Valley's ambitions to supply the world's people both business and personal services online. Although the Indian outsourcing firms have established their cloud computing servicing capacities, they have not offered themselves as the long-term storehouses of the world's information. Rather, they present themselves as the processors of that information, generally on an as-needed basis. China, too, is investing heavily in cloud services, but it is too early to say whether these services will attract large numbers of users outside China. I examine some aspects of the Chinese Internet industry in chapter 9.

How Law Made Silicon Valley

It is probably not much of an exaggeration that every company set up in a bedroom in Silicon Valley hopes to take over the world. There is reason for such optimism. Again and again, it is Silicon Valley firms that have become the world's leading providers of various web services—from social networks to search engines to game services to news reporting to payments. Why did this happen?

Popular explanations revolve focus on two features—money and education. It is not a coincidence that the heart of American venture capital is in Silicon Valley, where America's software industry is located. Both industries profit from each other in a symbiotic relationship. The availability of venture capital at an early stage allows these firms to build up their infrastructure, test their products, and market themselves. Venture capitalists must be willing to accept the failure of many of their investments. American corporate law helpfully supports the risk-taking represented by venture capital.

Silicon Valley also bestrides the great academic centers of Stanford University and the University of California, Berkeley, and is near the artistic and intellectual hub of San Francisco. With these universities in the vicinity, and other University of California campuses such as Santa Cruz and Davis nearby, start-ups and established firms find easy access to a local talent pool of leading designers, computer programmers, business managers, publicists, and innovators.

Other features of the United States more generally contribute to the leading role of American firms in global e-commerce. A large domestic American marketplace enables American firms to justify large investments. The enormous free trade zone of the United States, with its largely uniform commercial laws, makes it easy for a start-up to set up shop in one locality yet supply an enormous market. Until the recent enlargement of the European Union, the United States by itself was the world's largest free trade zone, in terms of the wealth of its population. The fact that the common language of this domestic market is English—increasingly the second language of much of the world—makes it easier to find people to localize a website for foreign markets. America's polyglot immigrant workforce also helps these corporations extend themselves around the world—including in the 60 percent of humanity that is Asia. Google's lunchroom in Mountain View, with its multiple different cuisines to serve that global workforce, epitomizes the Valley's global roots. The US government has championed free trade in services over the past few decades, helping open up such trade in a variety of forums, including the World Trade Organization, regional free trade agreements such as NAFTA, and bilateral free trade agreements. A culture of risk-taking and an acceptance of failure have also been crucial. Many of the leading American Internet firms were start-ups just a few years ago: Yahoo! formed in 1994, Google in 1998, Facebook in 2004, and Twitter in 2006. Steve Jobs's famous failure with the Next computer did not rule him out for further leadership in the industry.

An additional contributor to Silicon Valley's success is perhaps the most surprising. This last element is not based on the location of these enterprises in a particularly blessed corner of the United States and thus is not unique to Silicon Valley enterprises but applies to all net-work enterprises based in the United States generally. Both Congress and US courts have sought to provide a legal framework that embraces Web 2.0 enterprises. This permissive legal framework offers the United States as a sort of export-processing zone in which Internet entrepreneurs can experiment and establish services. In particular, the combination of (1) the First Amendment guarantee of freedom of speech; (2) the Communications Decency Act's Section 230, granting immunity to web hosts for user-generated information; (3) Title II of the Digital Millennium Copyright Act (DMCA), granting immunity to web hosts for copyright infringement; and (4) weak consumer privacy regulations has created breathing room for the rise of Web 2.0. That is, Silicon Valley has prospered with laws that exempted web hosts from liability for the actions of users yet did not interfere with web hosts who exploited user information extensively.

In Web 2.0, Internet service providers offer platforms for others to create, often for free. Human beings use these services for creative expression or more banal work, but they sometimes include material that violates someone else's rights or is otherwise prohibited by law. Will the net-work provider be liable for inevitable human misuse of the tools they supply? The wrongful material would, after all, be published on the net-work provider's site. Moreover, what if the misuse brings more users to the site and thus indirectly generates additional revenues from advertising? The possibility of liability in such cases might deter many from opening up such an open-ended shop. Thus, the DMCA offers immunity from copyright infringement for content supplied by users if the host service follows specified rules, such as taking down potentially infringing material upon notice. Meanwhile, Section 230 of the Communications Decency Act offers immunity from many other claims—including defamation and invasion of privacy.

The absence of privacy rights proved particularly important because of the business model used by many consumer-oriented websites. Web 2.0 providers earn money through advertising or through selling additional services. If the net-work provider can tailor advertisements precisely to the interests of the user, then it can justify higher advertising rates. In other words, the more the net-work provider knows about you, the more it can earn. Rules protecting user privacy can, accordingly, interfere with a company's ability to gather information about you. Thus, the absence of a broad array of effective privacy-enhancing restraints leaves net-work suppliers largely free to exploit user information for maximum profit. As long as the suppliers do not promise more privacy than they actually deliver, net-work companies in the United States can act with remarkable impunity with personal information, unless it falls into specific financial or health categories or knowingly involves children under the age of thirteen.

Law is crucial to the continued success of global e-commerce. The amazing revolutions in connection, including Facebook's social network, Google's information services, and the highly efficient business processes of Infosys and Wipro, all depend on the legal environment. In the next chapter, I turn to the rise of Bangalore.

3

EASTERN ENTREPÔT

Bangalore

Today an American family can outsource tutoring to an Indian engineer, tax preparation to an Indian accountant, and medical diagnosis to an Indian radiologist, and then sit for a portrait by an artist in coastal China.[1] An American corporation, for its part, can outsource human resources management to the Philippines, engineering to China, customer service to Jamaica, and regulatory compliance management and information technology to India.[2] Little seems immune: today even prayers for Kansans are outsourced to priests in Kerala.[3] Where China has become the factory to the world, India and other developing countries may become the world's back office.[4]

China once anchored the eastern end of the ancient Silk Road. The Chinese shepherded their monopoly in the manufacture of silk as a trade secret, decreeing death to anyone smuggling either live silkworms or the seeds of the mulberry trees needed to sustain these industrious creatures.[5] Europeans spun elaborate myths explaining the origin of silk, never suspecting that it might be the product of a humble worm. In his agricultural poems *The Georgics*, Virgil imagined the people of Asia, whom the Greeks called the Seres (the People of Silk), harvesting the fabric from trees: "The Seres comb from off the leaves / Their silky fleece."

Today, the Eastern epicenter of cybertrade is in Bangalore, though it faces challengers from Shanghai to Manila. What are the secrets of today's Eastern entrepôt to the Electronic Silk Road? Why did Bangalore, and India generally, emerge as a services powerhouse, and not China? What can other nations do to copy Bangalore's secrets? What are Bangalore's vulnerabilities?

The Rise of the Indian Multinational

The millennial turn had a literal significance for the cross-border outsourcing of services. Computer programs written decades earlier had been expected to be long obsolete before the clock rolled over to the year 2000. These computer systems were susceptible to catastrophic failure when the year struck 2000, a number for which many computer programs were not prepared. This problem became known as the Y2K bug, with the K borrowed from kilobyte (representing a little more than a thousand bytes, with each byte a unit of computer information). The millennial turn threatened the operation of everything from hospital records to the telephone. The task of reviewing millions of lines of computer code for this vulnerability was gargantuan. With their lower labor cost base, Indian software companies recognized an opportunity to attract new clients, especially from the United States. The relationships and experience developing from the millennial programming spurred Indian companies to expand their services domain. The *Economist* magazine declared, "Once the Indians had saved the world, they set out to conquer it."[6] Indian companies began to perform business processes such as procurement, finance and accounting, human resources, and data processing.[7] At Internet speed, Indian outsourcing pioneers grew into multibillion-dollar, multinational companies.[8]

The industry is broadly divided between information technology (IT) services and business process outsourcing (BPO). IT services consist primarily of software development and support. BPO services consist in performing a business process, such as accounting, customer service (including, famously, call centers), and human resources management. IT services, of course, are technically also business processes, but they are typically excluded from BPO calculations entirely because they constitute such a major share of outsourced services. There is a long history of outsourcing IT services to specialist firms. IT also opened the door to other services; Indian firms typically gained their initial entry into international services by providing IT services. IT services account for more than half of the services export revenues of the Indian outsourcing companies.[9]

Three firms lead the industry—Tata Consultancy Services (TCS), Infosys, and Wipro—though the industry also includes a host of other large corporations and small start-ups. The largest, TCS, is a subsidiary of the Tata conglomerate, with roots to a company founded by Jamsetji Tata in 1868. TCS was initially formed a hundred years later in 1968 to provide services to the Tata group of companies such as Tata Steel, but it soon began to serve customers outside Tata. TCS won contracts to supply services to European, American, and Indian customers over the 1970s and 1980s.[10] These contracts were often in financial services, perhaps unsurprising because of the early globalization and digitization of the finance industry.

Infosys was founded famously with just ten thousand rupees by seven entrepreneurs in Narayan Murthy's seven-hundred-square-foot apartment in Pune, India.[11] India's notorious License Raj was very much in evidence as these entrepreneurs began. Murthy recalls that "it took us nine to twelve months and as many as 15 visits to Delhi to get permission to import a computer."[12] However, because of the services nature of their business, such hurdles proved surmountable. Infosys's employees traveled to their customer's worksite and performed the services on location. (Even this was not without complication: in order to convert Indian rupees into the hard currency necessary for foreign travel, Infosys had to obtain the permission of the Indian central bank.) This "bodyshopping" was useful for another reason: the newness of the relationship meant that the clients had not yet developed confidence in their supplier. But with the foreign employees on-site, "the client could strictly control the parameters of the project and closely monitor the software development process."[13] GE became an Infosys customer in 1989. In March 1999, Infosys would become the first Indian company in history to list its shares on an American stock exchange. (By contrast, the first Chinese company to list its shares on an American exchange was Brilliance Automotive, which listed in 1992 on the NYSE; Hong Kong–based ChinaDotCom became the first Chinese company to list on the Nasdaq in July 1999.) It was a meeting with Infosys visionary Nandan Nilekani that convinced *New York Times* columnist Thomas Friedman that "the world is flat." Inside Infosys's Bangalore headquarters, where watchful clocks announced the time around the world, Nilekani argued to Friedman that the playing field for international competition was being leveled by electronic communications.[14]

Wipro's history offers a microcosm of India's own economic evolution. Wipro was founded as a vegetable oil company in 1947, the year of India's independence. The current customers of Wipro's highly sophisticated business services might be surprised to learn that Wipro is apparently an acronym for "Western India Palm Refined Oils." Its current CEO, Azim Premji, took the reins of the company at the age of twenty-one, when he, then a student at Stanford University, was called home suddenly to run the family business on his father's death.[15] He began expanding the business into new industrial and consumer sectors. Wipro formed a software services unit in the 1970s. In 1990, GE established a joint venture with Wipro to design, manufacture, and distribute a low-cost ultrasound machine. Over the coming years, ultrasound machines would certainly prove an important diagnostic tool for medical professionals in India, but they would also gain notoriety because of their widespread illegal use in gender-selective abortions.

The United States serves as the most important single market for these three companies. For the Indian IT-BPO industry, exports count for some $69 billion of a total of $100 billion in revenues in fiscal year 2012.[16] TCS generates slightly more than half of its revenue in the Americas (51 percent), with important shares also generated in the United Kingdom (19 percent), and the rest of Europe (11 percent). It generates less than a tenth of its revenues at home in India (8 percent). Infosys generates two-thirds of its income in North America (67 percent), with the bulk of the remainder generated in Europe (22 percent). India makes up little more than 1 percent of the company's revenues. Wipro, by contrast, draws nearly a quarter of its revenues from India (24 percent). Wipro's leading customer is still the United States, constituting nearly half (44 percent) of Wipro's revenues, and Europe makes up an additional quarter (24 percent).[17]

Legal developments, not technical developments alone, made the rise of these Indian multinationals possible. The Indian entrepreneur had historically faced a maze of regulation and prohibitions that hampered any global reach and forestalled international aspirations. Many enterprising Indians simply sailed for foreign shores more friendly to individual achievement, resulting in an enormous brain drain of highly educated individuals. *Forbes* characterized the British legacy for corporate India: "When the British gave India back to the Indians in 1947, they left behind a culture in which elected officials and civil servants, many of them the products of British schools, controlled the economy."[18] The License Raj that succeeded the British Raj continued extensive state controls on the economy but changed its philosophical underpinnings from imperialism to socialism. S. Ramadorai, CEO of TCS from 1998 to 2009, writes of some of the travails TCS faced in the 1970s as a result of the law. When his company wanted to import a product (such as computer systems), TCS had to undertake to export twice the cost of the imported inputs over a five-year period. Failure to meet this obligation would lead to the confiscation of the imported machine, as well as financial penalties.[19] To add to the risk, the United States, too, reserved the right to confiscate the machine if it was used in ways other than those approved of in the US export license. Because the Indian government did not permit Infosys to borrow in dollars, Infosys was forced to borrow in rupees, obtain a forward currency contract to protect itself against adverse exchange rate fluctuations, earn income in dollars from exports, convert the dollars to rupees, and then repay the loan in rupees.

In 1991, the Indian government, under then–finance minister (and now prime minister) Manmohan Singh, began to loosen the restraints on corporate India. The reforms "allowed firms to open offices abroad, travel easily, and hire foreign consultants."[20] The

Indian government also lowered import tariffs and made it easier for Indian companies to access capital markets. "Now we are our own masters," Anil Ambani of Reliance Industries declared.[21]

Economic liberalization proved crucial for firms such as Infosys. According to Murthy, "The Indian economic reforms of 1991 came as a heaven-sent opportunity for us at Infosys."[22] The liberalization paved the way for Infosys's 1993 initial public offering on the Bombay Stock Exchange (since renamed the Mumbai Stock Exchange by a more assertive regional government, which sought to restore what it claimed was the city's original name in the local language). Access to the capital markets permitted companies like Infosys to grow, allowing them to achieve the scale necessary to handle enormous applications for multinational enterprises.

Two American enterprises helped the fledgling Indian software enterprises, one by its presence, the other by its absence. First, the departure of IBM from India in 1977 created a vacuum that Indian companies stepped in to fill. IBM quit India rather than capitulate to new Indian laws that required local subsidiaries to be majority controlled by Indians.[23] This created a breach in servicing the computer hardware already installed in the country. Both TCS and Wipro benefited by beginning to service IBM hardware already deployed throughout the country. GE was the second enterprise that gave a fillip to the Indian IT industry. GE's early contracts with Indian firms gave these firms credibility at a time when many companies saw India as a "risky backwater."[24] GE provided not only credibility but cash: "At one point during the 1990s, Wipro's software unit, Wipro Systems Ltd., received 50 percent of its revenue from GE. At TCS and another leading technology company, Infosys Technologies Ltd., the figures were between 20% and 30%, the companies say."[25] Trade proved a positive sum game, as GE, famous for its efficiency, saved some $300 million a year.

As GE's early act of confidence in Indian enterprise shows by its rarity, Indian companies with global ambitions had to overcome a significant prejudice—the disbelief that an enterprise rooted in the developing world could provide high-quality services. As *Forbes* magazine described it in an early article on Infosys, "Despite a roster of big-name North American clients, Infosys was battling the crass Western perception that a smart, honest, reputable company could never come out of a country where cows still run in the street."[26] As Infosys's head Murthy puts it, "When in the early '90s we went to the US to sell our services, most CIOs [Chief Information Officers] didn't believe that an Indian company could build the large applications they needed."[27] Indian companies lacked the long track record of globalized American companies and thus had to prove themselves to skeptical customers.

Indian companies found an ingenious method to demonstrate their fidelity. They listed stock on the American exchanges. They did this less to raise capital than to bond themselves through a commitment to American disclosure law. As mentioned earlier, Infosys became the first Indian company to go public in the United States with its Nasdaq listing in 1999. Wipro followed in 2000 with a New York Stock Exchange (NYSE) listing. Wipro's long collaboration with GE was evident when GE's CEO Jack Welch joined Wipro's Azim Premji to ring the NYSE bell on the first day of Wipro's trading in the United States. By listing securities in the United States, these companies declared that they would subject themselves to the sword of American shareholder litigation. If subsequent events called their public accounts into question, they would face the wrath of American securities lawyers. This commitment would be sorely tested by Satyam Computer Services, whose chairman confessed in 2009 to greatly exaggerating the company's financial position. The Indian authorities replaced Satyam's board and appointed new officers within a month of the revelation. The US securities law bonding proved effective as Satyam paid $125 million to settle the claims of its US shareholders.

The most successful multinational corporations have diversified their markets, with footholds on every continent. The Indian multinationals, too, have diversified, increasing their presence in Latin America, east Asia, and Europe. TCS is perhaps the leader among Indian corporations in its global reach. It is rapidly expanding its polyglot workforce in Latin America, eastern Europe, and China, seeking to access the world's talent and serve the world's enterprises in their vernaculars.[28] TCS is offering its expertise, for example, to the government of Mexico, with a $200 million deal to manage IT services for the Mexican social security system. Mexico selected TCS after falling out with American services giants Accenture and Electronic Data Systems (EDS), which had previously provided IT services to the Mexican social security system.

One Infosys project demonstrates the global hopscotching of services today. Seeking to design software to manage a loan program for Spanish-speaking customers in the United States, an American bank hired Infosys, which had recently opened an office in Monterrey, Mexico. A Mexican team, the bank argued, would have both the language skills and the cultural knowledge to serve Hispanic Americans. As the *New York Times* observed: "Such is the new outsourcing. A company in the United States pays an Indian vendor 7,000 miles, or 11,200 kilometers, away to supply it with Mexican workers situated 150 miles south of the U.S. border."[29]

For all the focus on the Indian outsourcing giants, it is easy to lose sight that many of the world's biggest services outsourcing companies are American. Consider that nine of the ten largest IT outsourcing deals announced in May 2010 were awarded to American firms.[30] The largest IT outsourcing deal—for California's public health system—went to ACS, now a unit of Xerox Corporation.

Because seven of the ten largest deals involved US state or federal government agencies, there may well have been public pressure to keep the outsourcing onshore. Yet IBM even won a deal to provide back-office services for an insurance company in Brazil. IBM will now "be responsible for . . . issuing policies, registration updates, document transfers and claim management" for the Brazilian insurer. American companies have beaten Indian companies for contracts even in the Indian companies' backyard. Earlier in 2010, the Indian telecom firm Bharti selected IBM in a ten-year, $750 million deal.

IBM will likely perform much of its work for Bharti in Bharat (the Hindi name for India). IBM is heavily international not just in its revenues but also in its workforce. Like its major American services competitors, IBM routes significant parts of its global work to its staff in India. The *New York Times* even declares IBM a "postmultinational global corporation" because the firm not only sells to the world but also runs much of its operation from outside the United States: "The global purchasing and procurement unit is in China; human relations tasks like expense report processing are done in the Philippines; and back-office financial processing is done in Brazil."[31] IBM, having left India ingloriously in 1977, has now returned with a huge Indian workforce (its largest workforce outside the United States) and with major Indian clients. In 2008, *Business Week* provocatively asked, "IBM vs. Tata: Who's More American?" IBM, the business magazine noted, generated the bulk of its revenue outside the United States, while Tata Consulting Services generated the bulk of its revenues in the United States.[32]

Despite their ability to go toe-to-toe with leading American services companies in certain domains, Indian companies face a fundamental deficit in competing with their American counterparts: they are not yet trusted, household names. While Silicon Valley enterprises serve both corporations and consumers in India,

Bangalore enterprises earn the great bulk of their revenue from corporations alone. Wipro, Infosys, and TCS are relegated largely to the back office—or to the unseen phone—accents and corporate identities hidden to the greatest extent possible. With back-end outsourcing, consumers do not gain experience with a particular Indian company, and thus these companies fail to build a consumer brand.

The global dominance of Western media, which benefit from the economies of scale available in the wealthiest countries, helps cement this brand disparity. For many years, Google, likely the world's biggest advertising company, did not itself buy advertising. It had no need to. The media breathlessly announced every new product. Google ran its first television advertisement in 2009, a decade after its founding. Apple's hardware, and to a lesser extent its software, has received even more obsessive and fawning media attention.

Indian companies have not fared as well in the Western media. Much of the attention has been focused on the growing alarm over outsourcing, especially the threat to Americans who might lose their jobs to foreign competition. At the same time, Western media have oscillated between declaring the end of American jobs and the end of outsourcing. A 2004 story in *Business Week* argued that outsourcing was becoming "outmoded," a likely victim of rising wages in Asia. A 2010 story in the same magazine titled "The End of Outsourcing (As We Know It)" suggested that, because of cloud computing, "In the next five years outsourcing as we know it will disappear. The legion of Indian service providers will be sidelined or absorbed."[33] The hyperbole of the newspapers notwithstanding, American jobs and Indian outsourcing are likely to coexist, as are outsourcing companies and cloud computing enterprises. Indeed, services outsourcing companies often rely on remote databases held at the client site and thus have long practiced a form of cloud computing. Cloud computing represents the outsourcing of basic data storage and processing functions to a remote entity and thus reflects an opportunity for outsourcing companies generally.

The experience of other large Asian economies may be relevant. Japanese companies, too, once faced a reputation for cheap, inferior-quality products. Yet relentless efforts over decades to improve quality led Japanese products to be perceived as often better than rival American products. Chinese companies have had to overcome a perception for inferior products more recently. While Japanese companies have gone on to become household names (think Sony, Canon, and Nintendo), Chinese companies have not, even though Chinese subsidiaries of Taiwanese companies manufacture many of the items Americans use in our daily lives, including the iPhones and iPads that Americans adore. Lenovo and Haier cannot yet claim a place next to Dell and Whirlpool in the American household's lexicon. Whether India's services companies will follow Japan's path or China's remains to be seen.

The Human Networks Behind Net-Work

The rise of India as the epicenter of services outsourcing poses a puzzle: Why did India, and not China, Russia, or eastern Europe—all well-endowed with programmers and engineers—lead the world in supplying services electronically? While electronic networks made possible the new Silk Road in cyberspace, a kind of network as old as human migration has helped power this trade: diasporas.

Neither the revolution of information technology nor a particular millennial task nor even the imperatives of labor arbitrage explain adequately the evolution of the flow of trade in services. Helpful to the choice of India as a primary outsourcing destination was the ubiquity of Indian Americans in Silicon Valley, the heart of the information technology industry in the United States. An OECD study concludes that "diaspora populations [are] proving important in [facilitating trade in] areas spanning traditional medicines to audiovisuals."[34] The economist Hal Varian declares, "It is almost impossible for an entrepreneur to put a foreign development team together without some strong connections on the ground."[35] This is not merely an academic notion: Varian currently serves as Google's chief economist.

Also relevant are historical forces such as colonialism, which created both the language linkages between India's north and south and diaspora channels that facilitate trade in information services.[36] Personal relations remain important even in the global flows of network. Take, for example, the experience of a small San Francisco architectural firm that sought to outsource design work to Asia. The owner first attempted to outsource to firms in Southeast Asia that were "run by American ex-pats," but this proved unsuccessful. When a "young Indian architect joined our firm after finishing his Master[']s degree in the States," the firm began outsourcing—successfully—to the Indian company owned by that young architect's parents.[37]

As I mentioned in chapter 1, economists such as Ronald Coase described two modes of organizing production: hierarchy (the top-down structure common in corporations and governments) and markets (the arm's-length transactions entered into through freely negotiated contracts). More recently, economists have explored a third mode of organizing production—the network.[38] The network allows a loose coordination of tasks toward an overlapping goal.

Networks do not replace hierarchy or markets but rather support both, reducing informational deficiencies in this new remote trade regime. Networks are likely to prove especially important when charting new terrain. Lack of familiarity with a country and its cities, workers, educational institutions, and enterprises will necessitate a turn to alternative mechanisms to garner the information to engage in new transactions.

While ethnic networks might operate across continents to spur information flow, personal contacts arising out of geographic proximity still matter. Indeed, the rise of information centers such as Bangalore and Hyderabad, Silicon Valley and Seattle, attests to the continuing relevance of geography. Outsourcing has not been distributed evenly across the regions of the world with broadband connections. Scholars have suggested that geographic proximity might increase the "the availability of pools of specialized workers and the likelihood of knowledge spillovers from social and professional linkages among employees of competing firms facing similar problems."[39]

While the success of Indian Americans in Silicon Valley has long been touted, the prejudice they faced has been less well explored. Indeed, the journey of Indian Americans in corporate America is reminiscent in some ways of the journey of Indian corporations in global commerce. Consider the story of Kanwal Rekhi, whom *Fortune* names the "godfather of Silicon Valley's Indian mafia." Rekhi earned his fortune when he sold his company, Excelan, to Novell in 1989 for $210 million. But when he had founded Excelan with two other Indian Americans, the entrepreneurs had found it difficult to raise capital. According to *Fortune*, "Indians were widely regarded as great techies but inadequate managers. So when three Indians who lacked a white guy went to raise money from VCs, they faced lots of slammed doors."[40] Even if a particular venture capitalist does not himself (and it is almost always *him*self) share such views, the capitalist might worry about prejudices in the business world more generally. Accordingly, venture capitalists investing in "an Indian-founded company have brought in a non-Indian CEO, relegating the founder to a technical role."[41] Indian-Americans were seen as appropriate for the back office but not the front office, and certainly not the corner office.

Faced with such barriers, Indian Americans set up their own formalized network to support one another—The Indus Entrepreneurs, or TiE. Through TiE, Indian Americans with entrepreneurial dreams could meet people like Rekhi whom they could consider their "guru."[42] They also relied on alumni networks associated with the Indian Institutes of Technology.

Boston Brahmins and Bangalore Doctors

India has not, however, been uniformly successful in its outsourcing projects. An example from the lucrative field of medical outsourcing shows that even Bangalore can be rebuffed, based on both legal and consumer concerns.

In hospitals around the world, yesterday's photographic film is giving way to today's digital imaging.[43] Digitization of medical images facilitates review, reproduction, archiving, and error-checking while also enabling computer enhancement and speeding retrieval.[44] Digitization also permits radiology, once confined to review of films slapped atop lit boards in medical offices, to be conducted from a computer in the home or across the world—"anywhere with broadband access."[45] Crucial to this possibility is the standardization of communications and semantic protocols, which enable digital images produced on one system to be accurately stored, communicated, and interpreted across different hardware platforms.[46] Indeed, manufacturers, professional societies, and other interested parties have developed the Digital Imaging and Communications in Medicine (DICOM) standard for radiological data. One radiologist, supplying his services to the United States from Bangalore, reports: "'You can't reach over and slap [the radiologist] on the back, but every other aspect of the interaction is preserved.'"[47]

Hospitals now regularly outsource their nightshift radiology across the world "to be read by doctors in the light of day."[48] New firms have sprung up, responding to a "shortage of U.S. radiologists and an exploding demand for more sophisticated scans to diagnose scores of ailments."[49] One firm established in Idaho in 2001, NightHawk Radiology Holdings, listed its stock on Nasdaq in 2006 before being purchased by Virtual Radiologic in 2010 for approximately $170 million. NightHawk Radiology sent images from US hospitals to be read by physicians often located in Sydney, Australia. Another leading provider, Teleradiology Solutions, transmits images from US hospitals to be read by physicians principally in Bangalore.

But can a patient trust a doctor who lives in a different hemisphere? "Will a radiologist on another continent be as easily held liable?"[50] Can private medical records be protected as they travel around the world? How can the patient be assured that the foreign radiologist is adequately trained? Providers of such services have sought to allay these concerns. They hire only radiologists certified by the American Board of Radiology and licensed to practice in the United States.[51]

It was precisely the absence of such qualifications that foiled the most technologically sophisticated version of cross-border teleradiology, a service offered by Wipro. Wipro brought its considerable computing talents to the project, going far beyond the simple transmission of images and the return transmission of a report entailed by most nightshift services. The Wipro service, tested in collaboration with Massachusetts General Hospital, permitted Wipro's Bangalore radiologists not just to access the images of the patient taken that day or night[52] but the ability to "download prior studies, reports, and patient history with as much ease as if they were working in an

[Massachusetts General Hospital] reading room in Boston."[53] A radiologist in Bangalore sat at a 3-D workstation reading images of a patient at Massachusetts General Hospital and reviewed the patient's records before offering a diagnosis.[54]

The connections between India and the United States were coordinated by an Indian American radiology professor then at Harvard Medical School, Dr. Sanjay Saini. Doctor Saini emigrated from India to the United States when he was in high school. In connecting Boston to Bangalore, diasporic connections were clearly in play.

However, despite the technological feasibility of the enterprise, the project stumbled over three hurdles. First, Wipro failed to attract United States–licensed radiologists to Bangalore, and thus its radiologists were not licensed to read patient images. Wipro accordingly restricted its experiment to collaboration between Indian and US radiologists. The Indian radiologists "provide interpretations to Wipro-employed licensed radiologists in the United States, who in turn consult with the client radiologist."[55] The addition of a second radiologist creates a potential redundancy but also carries the benefit of potentially allowing for a second opinion and, possibly, a constructive dialogue between radiologists.

Second, Congress has restricted Medicare reimbursements to US-based physicians.[56] The regulations written under the statute go so far as to specifically bar subcontracting radiological services to India: "Payment may not be made for a medical service (or a portion of it) that was subcontracted to another provider or supplier located outside of the United States. For example, if a radiologist who practices in India analyzes imaging tests that were performed on a beneficiary in the United States, Medicare would not pay the radiologist or the U.S. facility that performed the imaging test for any of the services that were performed by the radiologist in India."[57] While the United States has committed under GATS to national treatment for "hospital and other health care facilities" with respect to consumption abroad (what is called "mode 2" under GATS), it has not committed to national treatment for crossborder health services ("mode 1" under GATS). (I describe the distinction between GATS modes in chapter 6.) The United States indicated that mode 1 offerings for "hospitals and other health care facilities" are "unbound due to lack of technical feasibility," presumably because the idea of a hospital implies a physical building. In any case, GATS exempts government procurement of services from the MFN, market access, and national treatment obligations. This means that the United States is free (at least under GATS) to discriminate against foreign health services providers operating over the Internet. Because of restrictions on foreign reimbursement, radiology outsourcing companies serving the United States from abroad thus typically rely on US-based radiologists to submit the claim and take responsibility for the reading, even if a radiologist based abroad provides an initial reading.

A third hurdle proved even more difficult to surmount. When the *New York Times* front page revealed the Indian radiologists assisting in reading patient images at Massachusetts General, there was a public outcry, and Wipro retreated.[58] Even while Americans have long become accustomed to Indian American doctors, who make up more than 10 percent of American physicians, there was concern when a significant medical service might be performed in India itself.

Ensuring that only US-licensed radiologists review the images would not resolve concerns about fraud, privacy, and the enforceability of agreements as private medical information crosses national borders. I return to these issues in chapters 6 and 7.

Even if part of the American public may currently be reluctant to have images read by doctors in Bangalore, other jurisdictions appear more receptive because outsourcing might improve the quality of radiological services available and/or reduce the costs of such services. Consider two examples. The Dutch company Radiologie-Uitslag.nl uses Indian and other radiologists to provide a second opinion to patients, in addition to the regular reading of the image. It allows individuals to receive the results of an MRI or X-ray in one day for 125 euros or in just six hours for 160 euros. The Singapore Ministry of Health has reviewed and accredited Bangalore-based Teleradiology Solutions to provide services to hospitals and diagnostic centers in Singapore. A national accreditation approach may offer a middle ground between rejecting crossborder teleradiology altogether and permitting hospitals to outsource at will.

Even though cross-border radiology has met roadblocks, a different type of cross-border trade in medical services is flourishing. Many individuals, and even corporations, are engaging in "medical tourism." The rich of the developing world have long come to the United States seeking medical care, but now Americans find that they can receive medical procedures abroad for a fraction of the price at home.

Document Review in New Delhi

If it is complicated getting a foreign doctor on the other end of your X-ray machine or your iPhone in the United States, it may be a bit easier getting a foreign lawyer. While the outsourcing of medical services via the Internet has yet to flourish, the outsourcing of *legal* services via the Internet seems to be growing at Internet speed. David Wilkins, director of Harvard Law School's program on the legal profession, characterizes the shift as a "historical movement."[59] Foreign lawyers, especially in India, are assisting American lawyers in legal tasks such as document review, legal research and writing, contracts management, and obtaining and enforcing patents and other intellectual property rights. Corporations especially may be driving legal process outsourcing (LPO), largely in search of cost savings.[60]

The practice of law is heavily regulated across the world and is generally restricted to those licensed by the local jurisdiction. Thus, outsourcing firms are careful to avoid performing work that might constitute the practice of law in a jurisdiction in which their lawyers are not duly licensed. Ethical obligations of the legal profession, too, might have posed an insurmountable hurdle to outsourcing of legal work. The model code of professional conduct used throughout the United States requires law firms to ensure that all lawyers conform to the rules of professional conduct and that all nonlawyer associates conduct themselves in ways compatible with professional conduct. Since an American Bar Association opinion interpreting the ethical obligations in 2008, local and state bar associations have generally agreed that outsourcing can be conducted in a manner consistent with professional rules, provided that the outsourcing lawyer remains ultimately responsible for the work and supervises it adequately.[61]

The San Diego County bar association considered a case in which a local firm employed an Indian firm to perform legal research, develop case strategy, prepare deposition outlines and draft correspondence, pleadings, and motions in a case. The ethics committee of the bar association concluded that "as long as the outsourcing lawyer is competent to evaluate the work performed by the outsourced contractor, retains control over the matter, exercises independent professional judgment, and retains ultimate responsibility for the work, the assistance contracted for does not constitute the unauthorized practice of law, whether the work is outsourced out-of-state or out-of-the-country."[62] The committee also concluded that because of the extent of the outsourcing of the legal representation in this case, the law firm had a duty to inform the client of the outsourcing relationship.[63]

The success of legal process outsourcing (LPO) depends on a careful assessment of the professional regulations in multiple jurisdictions. One leading firm in the industry, the Clutch Group, describes itself as providing "fact development and process management services" and not "legal advice."[64] Given the constraints on who can practice law, the opinions of the American bar associations have helped provide some assurance for firms in this area. Such a legal foundation for the trade may have helped bring the major US-based data provider Thomson Reuters into the industry through its purchase of the leading LPO provider Pangea3 in 2011.

Through legal services, one can begin to imagine a world in which service providers really are free to provide services across the world. Even if each jurisdiction requires one to demonstrate competence in its law and to be bound by its ethical rules, many lawyers around the world will be able to satisfy these conditions. To offer services in the United States, some could take the step of attending law schools accredited by the American Bar Association and then sit for the bar in the state or states whose law they wish to practice. This would most likely involve travel to the United States because thus far the ABA has approved only law schools in the United States, though the Peking University School of Law in Shenzhen, China, has applied for ABA accreditation. If these lawyers return home, either by choice or by lack of a visa to remain in the United States, they will still be able to offer legal services wherever they are members of the bar. Constraints on the practice of law generally do not require one to be physically present in the relevant jurisdiction, at least as long as the remote lawyer can gain the information he or she needs for competent representation. The most significant challenge for such lawyers may not be the law but rather attracting sufficient clients willing to trust foreign lawyers with local bar admissions. Perhaps the promise of lower fees or contingency fee arrangements might entice clients, but this suggests the increased competition faced by lawyers resident in the United States arising from net-work. Indeed, the United States has been at the forefront of seeking to open up free trade in legal services around the world, confident that American law firms are best prepared to meet global competition and take advantage of global advantage. As an American-educated lawyer who once worked in Hong Kong doing deals involving China and in New York conducting deals involving Latin America, I have experienced firsthand the high quality of American firms.

Keeping Filipinos Home and on the Phone

The Philippines has long sent its young men and women abroad for economic opportunities, generating $23 billion in remittances home in 2010.[65] Now it has emerged as a leading outsourcing provider, its young men and women prized for their "American style" English. In 2010, it became the leading call center destination in the world. The BPO industry now accounts for 4 to 5 percent of GDP, generating half the amount sent home by the estimated nine million overseas Filipinos. The BPO industry "keeps Filipino families together," observes Martin Crisostomo of the Business Processing Association of the Philippines.[66]

In developing this industry, the Southeast Asian country was "helped by an affinity for the language, culture and work ethics of the United States, its former colonial master."[67] Many of the call center workers are employed by captive subsidiaries of Western enterprises or local subsidiaries of global outsourcing enterprises like IBM, Accenture, Convergys, Infosys, and Tech Mahindra. For example, Aegis Global, an outsourcing firm based in Mumbai, employs nearly thirteen thousand Filipinos.[68]

Happy hour in Eastwood City, outside Manila, begins at 6:00 a.m. for call center workers seeking a drink after their shift.

Economic Development and the Electronic Silk Road

The nations of the ancient Silk Road as well as nations newer to the world stage are racing to supply trade through the new thoroughfares in cyberspace. In an article colorfully titled "Soccer, Samba and Outsourcing?" the *Wall Street Journal* announced that "Brazil appears poised to be Latin America's big winner in the global outsourcing boom."[69] Cities "from Buffalo to Belfast, from Beijing to Buenos Aires" vie to be outsourcing hotspots. Why are governments across the world so keen on becoming the next Bangalore?

The development of the outsourcing services industry has proved attractive for India. Indian net-work providers assist India's economic development in a number of ways. Let me identify five: (1) aiding employment and economic growth; (2) spurring education; (3) improving domestic processes; (4) promoting an entrepreneurial spirit and increasing opportunity; and (5) lifting Indian self-confidence.

Aiding Employment and Growth. Outsourcing is labor intensive, therefore employing many workers, most of whom are professionals. The Indian trade body Nasscom estimates that the domestic IT-BPO industry employs 2.8 million people. Nasscom further estimates revenues for Indian IT and BPO services to exceed $87 billion in fiscal year 2012, with the IT software and services sector (excluding hardware) accounting for $87 billion. Nasscom believes that this industry constitutes some 7.5 percent of the nation's GDP. Nasscom estimates Indian IT-BPO exports to reach $69 billion in fiscal year

2012, a quarter of India's total exports.[70] (Of course, a trade association's estimates of that industry's contribution to the national economy are by their nature self-interested.) Three of India's twelve largest publicly traded corporations (by market value) are TCS, Infosys, and Wipro, each a net-work enterprise.[71] Each of the big three employs more than 100,000 people, the bulk of them in India.[72]

The leaders of each of these three powerhouses all see their role as promoters of Indian economic and social development. Under Ratan Tata, Narayana Murthy, and Azim Premji, respectively of TCS, Infosys, and Wipro—these companies and their leaders contributed significantly to charitable enterprises. Philanthropic trusts established by the Tatas together own some two-thirds of the conglomerate.[73] Through the Infosys Foundation, Infosys contributes to healthcare, education, and rural development. Narayana Murthy titled his autobiography not with a statement about himself but rather with a noble ambition, *A Better India, a Better World.* Murthy cites three authors as his inspiration—India's Mahatma Gandhi, Germany's Max Weber, and, most surprising, Africa's Frantz Fanon. Citing Gandhi's dream of "wiping the tears from the eyes of every poor child," Murthy's declares his own "experiment"—"My experiment in using entrepreneurship as an instrument to create jobs and address the problem of poverty in India."[74] Azim Premji, who retains a substantial shareholding in Wipro, has established a foundation to aid primary education and has announced plans to give away the bulk of his wealth to charity.[75]

Spurring Education. The possibility of employment in the network sector leads individuals to make a personal investment in themselves—what economists call "human capital." They invest in the skills that allow them to enter these attractive service professions. Education in order to develop skills for international trade has long roots. The seventh-century Chinese Buddhist pilgrim

Xuanzang observed that "little boys in Samarkand were taught to read and write at the age of five, even if it was in the service of their commercial skills."[76] But unlike the trading depot of Samarkand, where girls might not be expected to become merchants, today both boys and girls can grow up to work in the net-work trade. Women represent some 30 percent of Indian IT-BPO employees.[77] However, women are poorly represented in the top management at leading Indian IT companies, as a glance at the photos of the officers and directors of these companies will show. TCS has but one woman among its twelve officers and directors; Infosys, two of twenty-nine; and Wipro, two of thirty-eight. American IT powerhouses are not much better—Apple counts but one woman of its eighteen top officers and directors. Google has three women among its thirteen directors and top officers; Microsoft has three women of seventeen; Facebook has only one of nine.

Even while it boasts many world-class research universities, especially in the sciences and in management, India lags in primary education. India ranks 107th among the countries examined in UNESCO's Education for All Development Index, precariously close to Niger's bottom ranking of 127.[78] By failing to provide sufficient education to boys and girls, India handicaps itself in its desire to be the back office to the world.

Improving Local Productivity. As in many developing countries, productivity in India is generally low. Productivity can be increased by better tools, techniques and education. The skills that outsourcing firms developed to supply the world can be increasingly applied within India itself. These enterprises have recognized that India, too, needs their services and, in a helpful bit of diversification, offers a rapidly growing market. Historically a promoter of the civil service, the Indian government for its part has been increasingly willing to outsource functions, for example, hiring an American firm run by a Czech immigrant to process visa applications of Americans traveling to India.[79]

Indian outsourcing enterprises have developed an obsession with performance metrics and process reviews. They are eager to demonstrate to potential clients that they meet international standards such as those set by ISO, the international standards-setting body. Many Indian firms have adopted the Six Sigma strategy for quality improvement, a program developed by Motorola and then embraced by General Electric's Jack Welch.[80] Bringing process review and optimization techniques such as Six Sigma to domestic industries previously protected from foreign competition promises to improve productivity. Moreover, Indian enterprises, which have often relied more on labor than technology, can benefit from the IT services offered by these enterprises.

Instilling Entrepreneurship and Increasing Opportunity. In the latter half of the twentieth century, commentators would condescendingly explain India's unremarkable economic growth rate of less than 4 percent annually as the "Hindu rate of growth."[81] India's millennia-old culture, with its entrenched hierarchies, could never grow at the pace of its neighboring tiger economies. Surprising many, however, economic liberalization beginning in 1991 doubled the rate of growth. The socialist economy was replaced by a more capitalist one. Where bright Indian students once hoped to join the vaunted Indian civil service, they now dream of joining a business or even creating one. Computer engineer Ashwin Hegde of Infosys observes this of his compatriots in Bangalore: "The bug is biting in Bangalore. . . . That's what everybody is thinking about all the time, starting your own company."[82] The emergence of a start-up culture demonstrated that popular accounts of Indian passivity and capitulation to karma were overblown. Because many kinds of IT-enabled services require less start-up capital than manufacturing, the opportunity to become a global trader has led many to build new businesses using India as a launching pad to the world.

It has also kept many Indians at home. There was a time when the majority of the graduates of India's prestigious Indian Institutes of Technology left for foreign shores in search of opportunity.[83] India's brightest and most entrepreneurial often left for better opportunities elsewhere. Few would return. Both Vinod Khosla, cofounder of Sun Microsystems, and Sabeer Bhatia, who founded the web-based email service Hotmail, were immigrants from India. Because of information technology, the brain drain of the past is giving way to opportunity in India. The Internet-speed success of the Indian services companies has demonstrated to Indians "that you can create substantial wealth in one generation," says Nandan Nilekani, managing director of Infosys. "For the first time, there is an option for Indian youngsters which does not mean going to the U.S."[84]

"Export Quality." Indian companies, like many companies in the developing world, have long labeled their higher-quality products "export quality," a term most American consumers are unfamiliar with. It denotes a product that meets world standards, and by implication, not the lesser standards prevailing at home. "Export quality" marked the few Indian products that would be good enough for Americans. With few exceptions (such as textiles), Indians were unaccustomed to matching American production quality.

The rise of net-work has led Indians to rethink their place in the world order. Since independence, India had protected local producers with tariffs designed to nurture infant industries. Its corporations accordingly lacked global ambitions, content to serve a huge domestic market. The panic in the West stemming from Indian competition in services shattered myths of Indian inferiority, long internalized within India. Indians' confidence in their own capacity to supply world-class services grew in the face of the realization that others now feared them. In the wake of the financial crisis precipitated by an inadequate US legal regime, even the American legal model's claim for superiority was battered.

Coupled with the rise of the Indian multinational is the rise of the Indian services professional. The idea that such an individual could compete globally for work with Americans and Europeans might have seem far-fetched just two decades back. Today, there may be few, if any, Fortune 500 companies that do not routinely outsource parts of their operations to Indians.

4

PIRATES OF CYBERSPACE

Can you stop the Internet? Is it possible to banish information from cyberspace? Or at least your part of cyberspace?

What if the information is on a computer on the other side of the earth but connected to the World Wide Web? The rise of the World Wide Web has made this a persistent problem for all the countries of the world. Indeed, we have already encountered one noted effort to ban cyberinformation—French efforts to stop Yahoo! from auctioning Nazi materials through its services. In that case, we saw a company voluntarily withdrawing most Nazi materials from its sites worldwide.

But what of companies that offer services from offshore locations precisely because such services are banned in the jurisdictions where consumers want them? These companies are more akin to pirates than to traditional Silk Road traders. History's safe harbors were not, as we might imagine, harbors safe *from* pirates but rather harbors safe *for* pirates. Such ports welcomed brigands, happy to sell them provisions, repair their ships, and gain their patronage. Can web entrepreneurs now find new safe harbors for their offerings, insulating them from the reach of the authorities of strict jurisdictions, yet still offering their service across the world?

The meme that information wants to be free has a potential corollary: the pirates of cyberspace cannot be controlled. Legal scholars David Johnson and David Post famously argued more than a decade ago that "efforts to control the flow of electronic information across physical borders—to map local regulation and physical boundaries onto Cyberspace—are likely to prove futile."[1] In this chapter we see that governments have sought to control information coming into their country with occasional success. Information may want to be free, but it can sometimes be chained.

Thus far in this book, we have met some of the world's best-respected net-work companies, from Apple to Wipro. In chapter 2, we met Silicon Valley enterprises, which leverage efficiencies of mass production, network effects, and first-mover advantage to become global traders. In chapter 3, we encountered Bangalore enterprises, which leverage efficiencies of mass production and labor arbitrage to become leading traders on the Electronic Silk Road. In this chapter we'll consider net-work enterprises that other countries deplore, whether fairly or unfairly. Here we meet companies from the Caribbean to Russia that leverage local regulatory laxity to become global traders.

I use the term *pirate* without any wish to tar all such enterprises as morally reprehensible. There is strong reason to think that many of these enterprises provide a socially useful function. Even Silicon

Valley enterprises might be seen as pirates in some cases, providing outlawed information to the people of repressive regimes. YouTube, Facebook, and Twitter transmitted information that the Hosni Mubarak dictatorship would have denied to the Egyptian people. Indeed, as we will see, in its desperation, Egypt's government turned off the Internet for the entire country.

In this chapter I describe five enterprises that have engaged in a kind of regulatory arbitrage: (1) the gambling enterprises of the tiny Caribbean island nation of Antigua and Barbuda, which hopes to become the Las Vegas of cyberspace; (2) Kazaa, a peer-to-peer file trading service; (3) The Pirate Bay, another peer-to-peer file trading service; (4) Russia's AllofMP3.com, which offered entire record albums for the price of one iTune; and (5) WikiLeaks, a site that seeks to reveal the world's deepest, darkest secrets. Each of these services asserts its legitimacy under the laws of its home country, but each is denounced as a pirate by authorities elsewhere. Like the pirates of yesteryear, these companies fly flags of convenience, claiming jurisdictional advantage and legal immunity by their choice of their home base.

Ultimately, however, their stories reveal that such enterprises are not entirely immune to legal process, at least where those they antagonize have the resources and perseverance to hound them, like Ahab, across the seas.

Gambling in Antigua

There was a time when American adventurers booked passage to Havana to place a bet. Restrictive laws across most of the United States necessitated travel to more permissive jurisdictions for those who wished to gamble. Today the Internet permits Americans to gamble on "foreign" card tables without leaving home. Recognizing this possibility, Antigua set out a decade ago to "become the Las Vegas and Atlantic City of online gambling."[2] It licensed online casinos and sports booking, charging $100,000 and $75,000, respectively, for each license.[3] Quickly this island of seven working stoplights became the principal haven for Internet enterprises offering gambling to Americans.[4]

Other jurisdictions followed suit. Spurred by an American entrepreneur, a Mohawk Indian community in Quebec set up computer servers on the banks of the Saint Lawrence River—near the American market and helpfully atop a "major fibre optic corridor."[5] Its principal client was the online gambling provider Party Gaming, established by an American lawyer and an Indian expatriate programmer, incorporated in the British overseas territory of Gibraltar, with a workforce in Hyderabad.[6] PartyGaming grew into a multinational corporation listed on the London Stock Exchange. At its height, it was worth more than $10 billion.[7] In 2005, almost 90 percent of PartyGaming's customers were in the United States, a country whose authorities believed that such gambling was illegal.

These money-making paradises would not remain undisturbed for long. American prosecutors, relying on a law enacted in 1961 to dismantle gambling operations run by organized crime, issued arrest warrants for online gambling operators. Attorney General Janet Reno warned, "You can't go offshore and hide. You can't go online and hide."[8] Confident that "no judge is going to let [an arrest warrant against him] stand" because he ran his business from Antigua, where online gambling was legal, online gambling proprietor Jay Cohen returned to the mainland to defend himself.[9] Cohen would spend a year and a half in prison, perhaps ruing his bad bet.[10] Fearing that a similar fate would befall her son should he return to the United States, the mother of Cohen's business partner did not tell her son of his father's death.[11] Cohen's lawyer saw the conviction as an affront to Antiguan sovereignty: "What they're doing is they're telling Antigua, which is a sovereign nation, 'You can't do this.'"[12] For its part, PartyGaming would lose billions of dollars in value when the United States enacted the Unlawful Internet Gambling Enforcement Act (UIGEA) in 2006. In 2011, it merged into another gambling enterprise, Bwin, based in Gibraltar.

Given the US authorities' commitment to enforcement, coming to the United States, even simply to change planes for another international destination, became a dangerous activity for overseas gambling executives. British gambling CEO David Carruthers might have regretted his 2006 layover in Dallas–Fort Worth International Airport, where he was arrested on his way from Britain to Costa Rica, where he ran an Internet gambling business. Like PartyGaming, Carruthers's firm was listed on the London Stock Exchange. Two months later, the chairman of London-based Sportingbet PLC was taken into custody when he arrived at JFK International Airport for a visit to the United States. As recently as 2012, the CEO of Irish gaming company Full Tilt Poker was arrested flying into JFK, charged not only with illegal gambling but also with running a Ponzi scheme in which he promised customers that their deposited funds were secure when they were not.

In passing the UIGEA, Congress recognized the limits of relying on gambling scofflaws (viewed from the American perspective) to retain legally unsophisticated travel agents. So Congress tried a different tactic: to go after the money flow to these foreign companies. The UIGEA required payment systems to identify and block funding of gambling transactions. Under pressure from New York attorney general Eliot Spitzer, Paypal had already desisted from serving Internet gambling customers in 2002. In response to the UIGEA, Visa, MasterCard, Discover, and American Express also identified and blocked Internet gambling payments.

Faced with these American threats to its thriving new industry, Antigua responded like any country that found its exports hampered by legal restrictions elsewhere: it filed a claim against the United States before the World Trade Organization. Antigua's claim was novel in at least two dimensions. It was the first in history brought squarely under the General Agreement on Trade in Services. Antigua's dispute was also the first to challenge international barriers to trade via the Internet. Antigua argued that the requirement of physical establishment in certain specified zones in the United States ran afoul of the national treatment obligation by disadvantaging foreign providers. Antigua further argued that the United States violated its commitment to provide market access to trade in "other recreational services." I discuss this dispute more fully in chapter 6, but for the moment it is sufficient to note that the WTO largely ruled in favor of the United States, accepting the American argument that online gambling might promote underage and problem gambling, as well as abet fraud and money laundering.

There was one hiccup in the American victory. The United States had failed to explain why it banned online gambling but yet permitted online horse racing gambling provided by US enterprises. This was inconsistent, at least on its face, with the American argument that online services were especially prone to undesirable activity. Despite the obvious inconsistency, the United States refused to budge, maintaining its horse-racing exception in the face of the WTO ruling. Antigua thus applied to the WTO to apply trade sanctions on the United States. But the United States is unlikely to worry about higher tariffs on exports to Antigua, the traditional trade remedy available under the WTO system. The loss of exports to Antigua would be but a pinprick to a giant. Antigua sought a slightly more painful remedy—the ability to violate American intellectual property rights in an amount roughly equal to the losses from the American trade law violation.

The WTO granted Antigua the right to retaliate by suspending Antigua's Agreement on Trade Related Aspects of Intellectual Property Rights (TRIPs) obligation to respect US intellectual property rights in an amount corresponding to the estimated lost revenues from online horse racing.[13] Antigua is thus officially free to copy Hollywood movies and the latest music—at least up to $21 million in value each year. Antigua is thus now truly a pirate of the Caribbean.

Next Stop, Kazaakhstan?

Kazaa, a peer-to-peer file trading system, was founded in the Netherlands by a Swede and a Dane but programmed from Estonia and eventually run from Australia and incorporated in the South Pacific island nation of Vanuatu.[14] Launched in 2001 by the Dutch company Consumer Empowerment, Kazaa soon faced a copyright infringement suit from the Dutch music publishing body Buma/Stemra. After an adverse November 2001 trial court ruling, Consumer Empowerment passed the hot potato along, selling Kazaa to newly incorporated Sharman Networks, headquartered in Australia and incorporated in Vanuatu. Kazaa's founders might have made a hasty decision. In 2002, a Dutch appeals court reversed the earlier ruling, holding that Kazaa provided a number of worthy uses and could not be held responsible for the members who used the service for copyright infringement.[15] The Dutch supreme court affirmed the appellate ruling the following year.[16] But the rulings came too late; the software's new owner, Sharman Networks, faced suits in both Australia and the United States. Even Kazaa's location on the other side of the world did not guarantee immunity from process in the United States. A federal district court in California ruled that it had personal jurisdiction over Sharman on either one of two separate grounds: (1) the large number of California users of its service, and (2) the fact that Sharman "is and has been well aware of the charge that its users are infringing copyrights, and reasonably should be aware that many, if not most, music and video copyrights are owned by California-based companies."[17] In 2006, Sharman reached a global settlement with the plaintiffs, agreeing to pay music studios $100 million and another undisclosed sum to movie studios.[18] It also promised to restructure its service to bar most copyright-infringing works.

Why did Sharman settle? Couldn't it have simply retreated to yet another jurisdiction? We can offer a conjecture: both the American and Australian lawsuits threatened Sharman's ability to raise revenues through advertising and other services. If it hoped to avoid a never-ending cat-and-mouse game that would undermine its ability to make money, Sharman needed to eliminate the legal threat hanging over it.

Of course, the same will not be true of all such services. So-called darknets, for example, promise to allow individuals to share information but mask the identity of all the parties involved. Such systems allow sharing among a small group of users who gain trust by sharing large quantities of high-quality, often illegal material.[19] Some have suggested that darknets make copyright law or censorship futile. But darknets require a significant degree of sophistication from users, thus reducing their potential market. To find the illicit online drug market Silk Road, for example, one needs to first install and configure the anonymizer Tor on one's computer.[20] Furthermore, while Silk Road has established Amazonlike reputation systems, suspicions may still hamper transactions in such a system. One does not know whether the anonymous person on the other end is a patient police officer pretending to be a longtime outlaw. Still, the prospect of open-source, not-for-profit peer-to-peer systems suggests that unauthorized distribution channels such as darknets will long remain a thorn in the side of law enforcement.

Kazaa's story has a happy ending, at least for its founders. Janus Friis and Niklas Zennström followed the Kazaa model to create the video and voice-over Internet Protocol service Skype, incorporating their London-operated company in Luxembourg and relying on Estonians for programming. In 2005, they sold Skype to eBay for $2.6 billion.[21]

From Russia with Love: An Entire Album for $0.99

Imagine that you are an executive of a Hollywood music studio. Consider your reaction to a Russian website that allows individuals around the world to download every song your studio owns for pennies on the dollar, all the while relying on Russian law to claim that it was entirely legal. This was in fact the reality for a number of years: "Sold by the megabyte instead of by the song, an album of 10 songs or so on AllofMP3 can cost the equivalent of less than $1, compared with 99 cents per song on iTunes."[22] For users, it seemed too good to be true: "From a consumer standpoint, AllofMP3.com was pretty close to the perfect music service—dirt cheap, easy to use. . . . Oh, and no DRM [digital rights management]."[23] The fact that AllofMP3 did not bother to license its content from your studio or any studio also meant that it could offer up a music catalog that covered music unavailable on licensed services; for example, it offered the entire Beatles catalog long before any part of that catalog appeared on iTunes. The end result: a bigger catalog than iTunes, for a fraction of the cost.

What made AllofMP3 especially troublesome for record companies was the possibility that it was legal under Russian law. According to its website: "The availability over the Internet of the ALLOFMP3.com materials is authorized by the license # LS–3M–05–03 of the Russian Multimedia and Internet Society (ROMS) and license # 006/3M–05 of the Rightholders Federation for Collective Copyright Management of Works Used Interactively (FAIR)."[24] This was not just the usual bluster of a shady business. The Russian license from the Russian collecting society arguably permits the online sale of music upon the payment of a 15 percent royalty to the Russian collecting society (the Russian Multimedia and Internet Society, known as ROMS), without requiring individual negotiation with copyright holders.[25] ROMS licensed the site and even backed it up, describing it as "quite legitimate."[26] ROMS collected royalty payments on behalf of record companies and artists, but it "had few takers" for the royalties obtained for AllofMP3 downloads.[27]

By 2006, the website, which claimed five million subscribers, had become one of the thousand most popular websites in the world.[28] AllofMP3 eschewed any responsibility "for the actions of foreign users" and advised them to consult local counsel while at the same time suggesting that downloading was in fact legal in the United States.[29] The website's backers themselves were not confident of the legality of the offering, refusing to publicize any physical address. The *New York Times* tracked down a responsible party to a Moscow address only by examining the site's domain name registration.[30]

Even a Moscow address may not prove an insurmountable obstacle for enforcement efforts within the United States. When the recording industry filed a copyright infringement suit against the site in 2006 in New York federal court, it sought statutory damages in the amount of $150,000 for each instance of copyright infringement, totaling $1.65 trillion (an amount that exceeded Russia's 2005 GDP).[31] It also sought the company's domain name. While the recording industry might have found it difficult to collect the monetary award, they might have had better luck against the company's ".com" domain name. This is because the company that operates the ".com" domain name registry, Verisign, is headquartered in Virginia. Verisign is likely to listen to a federal court order to remove or transfer a domain name.

The recording industry pursued yet another approach: blocking by the Internet service provider on the user side of the download. A Copenhagen court ordered Danish Internet service provider Tele2 to block access to the site on the theory that Tele2 would be liable for infringement if its customers used AllofMP3 to download music.[32]

The international music industry asked Visa and MasterCard to refuse to process payments to the site. When these companies complied, AllofMP3's owners sued the Russian financial agents for Visa. In 2007, a Moscow arbitral tribunal ruled that Visa could not refuse to process transactions for AllofMP3's successor site, AllTunes.com, because that site was legal.[33]

If the music studios could not stop the money, they could still put pressure on the site in other ways. In 2007, Russia happened to be negotiating entry into the World Trade Organization. WTO entry would mean that its exporters would face fewer tariffs and other trade barriers, but the United States could effectively block entry. US Trade Representative Susan Schwab explicitly linked WTO entry with protecting intellectual property rights: "I have a hard time imagining Russia becoming a member of the WTO and having a Web site like that up and running that is so clearly a violation of everyone's intellectual property rights."[34] Schwab's chief spokeswoman, Neena Moorjani, had even sharper words: "AllofMP3.com is the world's largest server-based pirate website," she declared.[35] Russian prosecutors charged Denis Kvasov, a former owner of AllofMP3, with copyright infringement. Kvasov faced a jail term of up to three years and a penalty of $500,000, payable to American music companies EMI, Warner, and Universal.[36] In 2007, however, a Moscow court acquitted Kvasov, ruling that AllofMP3 acted within Russian law.

Nonetheless, in July 2007, AllofMP3 was shuttered. Using a court order, Russian authorities severed the connection between the company, Media Services, and its Internet service provider, Master Host.[37] Tellingly, the action was reported to the media by the United States trade representative. By 2008, the recording industry had dropped its lawsuit, declaring the site defunct. Russia gained admission to the WTO in 2012.

Viking Pirates of the Twenty-First Century

The Pirate Bay is so accustomed to complaints from copyright holders that its home page includes a link titled "Legal Threats." The site's proprietors confidently assert that their actions are legal under Swedish law and that foreign laws do not apply to their Stockholm-based service, posting retorts on their website. When Hollywood studio DreamWorks complained that the site facilitated copyright infringement of its movie *Shrek 2*, The Pirate Bay's Gottfrid Svartholm responded with derision:

> As you may or may not be aware, Sweden is not a state in the United States of America. Sweden is a country in northern Europe. Unless you figured it out by now, US law does not apply here. For your information, no Swedish law is being violated.

> . . . It is the opinion of us and our lawyers that you are . . . morons.

Svartholm explains that The Pirate Bay supports freedom and that its services help disseminate important material that many people wish to censor or that traditional mass media do not show. Copyright holders argue that The Pirate Bay willfully abets copyright infringement. The site earns money from advertising. A visit to the site from a university computer in New Haven, Connecticut, in 2008 resulted in an advertisement for dates in that city.

In 2006, Swedish authorities raided the site's offices, seizing its servers. Despite the turmoil, The Pirate Bay restored service just three days later, unveiling a new logo (see fig. 1). The police eventually returned the servers, one of which the website donated to a Swedish museum. In 2009, the site's founders were convicted of violating Swedish copyright law and sentenced to terms of up to one year. In 2012, the site switched from a ".org" address to a Swedish ".se" address in order to lessen the risk of the seizure of the domain name by US authorities.

Figure 1. The Pirate Bay's defiant logo upon restoring service after a police seizure. Courtesy of The Pirate Bay.

Some copyright holders seem also to have employed "self-help" measures outside the law to attack The Pirate Bay. Such measures include seeding the site with corrupt files and launching denial-of-service attacks that make it difficult for users to access the site. There is risk in such an approach. Both denial-of-service attacks and uploading a site with corrupt files would likely run afoul of many national laws.

Copyright holders across the world have acted against the site through administrative and judicial processes in their home jurisdictions. They have targeted local Internet service providers, obtaining orders enjoining the ISPs from providing users with access to the site. According to Wikipedia, authorities in the following countries have, at times, ordered local ISPs to deny access to the site: Belgium, Denmark, Finland, Germany, India, Ireland, Italy, Malaysia, the Netherlands, the People's Republic of China, Sweden, and the United Kingdom. The blocks, however, are imperfect; a determined web user simply needs to point the browser to a new "proxy" address established by The Pirate Bay that has not yet been blocked.[38] A helpful list of proxy servers can be found at a site titled The Hydra Bay, recalling the Greek monster that grew two new heads for every head that was cut off.

Trying to Censor an Uncensorable Site

Imagine a way for anyone around the world who is privy to state or corporate secrets to share those secrets anonymously with the world. Governments and corporations might shudder to imagine their darkest secrets revealed for the world to see. Authorities, whether public or private, have little incentive to reveal their mistakes or their unethical or illegal conduct. Silencing the people who betray such secrets has provided the motive for countless murder mysteries.

When they founded WikiLeaks in 2006, the site's promoters knew that they were engaged in an activity that many governments would seek to suppress. Accordingly, Australian Julian Assange and a stealth group of other activists established a means for anyone across the world to pass secrets to them anonymously.[39] Assange stepped out in 2008 only as a spokesperson for the group. Wikipedia now recognizes Assange as the editor-in-chief of WikiLeaks. The network lacked any formal corporate organization. On their site, the nameless activists simply declared, "We help you safely get the truth out."[40]

The founders saw themselves as offering "a universal way for the revealing of suppressed and censored injustices."[41] In a sense, WikiLeaks represents the natural evolution of newspapers in an era of globalization and digitization. Newspapers have long prided themselves on scoops—being the first to divulge information that a few people have known, often much to the chagrin of the subjects of the story. But traditional newspapers have always been subject to state suppression. The breaking of printing presses and the shuttering of newspapers have been widespread since the dawn of the press. Even the US government famously sought to suppress the release by the *New York Times* of the history of American intervention in Vietnam, which revealed among other things the deliberate bombing of Cambodia and Laos. In the famous *Pentagon Papers* case decided in 1971, the Supreme Court rejected the effort to suppress the leak as inimical to the Constitution's free speech guarantee. Of course, there is probably no country in the world that can match American speech rights. And even US courts faced with efforts to reveal information about the War on Terror have been willing to abet suppression of "state secrets." But a global digital network of largely invisible persons could perhaps avoid the retaliation that might follow a shocking disclosure.

By establishing a network across nations, a website can pass a hot potato rapidly across countries. By relying on a digital network, the site can keep newsgathering and publishing costs relatively low while reaching people across the globe both as informants and as consumers.

In its earliest years, WikiLeaks annoyed a few governments and private corporations by divulging secret information. WikiLeaks exposed documents that suggested that former Kenyan president Daniel Arap Moi had laundered $4.5 billion. It leaked a Pentagon handbook that showed that psychological techniques that many described as torture were used against prisoners in Guantanamo Bay. It disclosed internal documents of the Church of Scientology.

In 2008, when the site revealed bank account records of Cayman Islands transactions involving a Swiss private bank, the bank sued. But where would it choose to sue a nameless, global network? The Swiss bank decided on the federal court in the Northern District of California. There the Swiss institution, Bank Julius Baer & Co., sought an order requiring WikiLeaks to desist in publishing the private banking details of clients. The federal judge, worried about the privacy of bank accounts, granted the request. The most surprising aspect of his preliminary decision was to accede to the bank's demand that the WikiLeaks.org domain be shut down. But how can one shut down a nameless, faceless website? It turns out that WikiLeaks' domain name provider, Dynadot, was based in San Mateo, California—within the Northern District of California. It may have been the connection with Dynadot that the Swiss bank was after in choosing to bring the suit in California. The district court granted the bank's request, ordering Dynadot to disable WikiLeaks.org temporarily while it considered the matter. WikiLeaks immediately found mirror sites around the world from which to post information, including WikiLeaks.be (Belgium),

WikiLeaks.in (India), and The Pirate Bay. Most interestingly, when the court ordered the domain name registrar to refuse to point WikiLeaks.org to the WikiLeaks' server, the *New York Times* and other news venues published the IP address of the WikiLeaks' Swedish web server, 88.80.13.160.[42] Equally notably, the Swedish servers that host the site were run by the founders of The Pirate Bay.[43] With more briefing on the case, the federal judge reconsidered his decision and quickly rescinded his order.[44]

The attack by Julius Baer foreshadowed the far wider and more vociferous response WikiLeaks would draw in 2010 when it began disclosing material related to the Afghanistan and Iraq wars, followed by US diplomatic cables. In releasing the Afghan documents, WikiLeaks partnered with mainstream print media to edit and interpret the material. It found willing partners in some of the world's leading names in journalism: the *New York Times*, the British newspaper the *Guardian*, and the German newsmagazine *Der Spiegel*.

Although WikiLeaks is not a commercial site and thus not in that sense a global trader, the response to it shows both the power and the limits of governments against a diffuse digital network. The attacks against WikiLeaks have come from various quarters, from private companies to sovereign governments. At the same time, WikiLeaks' principals and supporters, cyberexperts that they are, have proven both resourceful and clever in seeking to evade the sanctions imposed.

WikiLeaks' domain name registrar cut off its domain name on December 2, 2010. Perhaps surprisingly, WikiLeaks had again relied on an American registrar, though a different one. The domain name management service EveryDNS cut off WikiLeaks without a court order, instead citing denial-of-service attacks on WikiLeaks, which EveryDNS said were threatening the other half a million sites it served.[45] As before, WikiLeaks' principals simply promoted an alternative domain name—WikiLeaks.ch—linked to the IP address of their computer server. The choice of a dot.ch was likely neither entirely accidental nor based on convenience: Switzerland controls the .ch domain. Perhaps WikiLeaks hoped to benefit from the famous neutrality of their hosts.

That same day, Amazon stopped providing hosting services to WikiLeaks. Amazon reported that it, too, had experienced "large-scale DDoS [distributed denial-of-service] attacks," but stated that these attacks "were successfully defended against." It also cited violations of its terms of service, suggesting that WikiLeaks did not "own or otherwise control all of the rights to the content" that it was posting on Amazon's servers.[46]

The following day, PayPal, an American payment processor owned by eBay, stopped processing donations for the Wau Holland Foundation, which had been collecting monies for WikiLeaks. PayPal asserted that processing donations ultimately for WikiLeaks violated its "Acceptable Use Policy" because it was used for "activities that encourage, promote, facilitate or instruct others to engage in illegal activity." The vice president of PayPal later stated that they stopped accepting payments after the "State Department told us these were illegal activities. It was straightforward." Later the same day, he retracted that statement, saying that PayPal's decision was in fact based on a letter from the State Department to WikiLeaks.[47]

WikiLeaks' supporters responded by targeting the corporations that had denied service to WikiLeaks. Operation Payback involved a DDoS attack on these corporations. DDos attacks are typically launched through a "botnet"—a network of online "robots" (in this case, software programs) dispersed across thousands of computers. Typically, one creates such a botnet through a virus—indeed, this is the typical reason to create a virus—so that it will give one a sleeping botnet, to be activated when needed. The innovation of the WikiLeaks activists was that they created a voluntary botnet—in which individuals voluntarily downloaded the software program that created the botnet. But how does one get thousands of people to download software that makes their computer participate in a botnet? Via Twitter and Facebook, of course. Calling themselves "Anonymous," the loosely knit activists used social media to circulate information about the distributed denial-of-service response, including how to download the software. In one video, an announcer declares, "Corrupt governments of the world, we are Anonymous."[48]

In turn, evincing the never-ending cat-and-mouse game of Internet attack and counterattack, Twitter and Facebook shut down the accounts of Anonymous. And in the inevitable response, Anonymous shifted accounts.

There is reason to worry about corporations removing content they find undesirable on their own accord. Corporations will have the tendency to remove information their management disfavors, but worse, they may well seek to remove controversial material more generally. WikiLeaks' Assange has described the American corporate actions as the "privatisation of state censorship."[49]

WikiLeaks thus represents the cutting edge both of efforts to thwart undesired cyberactivity and to sidestep those blocks. Thus far, at least, WikiLeaks seems to be winning. The forbidden information remains widely and readily available. And it continues, in fits and spurts, to gather and release more underground information.

Controlling Cyberspace

Holding Internet service providers (ISPs) liable for the ephemeral copying that takes place when a music file is downloaded is certainly a broad strategy. The worry is that such an approach will cause ISPs to aggressively police what flows through their wires—barring otherwise inoffensive material in the process.[50] In the United States, the Digital Millennium Copyright Act offers immunity from civil liability for claims of copyright infringement against ISPs, as long as they meet the terms of a safe harbor. The DMCA's Section 512(a) immunizes ISPs for "routing . . . material . . . if . . . the transmission of the material was initiated by or at the direction of a person other than the service provider . . . [and] the service provider does not select the recipients of the material except as an automatic response to the request of another person."

But ISPs are hardly the only points of control. Other points of control include search engines, website hosts, and Internet routers, not to mention web users and website providers. Federal and state governments in the United States have targeted such points of control to reach illicit activity, including a federal government agreement with credit card companies to prevent illegal online purchases of cigarettes via credit cards; a congressional initiative to block illegal online prescription sales; and a Pennsylvania statute, later held unconstitutional, which would require ISPs to block child pornography sites.[51] Ronald Mann and Seth Belzley suggest that focusing on intermediaries (by placing liability on them) should only be pursued where cost effective: "The key question for determining the propriety of intermediary liability is the plausibility that the intermediary could detect the misconduct and prevent it [economically]." They explain: "When intermediaries have the technological capability to prevent harmful transactions and when the costs of doing so are reasonable in relation to the harm prevented, they should be encouraged to do so, with the threat of formal legal sanction if necessary."[52] However, just calculating relative costs of enforcement—the costs of intermediaries enforcing copyright versus the costs of copyright holders enforcing copyrights—neglects the price paid by such enforcement on values such as free speech.

Many countries have sought to employ various points of control to achieve their regulatory objectives. YouTube, for example, has attracted the attention of numerous governments. Thailand has objected to various videos posted to YouTube critical of the monarchy.[53] Even the United States has barred its military from posting videos to the site, citing bandwidth concerns.[54]

The emergence of a community titled "We Hate India" on Google's Orkut social networking service led to numerous efforts to respond, including attempts to block access to that community. The website includes a "picture burning the national tricolor [flag], bearing an anti-India message."[55] As if taking a cue from Justice Louis Brandeis, who promoted more speech as a response to false speech, a few Orkut members established new communities titled "I Hate Hatred" and "We hate those who hate India."[56] Others, however, sought to ban the anti-Indian community outright. A student group associated with a right-wing Hindu political party, the Shiv Sena, asked Indian cybercafés to block access to the anti-India community, going so far as to vandalize those that did not. The president of Bharatiya Vidyarthi Sena, one such student group, condemns Orkut, saying that it is "used by many destructive elements to spread canards about India, Hindus, our gods and cultural heritage." The complaint was even heard by a Mumbai court, though it does not appear that the complaint resulted in definitive action.[57] Orkut was briefly banned by Pune police in India after a series of violent events following the filing of a complaint by the Shiv Sena and related groups alleging that Orkut had allowed the posting of "slang, rude and vulgar language" about the Maratha warrior-king Chhatrapati Shivaji Maharaj.[58] The complaint centered on a mere 160-word posting on one of Orkut's multitudinous community web pages.[59] Indian authorities have also targeted ISPs in order to impede access to sites allegedly promoting hate or armed rebellion.[60] Unfortunately, the effort to block a dozen or so blogs has often led risk-averse ISPs to block access to all blogs hosted on various popular services, such as Blogger and Typepad. After complaints, ISPs have restored access to these services in favor of narrower censorship by blocking at the subdomain level. The OpenNet Initiative found that even the more refined attempts to block access to certain blogs were not entirely successful because the content migrated elsewhere.[61] OpenNet reports that Indian authorities sought to block an anti-Islamic website, but that again proved only partially successful, since one ISP refused to abide by the order. When the Mumbai police ordered the blocking of www.hinduunity.org for posting anti-Islamic material, they claimed to be exercising emergency powers to block material constituting a nuisance or threat to public safety. Most ISPs complied, but the largest one refused, arguing that the police lacked the power to issue blocking orders. As of March 2012, the website remains available in the United States but does not resolve to an accessible address in India, as tested on one Indian ISP. The domain name Hinduunity.org is registered to a person with a Post Office box in East Norwich, New York.[62]

Efforts to employ various control points to regulate information flow across the world will not prove uniformly successful. Determined web surfers may find ways to access forbidden information. There are numerous methods for bypassing government blocks of websites such as Orkut. The most popular requires the web surfer to access a website such as www.kproxy.com to reach an anonymizing proxy server, "a proxy server that removes identifying information from the client's requests for the purpose of anonymity."[63] Kproxy.com itself states that its site cannot be used "to transmit any unlawful, harassing, libelous, abusive, threatening, harmful, or hateful material of any kind or nature" or "for any illegal purpose including but not limited to the transmission or receipt of illegal material."[64] It will be difficult to stamp out entirely runaway information in cyberspace if there are determined disseminators and web surfers eager for the information sitting at computers around the world. In a dispiriting lesson for copyright owners, Hollywood brought a successful suit against one website to ban its linking to the DeCSS code that allows individuals to copy DVDs, but that code remains widely available.[65]

But yet another point is clear. The capacities of each state to regulate offerings from abroad will vary widely. Few countries will be able to hold accession to the WTO or some other international regime hostage to compliance with that country's legal regime. Very few will rival the United States' capacity in this regard. Countries such as China and Saudi Arabia might find success through control over routers and the Internet backbone or through employing large armies of censors. One common strategy will be to target Internet service providers as the locus for regulation, a strategy that will likely lead to the suppression of even some speech permitted in those restrictive jurisdictions. Another common strategy will be to target domain names.

The Domain Name System as Chokepoint

Complicating governmental efforts to enforce their rules in cyberspace is the "end-to-end" nature of the Internet. The end-to-end principle "holds that the intelligence in the network lies principally at its endpoints."[66] Rather than relying on a central, top-down hierarchy for disseminating information, like television, the Internet allows individuals worldwide to communicate directly with one another. The absence of a central authority to mediate information flows hampers regulatory efforts. Yet as the WikiLeaks case demonstrates, there is one crucial chokepoint for the Internet: the domain name system (DNS).

Information on the web is most readily accessible if it has a single, static address in cyberspace. The domain name system provides such a function. Just as in any property registry, the need for each web address to have a unique translation to a particular computer requires a single authority to manage that translation.[67] Currently that authority is the Internet Corporation for Assigned Names and Numbers (ICANN), a California not-for-profit corporation, which received its original authority through a 1998 US Department of Commerce contract. ICANN retains the power to set the rules for global domain name spaces such as ".com," ".net," and ".info" but does not claim authority over country domain name spaces. By convention, that authority is reserved for the governments of the countries themselves. Of course, there can be questions as to who the legitimate government might be. As an example, consider the awarding of the .ps domain name for the Palestinian Territories to the management of the Palestinian Authority.

Thus far, ICANN has chosen to apply its authority as a chokepoint only on behalf of trademark holders. ICANN has presided over an extensive dispute resolution system largely created and managed by the United Nations agency the World Intellectual Property Organization (WIPO). Under this system, in order for any person to register a domain name, that person must agree to arbitrate any claims that that domain name impermissibly infringes on a trademark holder's mark. This system extends ICANN's regulatory authority over all domain name registrants. ICANN's recent decision to allow new top-level domains (TLDs) promises to extend that authority in even more controversial ways.

An even more concentrated—and popular—point of control turns out to be the "root server"—the computer database that serves as the registry of domain names. For ".com" and ".net" domains, the root server has long been maintained by VeriSign in northern Virginia—in comfortable (or uncomfortable, depending on one's perspective) proximity to Washington, DC. More recently, the root server has been distributed across multiple jurisdictions, so it is harder to locate (or attack). The local Virginia federal court has attracted a large number of domain name disputes—especially those where the claims are brought *in rem* against a domain name held by a foreign party. Thus, the ultimate power over the ".com" and ".net" domains seems to rest, for US law purposes, with the federal district court for the Eastern District of Virginia, appeals from which are heard by the Fourth Circuit Court of Appeals and ultimately (though it has never taken a domain name case) the Supreme Court. The Pennsylvania-based Public Interest Registry manages ". org." In 2012, as noted, The Pirate Bay moved from an ".org" address to a Swedish ".se" TLD, hoping thereby to limit the reach of US authorities.

States and private parties can defect from the current domain name system: "If any country becomes disaffected with ICANN's management, it could opt out of it in favor of a parallel Internet system."[68] But because of network effects, opting out would reduce the value of cyberspace for all. Furthermore, it is difficult to persuade countless web users to modify their computers to point to the alternative DNS rather than the ICANN-managed DNS. One might imagine the European Union or China mustering the will and command authority to offer an alternative system, but the challenges would be enormous. A world with multiple domain name systems would make it difficult for Americans to talk to Europeans or Chinese to talk to Brazilians, and vice versa.

One final method of control might be mentioned. In 2011, facing rebellion, the dictator of Egypt, flailing for a means to shut off information flow in the country, found the Internet "kill switch." The government ordered the five major Internet service providers to shut off their service entirely. Traffic to the Google search site from Egypt vanished for the six days that the Internet was shut (see fig. 2).

Governments can ultimately control the Internet, at least through this blunt instrument. But turning off the Internet is the desperate measure of a government that is willing to wreak enormous economic damage. When the Mubarak regime was under siege, the Egyptian government initially spared the Internet access provider to the country's stock exchange, until it realized that dissidents were turning to this provider. Turning off the Internet can only be sustained in a largely undeveloped country whose government is willing to sacrifice the economic progress and knowledge advances that the Internet offers. North Korea, for one, bans its civilian population from accessing the Internet.

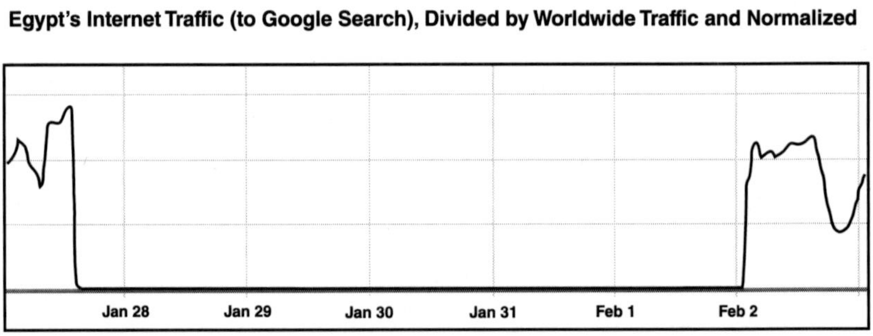

Figure 2. The Internet kill switch as evidenced by traffic to Google: Egyptian dictator Mubarak shuts off the Internet for his country to stall revolt. Courtesy of *Cornell Law Review.*

5

FACEBOOKISTAN

Who rules Facebookistan? The United States? France? Egypt? Mark Zuckerberg? Social networks by necessity span borders, following the transnational webs of human relationships. Who makes the rules that govern the ways that Facebook connects a seventh of humanity?

Facebook has become so powerful and omnipresent that some have begun to employ the language of nationhood to describe it. It boasts a community of a billion people. It circulates a currency that can be purchased in some forty-nine national currencies, from the Argentine peso to the Vietnamese dong. It dispatches a team of "diplomats" to reach governments around the world.[1] Its head of global communications previously served as press secretary for

President Bill Clinton. The *New York Times* reports a "Zuckerberg Law," where each year, people "share twice as much information as they shared . . . the year before." Facebook can boast of an "economy" consisting of the various third-party developers who engage in commerce using the Facebook platform. Facebook even holds a kind of a taxing power through its share of the revenues garnered via commerce on its site. Rebecca MacKinnon suggests that "Facebookistan . . . is run by a sovereign, who believes himself to be benevolent."[2]

For the growing numbers of people trusting their lifetime of intimate communications with friends and family to this service, the question of who controls Facebook is quite substantial. Facebook increasingly records our lives, mediates our interactions, and serves as a platform for businesses, media, organizations, and even governments to engage the world.

Facebook's global nature results in a dazzling array of possible regulators—from Afghanistan to Zimbabwe. More than 80 percent of Facebook users lie outside the United States, Facebook's home country. Will the array of possible regulators ultimately prove powerless, ineffective against this global service run (for most of its users) from afar?

The inquiry into Facebook's relationship with sovereign states allows us to interrogate some foundational issues of cyberlaw. By reviewing the interaction between one of the world's most important web enterprises and a number of nation-states, we can test the validity of early claims about the web. Is East Coast Code more powerful than West Coast Code, or vice versa?[3] Are national efforts to regulate futile against a company that operates offshore?[4] Will governmental efforts to regulate cyberspace be contested as illegitimate? Does cyberspace create separate fiefdoms, largely immune to sovereign-bound legal process?[5] Does voting "with one's feet"—or with one's clicks or taps—prove an effective disciplinary mechanism for wayward web masters?

At the same time, this inquiry furthers understanding about the globalization of contemporary corporations. Facebook represents a type of multinational corporation new to the world stage—one that raises issues different from those raised by earlier generations of multinational corporations. Earlier eras of corporate globalization saw companies turning to the world as markets for goods. Witness General Motors' cars and General Electric's turbines. These companies quickly globalized production of goods as well, establishing manufacturing subsidiaries or outsourcing manufacturing around the world. Hollywood studios, too, represent an important breed of multinational corporation, distributing their products around the world and occasionally outsourcing production as well. The multinational enterprises that make up Web 2.0 offer something different—not goods to be manufactured and distributed but rather a platform on which others can create and share.

This intertwines Facebook with issues of culture, religion, and politics around the world. Facebook founder and CEO Mark Zuckerberg acknowledges the firm's peculiar role: "We exist at the intersection of technology and social issues," he observes.[6]

Facebook is not the only Web 2.0 enterprise existing at the intersection of technology and social issues. Google, Yahoo!, and Microsoft are among the Internet companies with the breadth, capital, and power to challenge governments as alternative authorities. A focus on Facebook alone allows us to probe the position of major Internet enterprises in the international order.

Facebook, C'est Moi

Facebook now employs an "envoy to India" and an "emissary to Italy." *Slate* advises, "Now foreign countries should send diplomats to Facebook." One scholar observes, "When David Cameron became

Britain's prime minister, he made an appointment to talk to another head of state—Mark Zuckerberg."[7]

Facebook is hardly the only corporation with substantial power over people's lives. Since their original formulation as entities chartered by the king or queen, corporations have long enjoyed privileges and responsibilities associated with sovereigns. Corporations built bridges (and charged tolls), ran railways across cities and states, and managed universities. Granted an official monopoly on trade with India, the East India Company grew into history's most powerful corporation, becoming the de facto government for millions of people. The great chronicler of the twentieth-century corporation, Alfred Chandler, has called multinationals "leviathans," borrowing Thomas Hobbes's characterization of the omnipotent state.

Still, Facebook is different from the multinational corporations that have come before. A number of features make it different. First, its database of information about individuals is nearly unparalleled in human history. Second, it enjoys an enormous user base of individuals who can interact directly with each other. These direct relationships with a significant percentage of humanity and the power they give to Facebook have led many to employ the language associated with sovereigns to this company.

The close relationship between state and corporation is to some extent understandable. Each provides a good or service that individual persons would lack the capital to supply by themselves, with the state largely supplying public goods and the corporation largely supplying private goods. Each must deal with the possible abuse of minority stakeholders by those in power.

It is not the size of Facebook as a corporation alone that makes some deploy the language of nationhood to describe it. What makes Facebook different from so many other corporations, and more like a government, is how it is involved with so many aspects of our lives—including our business relationships, our friendships, and our families. Australian writer Julian Lee cautions: "If Facebook [were] a government agency, its power would be as undisputed as it would be frightening. For a single organisation to know as much as it does about the habits, interests and behaviour of 10 million Australians is unsettling."[8]

In some ways, Facebook is more involved with intimate aspects of our lives than governments of liberal states. In the United States, the constitutional right to privacy established in *Griswold v. Connecticut* and reaffirmed in *Lawrence v. Texas* removed the state government's right to interfere with certain relations in the bedroom. Liberal states generally maintain realms of private behavior—in which they may neither interfere nor monitor. Facebook limits itself somewhat—by banning some sexual material—but generally encompasses the breadth of our lives, even more explicitly so through its "Timeline" view of one's life.

Facebook has embraced the concept of the social graph and seeks to implement it across the world. The social graph refers to "the global mapping of everybody and how they're related."[9] Websites linked through this social graph can share information with each other, enhancing the user's experience by using information supplied by an individual's personal social network. At the same time, this means that an extraordinary amount of linked data and information passes through Facebook.

Facebook itself makes and enforces rules for the use of its platform. Enforcement consists in removing and/or banning individuals or groups for violating Facebook's terms (as determined by Facebook), deleting certain information, or sharing certain information with government authorities. To take one example, Facebook enforces a policy against nudity.[10] When individuals sought to post photos of breastfeeding mothers, Facebook initially deleted them. Its spokesperson explained, "I recognize breastfeeding is a natural thing to do, but many users want to foster diverse respect so we have come up with a set of community standards."[11] It reconsidered its decision to delete one breastfeeding photo after a reporter asked Facebook to explain the deletion. Like governments, Facebook is at times susceptible to public protest, as when it reinstated a photo of two men kissing after first removing it as a violation of the terms of use.

Facebook even briefly introduced a "governance" mechanism whereby users can comment on changes to Facebook's terms of use. Facebook promised that "if more than 7,000 users comment on the proposed change, we will also give you the opportunity to participate in a vote in which you will be provided alternatives." Facebook's management reserved the right to overrule the votes, however, unless "more than 30% of all active registered users voted"—a high hurdle, considering that its current user base is a billion people across the world. Still, the opportunity to participate in Facebook's governance was meaningful and could yet become more so over time.[12] By late 2012, Facebook had ended its experiment in governance.

Nation-states are likely not to leave Facebook entirely to self-regulation. Rather, they often seek to regulate Facebook because of four principal concerns.

- Facebook's practices implicate *privacy*—the sharing and processing of information about individuals. As James Grimmelmann writes, "By the time you're done [filling out your Facebook profile], Facebook has a reasonably comprehensive snapshot both of who you are and of whom you know."[13] Since Facebook users often post information about others (a natural human activity for everyone but the most solipsistic), Facebook holds information that people have not disclosed about themselves.

- Facebook might permit or censor *speech* in ways that raise regulatory concerns. Speech that involves religious, political, trade union, health, or sexual matters might be subject to diverse regulation across the world. Many countries, for example, regulate the health claims of drug manufacturers. Rules for defamation and hate speech will be implicated as well.
- States may wish to regulate the kinds of associations permitted by Facebook. Facebook grants individuals and enterprises the ability to form associations without official sanction or intermediation.
- States may wish to regulate the economic impacts of Facebook. Facebook is increasingly becoming a global bazaar. Rather than relying on advertising alone (which itself has economic impact), Facebook gains revenue from taxing the transactions occurring through its platform, taking 30 percent.

Each of these areas of law—privacy, speech, association, and economic regulation—vary dramatically across nation-states, increasing the risk of legal conflicts.

Some will suggest that nation-states should not seek to regulate Facebook because engagement with Facebook is entirely voluntary, in that one does not need to sign up at all if one does not like its terms. Indeed, there are many who have rejected Facebook and other social networks. Increasingly, however, one needs to open a Facebook account in order to receive information about an institution, a company, a store, to participate in a conference, or to receive information about activities nearby. Even if one forgoes all these opportunities, other people can still put up information about one on Facebook.

Faceoff: Facebook v. Nation

As Facebook goes global, have states melted against Facebook's juggernaut, or is Hobbes's Leviathan still potent? Writing of a faceoff between the German minister of consumer protection Ilse Aigner and Facebook's then-twenty-five-year-old founder Mark Zuckerberg, the *Economist* offers this acute observation: "It is hard to say who is the David," and who the Goliath.[14] I survey below efforts to use municipal law to influence Facebook.

United States. In its home jurisdiction, Facebook has been the subject of a number of federal and state regulatory efforts, as well as the defendant in a number of lawsuits. It seems sensible that the United States would be the jurisdiction with the most extensive efforts to regulate Facebook thus far. As the home of Facebook's principals, its key assets, its headquarters, and the site of its incorporation, the United States can be Facebook's most effective regulator, if it so chooses.

The most significant effort to modify Facebook's policies by the US government occurred in December 2011, when the Federal Trade Commission (FTC) sought to resolve a complaint against Facebook for its privacy practices. The FTC alleged that Facebook had failed to live up to its privacy promises, thereby engaging in "unfair or deceptive acts or practices . . . in violation of Section 5(a) of the Federal Trade Commission Act." The FTC alleged, for example, that Facebook had shared users' information in violation of its own privacy policies by doing such things as giving third-party applications access to information about a user's friends, even if those friends had not authorized such access. It also charged that Facebook would publish the list of one's friends, even when one selected a privacy setting to keep that information private. The FTC did not publish its complaint until December 2011, when it announced the proposed settlement. Under that settlement, Facebook agreed to not misrepresent the privacy or security of personal information about individual consumers and to obtain the user's "affirmative express consent" before materially modifying its privacy settings. Violations of the terms would result in fines of up to $16,000 per violation, per day. Some commentators characterized the FTC's proposed settlement terms as a "wrist slap."[15] But the settlement order included a crucial provision: an independent audit of Facebook's privacy and security practices conducted biennially for twenty years. The FTC had set a precedent for such audits in its earlier settlement with Google following the Buzz fiasco, when Google indirectly revealed to the world whom one emailed most often when it automatically enrolled these people in a social network together.

A smaller regulatory initiative, taken by a single state, shows both the possible multitude of regulators even within a single country and the extent of Facebook's reach into our relationships. This statute targeted Facebook users, as the focus of regulation, rather than Facebook itself. In 2011, Missouri passed the Amy Hestir Student Protection Act, a statute that included a section that quickly became known as the "Facebook Law." The law barred teachers from using "a nonwork-related website that allows exclusive access with a current or former student." In effect, this law outlawed teachers from using Facebook or other social media to communicate with students. This section was motivated by reports of teachers using online services to engage in misconduct with students such as explicit online messages. It responded to concerns that social media allowed teachers to reach students outside the classroom and without parental supervision. A storm of criticism was followed shortly by a lawsuit. The Missouri State Teachers Association sought to enjoin the contested portions of the statute as a violation of teachers'

First Amendment rights. The Missouri court granted a preliminary injunction based on the statute's "chilling effect on speech."[16] In October 2011, the Missouri legislature repealed the contested section of the law, replacing it with a requirement that each school board develop a social media policy "to prevent improper communications between staff members and students."[17]

Germany. Within Europe, Facebook has met its sharpest critics in Germany, a country with a deep commitment to privacy.

Facebook's "Social Graph" architecture allows any site to share information between the site and the Facebook platform, permitting readers of the German newsmagazine *Spiegel Online*, for example, to see what stories their Facebook "friends" like. Websites such as *Spiegel Online* often use a "Like" button to connect their visitors to Facebook, permitting users to promote a particular item with a single click. Many users might assume that no information would be passed to Facebook unless they pressed the Like button—but they would be wrong. An executive at a privacy software company offers a startling comparison: "What people don't realize is that every one of these buttons is like one of those dark video cameras. If you see them, they see you."[18]

Facebook admits that the company can see "information such as the IP address" of users who visit a site with a "Like" button.[19] But it asserts that it simply collects aggregate data: "According to Facebook, it simply counts the number of Internet Protocol (IP) addresses that visit sites with Like buttons."[20] The Facebook privacy policy, however, suggests that Facebook receives an array of data when a user visits a website that connects to the Facebook platform through such links as the Like button:

> We receive data whenever you visit a game, application, or website that uses Facebook Platform or visit a site with a

> Facebook feature (such as a social plugin), sometimes through cookies. This may include the date and time you visit the site; the web address, or URL, you're on; technical information about the IP address, browser and the operating system you use; and, if you are logged in to Facebook, your User ID.[21]

In August 2011, the data protection minister for the northern German state of Schleswig-Holstein, Thilo Weichert, declared that the Like button and other Facebook actions violated both German and European law. The state data protection authority led by Weichert, the Independent Center for Data Protection for Schleswig-Holstein (ULD), explained: "Whoever visits facebook .com or uses a plug-in must expect that he or she will be tracked by the company for two years. Facebook builds a broad profile for members and even a personalized profile. Such profiling infringes German and European data protection law."[22] The ULD thus directed websites based in the state to desist from connecting their site to Facebook through the Like button—subject to a penalty of up to 50,000 euros. The ULD also directed government agencies to shutter their own Facebook pages. The Schleswig-Holstein Tourism Agency was one of the entities that complied with the ruling, pulling its Facebook page. While noting that the tourism agency takes privacy very seriously, a spokeswoman for the agency also "bemoaned the loss of the tools provided by the social media platform, saying they had been useful for business."[23]

In response to these complaints, Facebook announced in September 2011 that it would abide by a voluntary code of conduct in Germany to protect user data, which, according to reports, was "the first time the site has agreed to such measures."[24] A possible approach is to adopt or adapt a voluntary code developed by

German media intermediaries under the auspices of the Federführung der Freiwilligen Selbstkontrolle Multimedia-Diensteanbieter (FSM).

Facebook has not smoothed its relations with all German authorities, however. In November 2011, the data protection authority of the German state of Hamburg said that it planned to initiate legal action against Facebook for a new feature that automatically recognizes faces in photos posted to the site. The Hamburg authority complained that Facebook had introduced this feature without seeking user consent. Indeed, in the United States, at least, the feature is activated by default, though an individual can disable it if he or she chooses. In 2012, Facebook suspended its automatic face recognition feature in Europe. By year-end, however, Facebook and German authorities were engaged in a new dispute: whether Facebook would permit pseudonymous speech.

Austria and Ireland. In July 2011, twenty-four-year-old Austrian law student Max Schrems, exercising his right under European data protection law, asked Facebook what information they had collected about him.[25] He received a CD with 1,222 pages of information. On these pages he found "everyone he had ever friended and de-friended, every event he had ever been invited to (and how he responded), a history of every 'poke' he had ever received, a record of who else signed onto Facebook on the same computers as him, email addresses that he hadn't provided for himself (but that must have been culled from his friends' contact lists) and all of his past messages and chats, including some with the notation 'deleted.'"[26] With this and other dossiers in hand, the group of activists calling themselves Europe vs. Facebook filed a complaint with Facebook's European regulator, the Office of the Irish Data Protection Commissioner. The group complained that Facebook was violating Irish and European privacy law by, for example, saving supposedly deleted data.

In December 2011, the Office of the Irish Data Commissioner announced both its findings and its resolution of the claims. The report did not focus on whether Facebook had broken European or Irish data protection law but considered whether Facebook had adopted what the commissioner believed to be the best practice for the social network in its European operations. Indeed, despite suggesting various changes to Facebook's policies, the report indicated that its recommendations "do not carry an implication that FB-I's [Facebook Ireland] current practices are not in compliance with Irish data protection law."[27] After cooperating with an extensive audit of its privacy practices, Facebook agreed to modify its policies in a number of ways, including anonymizing or deleting information gained through third-party websites connected to the Facebook platform, increasing the privacy controls available to users, and deleting information about advertisements clicked on by users after two years.

Facebook, Inc., itself was not the subject of the audit. Rather Facebook Ireland, Ltd., was the subject of the audit and the entity taking on obligations for changes. But despite the focus on the Irish entity, the Irish enforcement action has implications beyond Ireland and even beyond Europe. While the audit was focused on Facebook's Irish data-processing facility, the Irish data protection commissioner did visit Facebook's Palo Alto headquarters and meet with Mark Zuckerberg. Furthermore, because Facebook places responsibility for data about persons outside the United States and Canada with Facebook Ireland, Ltd., the home regulator of Facebook Ireland becomes, de facto, the regulator of Facebook across the world (outside the United States and Canada). Of course, this does not mean that other nations cannot regulate simultaneously. Indeed, even the Office of the Irish Data Protection Commissioner does not claim exclusive regulatory authority over Facebook even within Europe.[28] From the perspective of those concerned about protecting privacy, there are some advantages to this arrangement for those outside Europe. European data protection laws are stricter than US laws—and thus offer a stricter home regulator than the American alternative.

France. In *Hervé G. v. Facebook France*, the Paris Court of First Instance considered a claim brought by a French bishop against Facebook.[29] Bishop Hervé Giraud of Soissons claimed that a Facebook page titled "Courir nu dans une église en poursuivant l'évêque" (running naked in a church after the bishop) incited hate and violence against Catholics and thus violated the French hate speech codes. He also claimed that a photograph of him was used without his permission. The French court ruled in the bishop's favor on both grounds.[30] The photograph at issue was not at all scandalous but rather simply a portrait of the bishop.[31] The court ordered Facebook to remove the page and to pay 2,000 euros in damages, with a penalty of 500 euros for every day the page remained up. In addition, Facebook was ordered to identify the person who posted the page.

Facebook failed to appear before the court. Indeed, Facebook's French entity seems to have insisted that the complaint should be lodged with the Facebook parent entity rather than Facebook France. The bishop's attorney told the BNA news service that (in the news service's words) "Facebook France indicated to him that it had no connection to the litigious page and that the bishop would have to pursue Facebook.com in the United States."[32] Facebook did, however, take the page down.

Canada. One of the most thorough official examinations of Facebook's privacy practices to date was conducted by Canadian authorities. Faced with a complaint about Facebook's privacy policies, in 2009 the Canadian privacy commissioner undertook an investigation into those practices.[33] Assistant Commissioner Elizabeth Denham made a number of findings about the allegations, concluding that some allegations were well founded while others were not. With respect to the latter group, Denham made recommendations in a preliminary report, and in response, Facebook implemented a number of changes. It appears that Facebook also applied these changes to its American offering. In a sense, then, Denham became a privacy commissioner for Americans, too, since her recommendations were implemented in a manner that affects Facebook's operations for Americans as well as Canadians.

Facebook did not agree to all the recommendations, however. Facebook was asked "to implement technological measures to limit application developers' access to user information that is not required to run a specific application."[34] It refused to do so, instead proposing to give users specific consent for each category of information shared with third-party applications.

In *St-Arnaud v. Facebook, Inc.*, the Montreal Superior Court considered a privacy-based challenge against Facebook. The petitioner, Patrice St-Arnaud, sought to have the court certify a class action brought by Quebec residents who claimed they were harmed by Facebook's privacy practices. Facebook argued that Quebec users of its service had agreed to resolve disputes exclusively in its home jurisdiction in Santa Clara County. The submission to jurisdiction clause in the terms of use read as follows: "You will resolve any claim, cause of Action or dispute ('claim') you have with us arising out of or relating to this Statement or Facebook exclusively in a state or federal court located in Santa Clara County." St-Arnaud argued that the clause was part of an abusive adhesion contract and should therefore be unenforceable.[35]

Relying on the decision by the Supreme Court of Canada in *Dell Computer Corp. v. Union des consommateurs*, in which the Canadian Supreme Court had held that hyperlinked terms of use were properly notified to the user and therefore enforceable, the Montreal Superior Court held that St-Arnaud was bound by the Facebook terms.[36]

St-Arnaud offered an alternative, and seemingly promising, argument. The Civil Code of Quebec declared that waivers of the jurisdiction of local courts were not valid in consumer contracts. The Montreal Superior Court ruled, however, that "Facebook does not have a consumer relationship with its Users," because "access to the Facebook website is completely free." A consumer contract is "premised on payment and consideration," and must be "onerous."[37] Thus, St-Arnaud could not take advantage of the mandatory Quebec law to maintain an action in Montreal, despite Facebook's terms of use. There is no guarantee that the court would reach the same conclusion if Facebook began charging consumers for its popular services.

Although Quebec consumer protection law might not be applicable to Facebook, Facebook itself may have had an impact on Canadian law. The pressure of Twitter and Facebook and other social media services based outside Canada seems to have resulted in the Canadian government rescinding its ban on election night release of early election results.[38] In place since 1938, the law was designed to prevent what was seen as improper influence on voting in western provinces by the results of voting in eastern provinces. The Canadian supreme court had upheld the restriction in 2007 as a speech constraint that was within parliamentary power.[39] In January 2012, the Canadian government announced its reversal of the 1930s law via a twenty-first-century medium, Twitter.

China, Syria, Tunisia, and Egypt. Although many governments in liberal states have found Facebook an irritant, a few governments see it as a mortal threat. In July 2010, a newspaper associated with the Chinese Communist Party carried the front-page headline: "Facebook Could Be a Spy Tool." A report by the Chinese Academy of Social Sciences (CASS) concluded, "Facebook and certain other social networking sites may be exploited by Western intelligence services and used for subversive purposes.... Its special political function can be a threat." The report went on: "In the name of freedom, some organisations or people are encouraging revolt."[40]

China blocked Facebook in July 2009 across the country after unrest in the northwest province of Xinjiang. The site remains blocked as of this writing. According to a report by Sohu.com, Mark Zuckerberg held several meetings with Baidu CEO Robin Li to discuss a possible linkup to develop a Chinese offering for Facebook. Thus far at least, these discussions do not appear to have borne fruit.

In 2009, Syria blocked access to Facebook after Facebook permitted residents of the Golan Heights to claim Israel as their country of abode.[41] Facebook had responded to earlier protests of its policy of requiring residents of that area to specify Syria as their country of residence. Critics suggested that "the Syrian government was simply looking for a pretext to block Facebook because it fears the influence of the social networking site."[42] Syria restored access, only to deny it again in early June 2011 in response to widespread protests. Again, Syria restored the Internet, though the civil strife continues as of this writing.

In Tunisia, weeks before the Ben Ali dictatorship fell, it was reported that the government was trying to "steal an entire country's worth of passwords."[43] Dissidents "found their Facebook pages taken over without their knowledge."[44] Back in California, Facebook treated the hacking as "a black and white security issue and less of a political issue."[45] Access to Facebook was insecure because Facebook had not offered more secure communications options. As the *Wired* "Threat Level" blogger wrote, "The dangers of that design decision became very clear earlier this month when the Tunisian government, via the country's largest ISP, inserted rogue JavaScript into the html of Facebook.com's homepage as users loaded it, in order to steal passwords of activists. It used those passwords to delete accounts and pages critical of the regime."[46] In response, Facebook allowed users to use https, a more secure method of accessing Facebook, throughout its site. Facebook also devised a clever method to foil government infiltrators of dissident accounts. It required anyone logging in to an account to prove his or her identity by identifying that person's friends.

Facebook proved crucial because Tunisians wanted to share videos of the government's repression and the government had blocked other video sites.[47] Videos posted to Facebook helped disseminate information widely among the Tunisian population: "The videos—shot shakily with cameraphones—created a link between what was happening on the streets in the poor areas of the country and the broader Tunisian population. . . . Those videos, and the actions they recorded, became the raw material for a much greater online apparatus that could amplify each injury, death, and protest."[48] Today, the small-town fruit-and-vegetable peddler named Mohamed Bouazizi who tragically immolated himself to protest conditions in his country is known the world over. Video of Buoazizi's mother's protest following his death was broadcast on television by Al Jazeera, which "had picked up the footage via Facebook."[49]

Facebook, of course, seeks to keep its services as widely available as possible. Dan Rose, who is responsible for Facebook worldwide business development, states, "We try very hard to keep Facebook available wherever people want to access it." He continues, "We have outreach and relationships with governments all around the world. We can only do what we can do."[50]

Of course, perhaps the most important use of Facebook thus far has been its use by the Egyptian revolutionaries. Wael Ghonim, the Google Middle East executive who helped spark the revolution using Facebook, thanked Mark Zuckerberg after Hosni Mubarak fell:

> I want to meet Mark Zuckerberg one day and thank him. . . . I'm talking on behalf of Egypt. . . . This revolution started online. This revolution started on Facebook. This revolution started . . . in June 2010 when hundreds of thousands of Egyptians started collaborating content. We would post a video on Facebook that would be shared by 60,000 people on their walls within a few hours. I've always said that if you want to liberate a society just give them the Internet.[51]

Ghonim's account suggests that Facebook had an impact—and that local authorities lacked the power over the social media service that they would have liked. As we have seen, the Mubarak government demonstrated its fear of Facebook and other social media by completely switching off the Internet for the entire country.

The above review of points of tension between the law and Facebook in countries across the world reveals that neither the local government nor Facebook always prevails. We see Facebook bending its course—for example, agreeing to independent privacy and security audits. We also see governments changing theirs—take, for example, Canada, rescinding a 1938 election law, or, more dramatically, Egypt's Hosni Mubarak yielding power in the face of mass demonstrations nurtured by social media.

The Jurisdictional Dance

Richard Ford compares jurisdiction to dance. Like dance, Ford tells us, jurisdiction exists through its performance.[52] But he also means an almost literal dance across the border, like that of the von Trapp family crossing the border into Switzerland. With Facebook, we see both the company and governments stumbling over borders, uncertain which way to step or who should lead. The jurisdictional dance here is hardly graceful but, rather, is characterized by what we might call jurisdiction confusion.

Let us return to the disliking Like controversy. When the data protection authority in the German state of Schleswig-Holstein ruled that the Facebook web analytics were illegal under German law, it sharply limited its ruling. It imposed its prohibition on the Like button only to "website owners in Schleswig-Holstein," by which it seemed to mean websites owned by persons located in that German state. It did not command Facebook itself to no longer collect information from Facebook's social graph affiliates in the absence of affirmative actions by the user to share information with Facebook. That is, even though the data protection authority ruled that Facebook's practices violated German and European law, it did not tell Facebook to stop but restricted its ruling to German entities in its state.

Why did the German state authority pull its punch? A clue might be found in its public statement explaining its ruling. There the authority noted that "Facebook . . . does not have an establishment in Germany."[53] Under the European Data Protection Directive, the physical location of the establishment is relevant to the assignment of both the law and the regulatory authority. Under Article 4 of the directive, the national law applicable to a data processor is the law of the state of the establishment of the data controller. The directive makes the establishment accountable to its local data protection authority. Because Facebook's European headquarters were in Ireland, this might suggest that the Irish data protection authority would be Facebook's appropriate regulator.

Facebook insists as much. The German newspapers explained that "Facebook had previously said it needed to obey only Irish law as it maintained a European headquarters in Dublin." This explains why the Austrian group brought its complaint against Facebook to Ireland. Uncertainty and confusion are the order of the day. When Ilse Aigner, the German consumer protection minister, announced that she would advocate "strict bloc-wide rules on facial recognition, geodata and the profiling of individual Internet users," the German newspaper noted that it "remain[s] unclear how the new rules . . . will be applied to international companies based outside of the EU."[54]

In the context of web services, European law itself opens up the possibility of jurisdiction confusion. On the one hand, the Brussels regulation on jurisdiction allows one to sue for torts "where the harmful event occurred."[55] On the other hand, the European Union's Directive on Electronic Commerce declares that "information society services should in principle be subject to the law of the Member State in which the service provider is established." The preamble to the Directive reads as follows: "In order to effectively guarantee freedom to provide services and legal certainty for suppliers and recipients of services, such information society services should in principle be subject to the law of the Member State in which the service provider is established."[56] The two commands are, of course, not necessarily incompatible. A web user might have the right to sue a website in his or her local court yet be required to sue under foreign law, specifically, the law of the company's domicile. But choice of forum and choice of law are usually tightly linked.

In the consolidated cases of *eDate Advertising GmbH v. X* and *Oliver Martinez v. MGN Ltd.*, the European Court of Justice faced this quandary directly. The two cases involved efforts by individuals to sue websites based in other European countries. Understandably, in each case, the individuals filed suit in their home jurisdiction. In the first case, a German individual sought to stop an Austrian dating website from disclosing the fact that he had been convicted of murder (the individual was now free on parole). In the second case, French actor Olivier Martinez sought to stop a London website from alleging that he was dating the Australian singer Kylie Minogue.

The court sought to thread the needle—allowing the company to be governed by law no stricter than that in its state of establishment yet permitting European citizens to bring suit in local courts for the harms arising to them locally. The court, in effect, separated the choice of law and jurisdiction inquiries—allowing suit where the consumer lives yet limiting protections to those offered in the service provider's home jurisdiction.

Facebook for its part often seeks to resist local efforts to assert jurisdiction: in the French bishop's case, Facebook's French entity seems to have insisted that the complaint should be lodged with the Facebook parent entity, rather than Facebook France. The bishop's attorney, Thierry Massis, told the BNA news service that (in the news service's words) "Facebook France indicated to him that it had no connection to the litigious page and that the bishop would have to pursue Facebook.com in the United States."[57]

For their part, the privacy regulators are mindful of their limitations. Complaining that Facebook's Like button on non-Facebook sites allows tracking of users, the data protection authority in the German state of Schleswig-Holstein noted that it was a "small privacy agency."[58] The fact that the Irish authorities serve as Facebook's principal regulator for all of Europe may redound to Facebook's advantage. Given Facebook's importance to both Irish employment and to government revenues, authorities will want to be careful not to risk their golden goose. A 2012 study commissioned by Facebook suggests that Facebook has contributed some 400 million euros in value to the Irish economy.[59] Irish authorities have taken to touting Facebook's decision to locate its European headquarters in their country, as shown by an advertisement run by the Irish government in an Atlanta airport, using Facebook's presence to try to attract additional foreign direct investment (fig. 3).

Often the consequences for failure to observe local law are far from severe, even in Germany. When Johannes Caspar of the Hamburg data protection authority initiated legal proceedings under Germany's strict privacy laws, he noted that "*Facebook could be fined tens of thousands of euros* for saving private information of individuals who don't use the site and haven't granted it access to their details."[60] For a company with revenues in the billions of euros, such a fine might seem fairly minor.

Recall that in the French bishop case, even though Facebook failed to even appear in the French trial court to defend itself, the judgment entered against it included only a fine of 2,000 euros plus 500 euros for each day of noncompliance after the judgment—likely less than the costs of hiring a lawyer to appear for the day. While the Irish data protection authority was considering the Europe vs. Facebook complaint, reports suggested that Facebook might be subject to a fine of just 100,000 euros. In fact, Facebook's settlement with the Irish authority included no monetary penalties.

The threatened consequences for noncompliance might be so mild as to be charming: Miffed at Facebook's privacy policies, the German federal minister of consumer protection, Ilse Aigner, concluded her letter to Mark Zuckerberg urging Facebook to change policies that she believed violated German law with these words: "Should Facebook not be willing to alter its business policy and eliminate the glaring shortcomings, I will feel obliged to terminate my membership."[61]

While lawyers in the United States divide jurisdiction into subject matter jurisdiction (does the court have the authority to hear this kind of legal dispute?) and personal jurisdiction (does the court

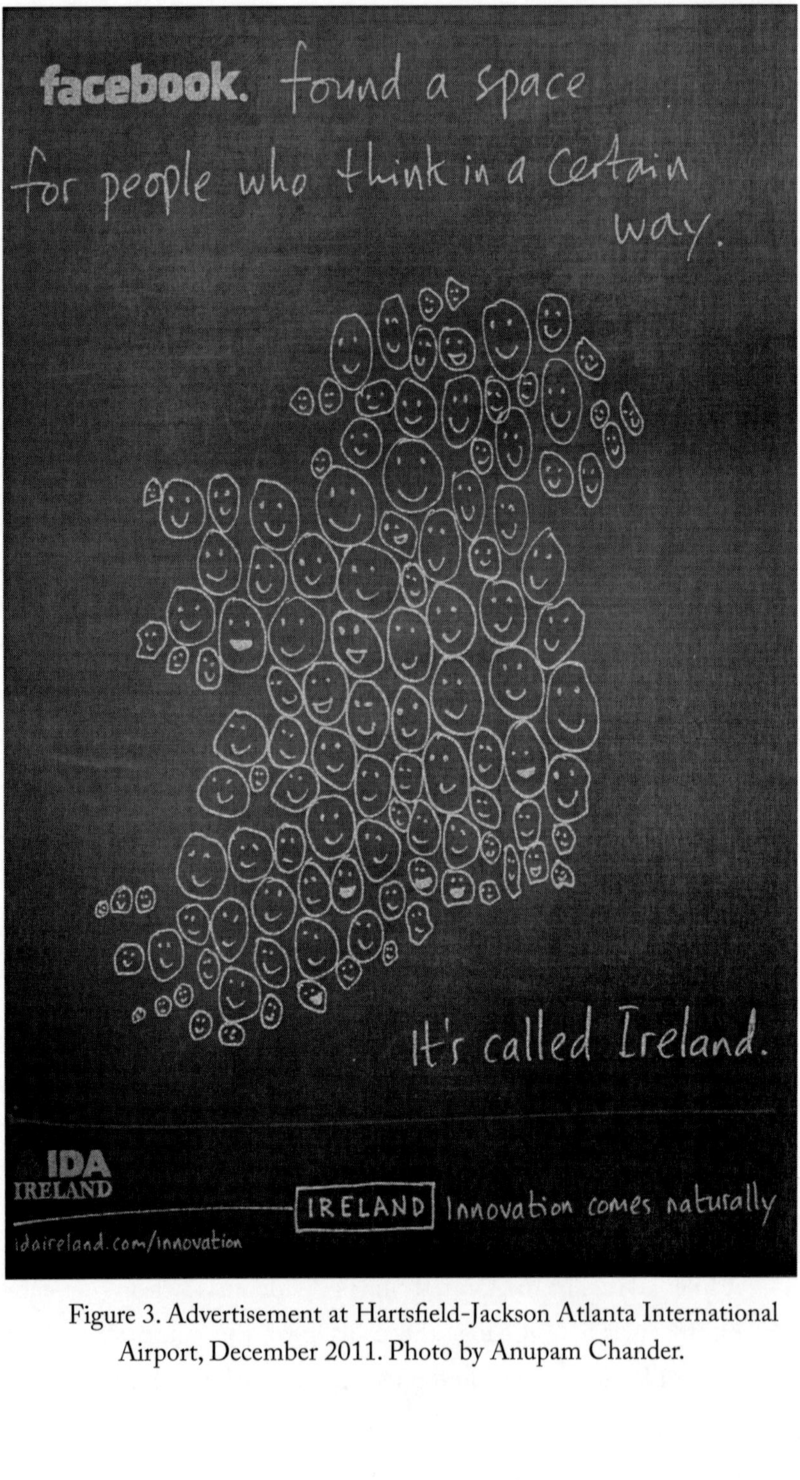

Figure 3. Advertisement at Hartsfield-Jackson Atlanta International Airport, December 2011. Photo by Anupam Chander.

have the authority to adjudicate a claim against this defendant?), international lawyers divide it in a different way—into legislative jurisdiction, adjudicative jurisdiction, and enforcement jurisdiction. The last division corresponds to the separation of powers familiar to students of American political structure, though international law does not require each of the three jurisdictional powers to be exercised by different agencies. Because of the division of the world into territorial sovereigns, exercises of jurisdiction are regulated by international law. International law's territoriality principle permits federal and state courts to exercise jurisdiction over occurrences in their territory, but events in cyberspace are by their very nature hard to locate either here or there. Asserting jurisdiction based on substantial effects in a state's territory is a corollary of the territoriality principle itself. As Christopher Kuner notes, "The effects doctrine has been vehemently criticized, but seems to have become widespread, at least with regard to assertions of jurisdiction over conduct on the Internet."[62]

If each state asserts jurisdiction over the same website, it is inevitable that the rules for users across the world will vary. In chapter 8, I label this legal *glocalization*, with a site localized to conform to varying rules in different jurisdictions. Even Facebook does this to a minor extent by offering Germans a special set of terms of use and, as we have seen, turning off its automative face recognition in Europe.[63] However, states asserting jurisdiction based on effects must consider rules of proportionality. Such assertions should be tempered, with forbearance a wise course unless the interests are sufficiently strong to justify intervention. The risk is that excessive interventions will jeopardize the worldwide nature of the web, hampering communications across borders—a risk I return to in chapter 8.

Who Should Rule Facebookistan?

Let's move from the description of the current state of the law to the normative question of who should rule Facebookistan? Consider a number of possibilities:

1. Country of origin—letting the home country of the corporation be its exclusive regulator;
2. Countries of reception—letting the home countries of its users regulate;
3. United Nations or other treaty-based entity—granting exclusive regulatory authority to an international treaty–based entity;
4. Self-regulation by Facebook's officers; or
5. Regulation by its users.

Each approach has its virtues. The country-of-origin principle is efficient and clear, reducing costs for compliance. The countries-of-reception principle is fair to users, who will often lack the knowledge and resources to bring claims against an enormous enterprise in a distant jurisdiction. A United Nations or international treaty–based approach would involve all the governments of the world in creating a single regulatory regime. Self-regulation would be ideal for corporations, allowing them to maximize profits, subject only to a loss of consumers from potential disagreements over policies. Regulation by users would give them maximum control over the site.

Each also carries flaws. The country-of-origin principle might lead corporations to race to the bottom, locating the country with the least rules from which to operate. The countries-of-reception principle would subject the corporation to multiple and sometimes conflicting regulations. As regards a treaty-based regime, it is difficult to imagine agreement on a single set of rules for intellectual property, privacy, security, defamation, pornography, and hate speech. Self-regulation might lead to exploitation of consumers, especially if consumers were not fully aware of what happened in an opaque system. Regulation by users might yield policies that fail to generate sufficient income to provide a powerful service.

For now, the most likely disciplinary mechanisms for Facebook are governments and the website's many users.[64] Albert O. Hirschman famously characterized two options for the disaffected member of a community—exit or voice.[65] Rebecca MacKinnon offers the example of Lokman Tsui, who in May 2010 quit Facebook to protest its privacy practices. Yet a year later Tsui returned (even though he was then joining Google as a full-time employee). Facebook had become such a valuable tool for staying in contact with people with whom he had "weak ties" that leaving it was far more detrimental for Tsui than it was for Facebook.[66] Voting with one's feet might yet prove an important disciplinary mechanism if there is a viable and popular alternative to Facebook, such as Google Plus or a foreign alternative such as Mixi or Tuenty. As I have indicated earlier, voice has shown occasional success in changing Facebook's policies.

Facebook's terms of service would have its users resolve disputes with Facebook on Facebook's home turf in California.[67] It should be noted that California law offers far more consumer protections than the laws of some other states. Both a California state appeals court and the Ninth Circuit Court of Appeals have refused to enforce forum selection clauses which aimed to send California consumers to Virginia state courts.[68] But even if California law offers a robust set of consumer protections, many users around the world may lack the resources to bring claims in California. Furthermore, California law may provide greater protection for speech than the laws of other jurisdictions that may protect privacy or reputations in greater measure. Finally, any contractual choice of law or forum would of course not be applicable to torts.

Now that it is a publicly registered corporation in the United States, Facebook will face yet another kind of public scrutiny—that of its public shareholders. A corporation that offers securities to the public must disclose information that is material to the investment decisions of those who might buy its securities. The disclosures become useful not only to those who might invest but also to the general public, who may have interest in the firm for other reasons. Facebook will have to inform its investors what actions might put it in legal jeopardy in a financially material way.

Return to the notion of Zuckerberg's law: "'When we started Facebook, we built it around a few simple ideas,' said Mr. Zuckerberg. 'When people have control over what they share, they want to share more. When people share more, the world becomes more open and connected.'"[69] But Zuckerberg's law for a digital world will at times run afoul of the laws of countries of earth and blood. Both Facebook and governments must negotiate a reasonable path through this difficult jurisdictional terrain.

The fact that Facebook transcends national borders rather than being Balkanized into different networks (or "-stans") for each country in which it operates is a key aspect of its usefulness. After all, human beings do not confine their relationships within national borders. At the same time, Facebook gains income from serving as many people as possible, including those outside the United States.

The laws of various states—from the United States to Canada and Europe—have influenced Facebook's operations. In turn, Facebook has influenced the law, putting pressure on authoritarian governments worldwide. At the same time, US law permits a large measure of freedom for Facebook to set the terms of Facebookistan.

European and Asian states, by contrast, impose greater obligations on their social network spaces. The answer to the question of who rules Facebookistan—nation-states, Facebook—is, in the end, all of the above.

6

FREEING TRADE IN CYBERSPACE

At the core of every cybertrade controversy described in this book is a provider in one jurisdiction supplying services to consumers in another. In each case there may be a conflict of laws between the provider's jurisdiction and the consumer's. The provider may lack legal precedents or authoritative guidance and must innovate not only technological methods and business models but also legal structures.

Four distinctive legal challenges of electronically tradable services, or Trade 2.0, become apparent: (1) legal roadblocks to the free flow of net-work; (2) the lack of adequate legal infrastructure, as compared to trade in traditional goods; (3) the threat to law itself posed by the footloose nature of net-work and the uncertainty of whose law should govern net-work transactions; and (4) the danger that local control of net-work might lead to either *Balkanization*—the disintegration of the World Wide Web into local arenas—or *Stalinization*—the repression of political dissidents, identified through their online activity by compliant net-work service providers.

In this and the following chapters, I discuss a framework to simultaneously liberalize and regulate Trade 2.0 in order to ameliorate the difficulties identified above. To liberalize trade, I introduce two principles: technological neutrality and dematerialization. *Technological neutrality* would require that online versions of a service be tested under the same legal regime as the offline version of that service, thus not permitting discrimination against the online version of a service. *Dematerialization* would require governments and services-standards bodies to replace physical in-person requirements with online substitutes wherever possible.

To respond to the risk to law of net-work trade (the third challenge), I suggest the necessity at times of *glocalization*—abiding by the local law of the jurisdiction in which a service is consumed where that law does not conflict with international law. But the assertion of local law invites the unwelcome consequences of Balkanization and Stalinization. To respond to the problem of Balkanization, countries will need to reinvigorate efforts for *harmonization*—seeking to agree on the common legal standard or tolerating deviations from local rules. To respond to the problem of Stalinization, companies themselves must adopt policies to "do no evil" and comport with human rights law. In this chapter I focus on the technological neutrality principle. I set out my arguments for the dematerialization, glocalization, harmonization, and do no evil principles in the remaining chapters.

An example might help illustrate these principles. If Yahoo! offers auction services, governments should not evaluate those services on a stricter basis than live, in-person auction services because this would have the effect of discriminating against foreign suppliers of auction services (technological neutrality). If auctioneers are required to have licenses, these should be available to the extent possible remotely, as should contracting and even dispute settlement (dematerialization). Where there is a strong societal commitment to outlawing Nazi paraphernalia, Yahoo! should not offer such material to those jurisdictions (glocalization). Where possible, countries should seek to work together to develop common standards or, alternatively, should recognize each other's legal regimes as sufficient (harmonization). Yahoo! should refuse to use the information it garners about its users (such as the listserves they subscribe to) to assist totalitarian governments (do no evil).

At times, these principles remain in a productive tension with one another. The trade liberalization envisioned in technological neutrality, dematerialization, and harmonization contrasts with glocalization, which poses legal hurdles to trade. But the occasional insistence on local law will help the cause of free trade more generally, just as local health and safety standards do not automatically fall in order to facilitate trade in goods. Abiding by the demands of local law may help staunch a protectionist backlash against foreign service providers. If foreign service providers are seen as abusing local persons and defying local law with no legal recourse, there will be calls for strong import restraints against Trade 2.0.

But restraint in insisting on local law is necessary. Excessive local regulation leads to the Balkanization of the Internet, making commonplace the dreaded warning, "This material is not available in your country." Both glocalization and harmonization represent efforts to regulate Trade 2.0 rather than declare such trade to occur in a law-free zone.

What if a country requires a foreign service provider to turn over information on dissidents? Respect for a jurisdiction's law is especially inappropriate where the law violates international human rights law. Because they traffic in personal information, net-work providers cannot ignore human rights. Cyberspace should help dissidents in totalitarian countries learn about the world and share information with others both outside and inside their country—not expose them to certain prosecution or vicious reprisal. Respect for local law entailed by glocalization might seem to run counter to the do no evil principle. However, because glocalization can only be justified by popular sovereignty and is limited by international law, including human rights law, it cannot justify comporting with demands for political repression.

In this and the following chapters, I discuss legal reform projects to accommodate Trade 2.0—how we can *free trade*. In later chapters, I turn to the steps we can take to ameliorate the threat to domestic regulation posed by Trade 2.0—how we can *protect law*.

While trade in goods and trade in services share the same underlying economic rationale, the two differ in key respects that may be relevant to law.[1] Consider the following list of differences between Trade 1.0 and Trade 2.0, keeping in mind that these are often differences in degree rather than kind:

- The tangibility of goods makes it easier to measure the performance of a production contract.[2]
- Services may be more likely than goods to implicate local cultural norms.
- Services may be more "footloose" than manufacturing because of lower capital-intensity and sunk costs.[3]
- Services often involve the transfer of sensitive personal data.
- Firms in both the manufacturing and services sectors can outsource service functions, while only those in the manufacturing sector can outsource manufacturing.

- Services employ white-collar professionals who have historically not faced widespread international competition.
- The measure of the quality of a service often involves not just the appraisal of the outcome but also the appraisal of the process by which the service was produced.[4]
- Unlike electronic services, goods can generally be controlled at border checkpoints.
- We have longer experience in identifying and restraining tariff and nontariff barriers to trade in goods than to trade in services.

Unlike trade in goods, the regulation of services occurs not at customs houses on dry docks at border ports but rather in administrative offices scattered inland. It consists, for example, in certification and licensing rules, rules about government procurement, geographical and quantitative restrictions, and rules for membership in private associations.[5] International trade law has long recognized that internal regulations, not just border rules, might serve as barriers to trade in goods,[6] but the even more extensive diffusion of regulatory authority over services heightens the challenge for discerning protectionist from other regulatory objects in services. Dispersing regulatory authority through city and county halls, the chambers of self-regulatory associations, and state and federal administrative and legislative units renders the task of liberalizing trade in services particularly difficult.

The infancy of such efforts poses yet another challenge. Where liberalization of trade in goods has a long, rich history, the global effort to dismantle barriers to trade in services is barely a decade old. The General Agreement on Trade in Services introduced services to the binding agenda of global trade liberalization in 1995. GATS, however, is far less demanding than its older cousin, GATT (the General Agreement on Tariffs and Trade), which was born from the ashes of a world war. Where GATT requires national treatment for suppliers of goods unless an exception has been carved out, GATS requires only the inverse: it permits discrimination against foreign service providers, except in those few sectors specifically designated by a state party for liberalization (this is called the "positive list" approach).[7]

Increasingly, regional trade arrangements offer stronger mandates to liberalize trade in services. Europe's ambition to create a single European market remains the leading effort to dismantle barriers between countries. Free trade in services is also one of the pillars of the North American Free Trade Agreement and the Dominican Republic–Central America–United States Free Trade Agreement (CAFTA-DR), as well as a goal of regional arrangements including those set up by the Association of Southeast Asian Nations, the African Economic Community, and the South American trading block, Mercosur. All of the bilateral free trade agreements ratified recently by the United States—with Australia, Bahrain, Chile, Colombia, Morocco, Oman, Peru, Singapore, and South Africa—include broad obligations to liberalize services.[8] Unlike GATS, in which a country has an obligation to allow free trade in a particular services sector only if it specifies that sector in the country's GATS adoption schedule, these bilateral agreements adopt a positive list approach to the sectoral commitments to liberalize trade in services. Such an approach assumes that *all* services are covered *except* those that are specifically excluded.[9] The reach of these services agreements will thus likely prove especially broad.

Perhaps unsurprisingly, the first WTO dispute squarely involving services, *Measures Affecting the Cross-Border Supply of Gambling and Betting Services (United States—Gambling)*, centered on the Internet.[10] This decision lays the groundwork for extensive liberalization of net-work trade. Indeed, we begin to see the fruits of this liberalization in the second major WTO dispute involving Internet-mediated trade, *China—Measures Affecting Trading Rights and Distribution Services for Certain Publications and Audiovisual Entertainment Products (China—Audiovisual)*, also discussed below.

United States—Gambling

Countries that want to discriminate against foreign online service providers hold at least two arrows in their quiver. They can argue that they never committed to liberalize that service (or its online version only) in the first place and thus cannot be held to account for any discrimination against it. Alternatively or additionally, they can claim that online services raise concerns that offline versions of that service do not. We saw both these arguments deployed in the *United States—Gambling* dispute, and versions of them deployed in the *China—Audiovisual* case as well, along with a host of more specific defenses in each case.

Both of these arguments are premised on the notion of regulatory autonomy, that is, the fundamental ability of each state to govern itself. The central tension in the world trade order is that between a country's authority to regulate commerce within its borders and that country's commitments to liberalize imports and exports. The perennial difficulty for trade law is smoking out situations where domestic regulatory objectives mask (intentionally or unintentionally) policies that undermine that country's liberalization commitments for trade.

Controversy over whether a country committed to liberalize a particular service might seem inexplicable; after all, should not the parties to the trade agreement know what economic activities each side has agreed to liberalize? The difficulty lies in the fact that it is often possible to characterize a particular service in multiple ways—some liberalized and some not. Thus, this most basic of disputes—not "Did a country violate its commitment?" but "Did it make a commitment in the first place?"—will prove a consistent thorn in the side of net-work. More important, changes in tradability make possible crossborder competition in services that nation-states may not have anticipated when they wrote their liberalization schedules (which for the founding WTO members occurred in 1994, when the Internet was just entering popular use).

In the *United States—Gambling* case, the United States argued that it had never agreed to open up trade in gambling services, specifically excluding "sporting" from its liberalization commitment. Antigua, by contrast, saw gambling as part of the American commitment to open up "other recreational services." The WTO Appellate Body recognized that the word *sporting* could at times include gambling but examined preparatory material that indicated that the United States had fashioned its schedule according to a classification list that placed gambling under "other recreational services," and not "sporting." It reasoned that the other parties to the negotiations would have understood that gambling was covered.

The United States went on to argue that even if it had committed to liberalize gambling, it had met its obligations. After all, Antiguan corporations were welcome—like any American national—to provide gambling to Americans. They just had to set up shop in Las Vegas or another permissive American jurisdiction.[11] The United States also insisted that, because of their differing consumer experiences and regulatory risks, offline gambling and online gambling were two distinct services, and thus opening up one and not the other did not effectively deny national treatment. And the market access requirement, the United States argued, did not bar a *total* prohibition on a particular service.

Seized of the dispute, the Appellate Body confined its analysis to the market access complaint, finding it unnecessary to resolve the national treatment complaint. The United States argued that its rules against online gambling were merely rules regulating the form or manner of how services are delivered, not quantitative constraints on services or suppliers.[12] Under this reasoning, the United States would meet its market access commitment for a service even if it barred the provision of that service online. The Appellate Body held that a blanket prohibition operated as a "zero quota" and thus presented a quantitative restraint prohibited by the market access commitment.

Although it lost on these first two arguments, the United States had a final argument, the last arrow in its quiver, and this one found its target. GATS permits derogation where "necessary to protect public morals or to maintain public order."[13] This clause serves as a crucial regulatory safety valve, ensuring that liberalizing commitments do not unintentionally jeopardize important local public policies. The Appellate Body accepted the American contention that the restraints on online gambling were necessary to protect concerns related to "(1) organized crime; (2) money laundering; (3) fraud; (4) risks to youth, including underage gambling; and (5) public health." Gambling via the Internet posed special concerns: "(i) the volume, speed and international reach of remote gambling transactions; (ii) the virtual anonymity of such transactions; (iii) low barriers to entry in the context of the remote supply of gambling and betting services; and the (iv) isolated and anonymous environment in which such gambling takes place." The Appellate Body agreed that the "distinctive characteristics" of online gambling justified the US discrimination against it.[14]

But the United States stumbled in an inconsistency: US law "authorizes *domestic* service suppliers, but not *foreign* service suppliers, to offer remote betting services on horse races." Post-ruling, the United States has stubbornly resisted resolving this inconsistency. As we saw in chapter 4, Antigua has received permission for retaliatory sanctions for this violation, consisting in permitting infringements of American intellectual property rights—becoming a legal paradise for the infringement of US intellectual property.[15]

Net-work providers share an Achilles' heel: because their services are not delivered face-to-face, the authentication clues available through in-person presentation are unavailable. Their remote nature thus leads to concern about fraud by suppliers (either in representing their credentials or in failing to perform the service as promised) or potential anonymity among consumers (leading to concerns about underage or otherwise inappropriate consumption). Can a state simply assert these concerns to protect its local suppliers, who after all can provide services face to face with greater ease than foreign suppliers? If so, this would mark the death knell of crossborder net-work.

At first glance, *United States—Gambling* poses exactly this roadblock to net-work. After all, the Appellate Body held that the risks particular to electronically mediated services might justify ignoring a country's free trade commitments (so long, that is, as the country bars all electronically mediated services, not just those provided by foreigners).[16] The WTO upheld a state's banning of online suppliers (both domestic and foreign) because of the risks of underage and pathological gambling, fraud, and money laundering. But even in largely dismissing Antiguan claims for access to the US market, the decision laid the groundwork for a substantial erosion of barriers to net-work.

The "chapeau" to GATS article XIV permits a public order–based violation of trade commitments only if it is not in fact a "disguised restriction" on trade in services.[17] A country may not maintain an infringing trade barrier if there is a "reasonably available alternative" that allows that country to maintain its public order or morality objectives.[18] Antigua might have demonstrated practical alternatives to the American prohibition to achieve the desired regulatory goals. Antigua could have shown that it had redoubled its financial crime efforts, strictly enforcing international anti-money-laundering principles, such as the international standards offered by the Financial Action Task Force.[19] Antigua could have required independent auditors from large international firms to audit compliance by Antiguan gambling operations, helping to assure users that the computer systems and financial payouts were sound.[20] Antigua could have shown that the steps it requires to add money to a gambling account (such as bank wire transfers) would prove nearly insurmountable for youth. And it could have required that gambling providers make available services for gambling addicts, including mechanisms for allowing people to limit losses or to lock themselves out.[21] But Antigua did none of these things. Rather, Antigua mistakenly relied on America's stubborn refusal to discuss alternative means to achieving its regulatory goals.

Perhaps the strongest rebuttal to the American argument that an online service was inherently risky comes from the US Supreme Court. In the case of *Granholm v. Heald*, the Supreme Court considered a challenge to Michigan and New York regulations barring out-of-state wineries from selling directly to Michigan and New York residents.[22] The challenge involved what constitutional lawyers call the "dormant commerce clause." The dormant commerce clause creates a free trade area *within* the United States, preventing states from unduly burdening interstate commerce. In *Granholm*, as in *United States—Gambling*, the defenders of trading restraints argued that these restraints were necessary to preserve local values. New York insisted that its rules barring the retailing of alcohol via the Internet were "essential" to "promoting" no less a value than "temperance," as well as the more mundane goal of "collecting applicable taxes." Requiring alcohol to pass through state-sanctioned distribution channels, New York argued, allows it "to effectively monitor alcohol distribution and enforce its liquor laws."[23]

The Supreme Court was not persuaded. New York and Michigan "provide[d] little evidence for their claim that purchasing wine over the Internet by minors is a problem." The states could have minimized risk "with less restrictive steps," such as requiring "an adult signature on delivery." The Court held that New York's "regulatory objectives" could be achieved "without discriminating against interstate commerce, *e.g.*, by requiring a permit as a condition of direct shipping." The states' "other rationales, such as facilitating orderly market conditions, protecting public health and safety, and ensuring regulatory accountability . . . [could] also be achieved through the alternative of an evenhanded licensing requirement." The fundamental question, the Court asked, is whether a state's discriminatory regime "advance[d] a legitimate local purpose that cannot be adequately served by reasonable nondiscriminatory alternatives." While *Granholm* involved trade in goods, not trade in net-work services, both cases involved trade mediated largely by the Internet. The Supreme Court's "reasonable nondiscriminatory alternatives" formulation comes strikingly close to the WTO's "reasonably available alternative"; both give the tribunal the ability to strike regulations that unnecessarily restrain competition from outside producers. The convergence in the Supreme Court and WTO formulations is not a coincidence: though poles apart in their history and status, both institutions promote commerce among jurisdictions while protecting the power of those jurisdictions to regulate themselves.[24]

Of course, even the most robust alternative for achieving the regulatory objectives may not prevent all potential wrongdoing. But neither would an outright prohibition of online gambling accomplish perfectly the regulatory goals. After all, underage persons can sneak their way into casinos; gambling addiction predated the Internet; cash in casinos can be more anonymous than an offshore bank account, which requires extensive security measures; and organized crime is not entirely unknown in American gambling history. The question is whether the proposed alternative achieves the "desired level of protection," not whether it promises one hundred percent compliance.[25] In the *United States—Shrimp* dispute, the WTO Appellate Body held that an importing nation's insistence on a "single, rigid, and unbending requirement" would constitute "arbitrary discrimination" within the meaning of the GATT article XX chapeau.[26] Contrast District Judge Marilyn Hall Patel's standard for Napster, in which she required the online service to remove 100 percent of copyright-infringing material, a standard that Napster rightly insisted was impossible to satisfy and that was not met even by offline distribution systems.[27] The appropriate standard should be one *where the online service should be required to achieve the regulatory goals at rates roughly equivalent to those achieved by offline versions of the service*. This is a principle of *technological neutrality*.

Such steps would likely raise the costs of doing business electronically as well as the costs for governments of enforcing compliance. At times, the costs today may be so high as to make net-work economically infeasible. Perhaps governments might be willing to reduce compliance rates in some cases in view of the liberating and economizing possibilities of the electronic medium.

GATS does allow countries to liberalize trade only with respect to certain modes of delivery of a foreign service over others. The principle of technological neutrality that I assay here would come into play only when a country has committed to liberalizing a particular service with respect to *mode 1*, crossborder trade. In such a case, to demand higher standards for electronically provided services than services delivered in person is to engage in outright discrimination. Such discrimination would likely violate the GATS national treatment commitment[28] because foreign suppliers would be at a natural disadvantage in supplying face-to-face services because they are less likely to have representatives on the ground. Where the discrimination against the online service acts as an effective barrier to online supply, it could, as in *United States—Gambling*, violate the GATS market access requirement.

This is an especially grave threat to net-work. After all, due to the non-face-to-face nature of the medium, it is easy to challenge net-work as potentially promoting fraud. But to insist on the complete absence of fraud on Internet-mediated services would be to conjure a preexisting world of face-to-face transactions devoid of fraud. Fraud and other regulatory leakages are a persistent fact of commerce and are not unique to Internet commerce. Trade law should not allow countries to insist on a regulatory nirvana in cyberspace unmatched in real space. Such discrimination against the electronic medium will likely disadvantage foreign suppliers, which are less likely to have the resources to deploy service providers on the ground.

China—Audiovisual

The United States was on the other side of many of these issues when it brought a complaint against China in 2007 for controls on the distribution of publications and audiovisual products, including controls on the distribution of material online. The United States charged that these controls, which required such products to be distributed by Chinese state-owned entities, violated China's

GATT and GATS obligations, as well as the extra WTO obligations that China had taken on as a price of its late WTO entry in 2001 (six years after the WTO was formed). The Chinese controls imposed greater burdens on foreign audiovisual products and publications than ones produced domestically. They also constrained rights to distribution to state-owned entities, ostensibly to support the extensive Chinese censorship regime.

As in *United States—Gambling*, the respondent in the dispute argued that it had never committed to liberalize the particular service at issue. China conceded that it had indeed committed to liberalize distribution of "sound recording distribution services" but argued that *electronic* distribution of audio products were not "sound recording distribution services."[29] The Appellate Body disagreed, noting that China's market access and national treatment commitments with respect to such services were written generally, not specifically excluding distribution in electronic form. Thus, China's commitment "would encompass distribution in electronic form."[30] With this language, the Appellate Body signaled that liberalization commitment for any particular service would be interpreted to include delivery of that service electronically—unless the Member State had specifically indicated otherwise in its liberalization schedule. The Appellate Body also stated that commitments should be interpreted in a dynamic fashion, rather than strictly interpreted according to the ordinary meaning at the time the commitment was made. The tribunal explained that an originalist approach would "mean that very similar or identically worded commitments could be given different meanings, content, and coverage depending on the date of their adoption or the date of a Member's accession to the treaty."[31] By subsuming an electronic version of the service within a services commitment and by interpreting treaty commitments in a dynamic form, the treaty can take account of changing technologies.

Faced with the finding that it had indeed violated commitments in its WTO accession protocol by requiring that audiovisual products be imported through specified state-owned enterprises, China argued that the requirement was necessary to protect public morals. Following the reasoning of *United States—Gambling*, the Appellate Body disagreed. The Appellate Body concluded that the United States had offered a reasonably available alternative to the trade restrictive measure—censorship by the government directly, rather than through state-owned enterprises. Thus, China's breach could not be justified in the name of public morals.

Even if the law technically permits online service providers to supply services across borders, online service providers may still fail because of physical constraints. In the next chapter, I describe another key principle to free Trade 2.0, what I call *dematerialization*. The infrastructure of services delivery must be reformed to permit services to be supplied remotely, consistent with the requirements of consumer protection.

7

HANDSHAKES ACROSS THE WORLD

The merchants traversing the Silk Road were not anonymous agents of globalization. Rather, they were repeat players, connected to one another through personal histories and kinship networks. Goods delivered via this route would pass through many hands, from entrepôt to entrepôt, with each leg of the journey often dominated by particular tribes. In this chapter, I argue that the characteristics that permit net-work trade might be deployed to create a robust infrastructure for such trade: real-time information transfer, low information and other transactions costs, the ability of individuals around the world to collaborate, and electronic identification. Perhaps the electronic version of the wax seal or chop, used to signal authority, could even improve on the original.

The architecture of real-world transactions helps promote security, privacy, monitoring, trust, and enforceability between parties, which in turn fosters marketplace contracts with strangers. In order to foster trade in services, governments, corporations, and state and industry associations will need to re-create security and trust in cyberspace. They will need to establish the electronic counterparts to handshakes, ink signatures, demeanor evidence, word of mouth, and the ready ability to seek legal redress. In this chapter I argue for a *dematerialized architecture* for cyberspace trade and describe incipient efforts toward that goal.

Even were legal restraints on crossborder net-work entirely eliminated, local service providers would retain a natural advantage. Local persons are more likely to have obtained any certifications and licenses necessary to provide a service in the jurisdiction. They are also more likely to have access to any regulations governing the service. Parties that meet face to face have the advantage that they can rely on the physical clues that promote trust among counterparties.

Despite this, mail-order contracts became increasingly commonplace in the last half-century, demonstrating that face-to-face transactions are not entirely indispensable for large-scale commerce. Even more dramatically, global supply chains now dominate the production of goods, proving the possibility of commerce across national borders, time zones, and oceans. Yet, undergirding these global supply chains are developments in the legal infrastructure, both between states and within states. Bills of lading and procedures for documentary credits established a framework for shipping a good and receiving payment. The International Chamber of Commerce (ICC) helped standardize shipping terms through "Incoterms." The United Nations Commission on International

Trade Law (UNCITRAL) promoted "uniform rules which govern contracts for the international sale of goods" through the Convention on the International Sale of Goods (CISG).[1] That convention regulates the formation of a contract, the obligations owed by buyers and sellers, the passing of risk of the good during transit, and remedies for breach.

Many of these standards and rules cannot be applied to services. As its title indicates, the CISG is the Convention on the International Sale of *Goods*. Shipping terms referring to risk passing when a load crosses the ship's rail have little meaning in cyberspace. Documents evidencing the loading of a truck or ship cannot be easily adapted to products delivered electronically.[2] The principal promoters of the international legal framework for goods, UNCITRAL and the ICC, have accordingly extended their work to electronic commerce and services. For its part UNCITRAL has been proved especially useful for domestic and global e-commerce, though few may even be aware of its existence or think of a UN body as promoting commerce. UNCITRAL developed an e-signature initiative that served as a model law for the United States and other nations, helping validate contracts made electronically.[3] While it may be hard to believe in today's world of ubiquitous e-commerce, not long ago it was unclear whether a contract entered into electronically could be enforceable.

Trade 2.0 will require electronic substitutes, where possible, not only for signatures but also for handshakes, facial identification, bureaucratic offices, education, testing, and even administrative and judicial hearings. This is the *dematerialization* of the services infrastructure, the systems and practices that foster trust, promote social goals, and resolve disputes.

Net-work will flourish as the need for physical presence in order to provide a service recedes. Regulated professions (for example, law, medicine, accounting, and architecture) require the service provider to obtain educational credentials, pass an examination, and conform the service to certain rules, or some combination of the above. The international trade order seeks to reduce at least the difficulties of ascertaining the local rules. GATS hopes to make obsolete the ritual pilgrimage to numerous governmental offices to obtain rules and applications applicable to a particular service. WTO member states must publish regulations governing any service covered by their specific commitments[4] and establish inquiry points where foreign service providers can obtain information about such regulations.[5] Canada helpfully posts this information online,[6] and many other countries provide an email contact point.[7] Through this transparency requirement, GATS will foster trade by enabling foreign service providers to develop the ability to conform to local rules.

The European Union's Services Directive goes substantially further. Not only does it mandate that information on service regulation be supplied electronically,[8] but it requires member states to "ensure that all procedures and formalities relating to access to a service activity and to the exercise thereof may be easily completed, at a distance and by electronic means, through the relevant point of single contact and with the relevant competent authorities."[9] Accordingly, each of the twenty-seven EU member states, as well as three of the four European Free Trade Association states, have created a "Point of Single Contact" to serve as a portal for foreign service providers hoping to provide services to that state. These portals promise to inform foreign service providers of the rules to provide a service within that jurisdiction and to offer the possibility of completing administrative procedures online, rather than presenting themselves in person at the offices of different authorities in different countries. With this mandate, the EU will lead the way toward dematerialization, in the process establishing standards that the rest of the world will likely use as models.

Where a service is licensed, governments should consider whether a foreign credential should be recognized as a substantial equivalent—thus eliminating the need for the service provider to obtain the necessary license through physical presence in a foreign country. Certain educational processes may be harder to mimic. The magic of walking the corridors of a law school may be difficult to re-create virtually, though Harvard's innovative Charles Nesson has tried by teaching a class in a virtual re-creation of Harvard's Austin Hall.[10] Law schools are, however, experimenting with distance learning. Thus far, the American Bar Association has not accredited any fully online law schools, though graduates of online law schools (even unaccredited ones) may sit for the California bar under that state's rules. Graduates of the for-profit Concord Law School have done so, with a reported first time pass rate since 2003 of 36 percent, with merely 32 percent passing in July 2011.[11]

Even largely unregulated services will benefit from the creation of a trust infrastructure in cyberspace, enhancing consumer confidence in the service. Systems for providing authentication, security, and privacy will alleviate consumer concerns about online activity.

Allowing aggrieved parties to an international transaction to settle disputes via the Internet would substantially reduce impediments to trade. The WIPO-initiated domain name dispute resolution system demonstrates the possibility of a cybertribunal that efficiently processes international disputes while dispensing with physical presentations or evidence.[12]

India established the Cyber Appellate Tribunal and empowered the tribunal to regulate its own procedures, dispensing with the national code of civil procedure.[13] Although this is promising, the procedures include the antiquated requirement that each person seeking redress submit "six complete sets [of the complaint] in a paper-book form along with one empty file size envelope bearing full address of the respondent."[14] Even the e-filing option includes a note to "take printout of word file and submit six (6) copies of this application along with printouts of annexures with each application and single demand draft."[15] It thus should hardly be surprising that the tribunal has handled only a dozen or so cases since 2009. The few cases that have been decided do not demonstrate a clear bias toward local complainants, but they also suggest that the basic procedures have yet to be worked out. For example, the tribunal rejected a number of cases brought against "Gmail.com" seeking to compel information about the identity of a Gmail user. Noting that perhaps Google Inc., and not Gmail, was the proper defendant, the tribunal ruled that the complainant should have first filed a claim with the appropriate adjudicating officer under the Information Technology Act of 2000. The Indian government has named the secretary of the Department of Information Technology of each of the states or of the union territories as the adjudicating officer, but there is little information on how to actually file a complaint through such persons. The government has posted a list of emails for each of the secretaries for each state or territory, some of which notably use Hotmail, Yahoo!, or Gmail services.

Governments do not necessarily have to provide international dispute resolution services themselves because private parties can offer to resolve disputes. It may be that any particular website, such as eBay or Facebook, might require its users to contractually agree to abide by the judgments of a private dispute resolution provider, but such contracts cannot, of course, bind third parties. Furthermore, where the agreement to submit to binding dispute resolution is made through terms of service that are rarely reviewed by users, there are reasons to be cautious about ready enforcement, especially when the rules may undermine consumer protections.[16] Service providers might themselves volunteer to be bound by a global electronic dispute resolution mechanism, in order to increase confidence of their users and clients through submission to a neutral and readily accessible third party for dispute resolution. Because many online disputes might arise from contractual relations, dispute resolution schemes can be pre-established by contract.

Dematerialization does not require automation; human beings would still need, for example, to conduct conformity assessments with the regulatory standard.[17] Dematerialization might also be approximated by enabling foreign service providers to meet requirements through processes that can be engaged in at numerous locations worldwide. Certification tests can be administered in a variety of secure locations around the world. The Law School Admissions Test (LSAT), to use a familiar example, can be taken in more than sixty foreign countries, including Australia, China, Egypt, and Vietnam.

If regulations require physical presence for a signature or some other process, they might violate international trade law. If a country has agreed to liberalize trade in a particular sector, such physical presence requirements encumber foreign traders' ability to provide that service, imposing special travel costs on the foreign trader, not to mention the serious obstacles of obtaining visas. Regulations that require a physical presence might be subject to GATS challenge on at least two grounds: (1) a violation of the national treatment obligation because a physical presence requirement confers advantages on local providers; and (2) a violation of the market access commitment, where mode 1, the crossborder supply mode, has been committed to liberalization. As we saw in the discussion of *United States—Gambling* in the last chapter, a nation insisting on physical presence can plead the need to protect public morals, maintain public order, or protect life, but that plea can be tested for a "reasonably available alternative." As the legal and technical infrastructure of net-work grows through increased dematerialization, a physical presence requirement will be harder to defend.

While dematerialization will mean that a local service provider will face competition from abroad, it simultaneously expands that provider's potential market. For consumers, dematerialization will mean a wider selection of service providers from which to choose, improving quality or price, or both. A handshake, a pat on the back, and eye contact are all activities that help define our humanity, but they may not be always possible or necessary for all transactions that make up our contemporary lives.

8

GLOCALIZATION AND HARMONIZATION

The footloose nature of net-work increases the likelihood that a service provider might relocate to take advantage of regulatory environments it finds favorable. The fear is that this mobility might lead to a race to the bottom, as providers search out the jurisdiction with minimal or even no regulation.[1] Will service providers relocate to offshore havens where they can escape law yet still offer services via the Internet? This is not merely a theoretical possibility, as we saw in chapter 4. Antigua did not attract gambling operators only on the strength of its ample sunshine and beautiful beaches.

The bottom of such a race might well be found in the self-declared principality of Sealand. Established on a floating platform used for British air defense during World War II, Sealand provided "the world's first truly offshore, almost-anything-goes electronic data haven."[2] Through its web hosting company, forthrightly named "HavenCo," Sealand offered "the 'freedom' to store and move data without answering to anybody, including competitors, regulators, and lawyers."[3] *Free*, as in *without regulation*.

Do Sealand and its ilk spell the death of law? Might entire countries set themselves up as Sealands, offshore havens from law itself?

Thus far, with few exceptions such as online gaming, net-work has not migrated en masse to offshore regulatory havens.[4] More important, there may be significant virtues in the regulatory competition that might arise from multiple jurisdictions with diverse regulations (including no regulation). Where earlier scholars saw regulatory competition as inexorably resulting in a calamitous deregulation, today's scholars have identified potential virtues in the process. Rather than a race to the bottom, they predict a race to the top or, alternatively, a race to the global welfare-maximizing ideal.[5] Regulatory competition might pressure regulators to bring regulation to global standards or allow private parties to locate the best-tailored rules to govern a particular transaction. Competition might lead to the optimal regulation, maximizing social welfare. Regulatory competition "has the potential to discourage harmful regulatory laxity as well as extreme regulatory rigor."[6] The Internet might turbocharge regulatory competition: by permitting individuals to select service providers from around the world, the Internet might greatly enlarge the domain of laws subject to regulatory competition, effectively making optional what had been mandatory services law.

The optimistic story of regulatory competition in cyberspace faces at least two objections. First, states are unlikely to be sanguine about the widespread avoidance of local law. The possibility of the evasion of mandatory law is the focus of the first half of this chapter.

Second, the race to the optimum is likely only where a company will internalize the costs of either regulation or deregulation.[7] Many argue that this is the case with respect to the choice of where to incorporate a business, where the promoters' decision to incorporate in a jurisdiction with lax shareholder protections makes it more difficult to convince people to invest in that business.[8] But this happy scenario will not often obtain with respect to services regulation. Take for example government protections for personal information collected by corporations: because of limitations and biases in human cognition and also because of collective action problems, we should not expect private markets to achieve efficient practices regarding the use and disclosure of customer information.[9] Few of us take the time to fully understand privacy policies; furthermore, privacy realities may be entirely invisible despite lots of effort. Thus, companies may not fully internalize the costs of their information use and disclosure practices and might choose regulatory regimes with little or no privacy protections. This same defect may exist with respect to a wide swath of services regulation. To make matters worse, the country that deregulates may not suffer the brunt of the ill effects of deregulation if the principal markets for the deregulated service are abroad. The offshore haven might sit back and collect taxes while letting the social costs of the activity fall on distant lands. Although the regulated jurisdictions might seek to bargain with the haven for a more congenial outcome (or, borrowing from an earlier era, even engage in gunboat diplomacy), the fruits of such negotiations are uncertain at best.[10]

Such a race to the bottom arises because of the existence of highly *liberal* regimes, lacking consumer and other protections. There is a second potential race to the bottom in net-work, this one arising out of the reality of highly *repressive* regimes. Companies may submit to the repressive demands of totalitarian regimes in order to supply services to their populations. In the competition to supply such markets, companies might race to the bottom by censoring the information they supply and even spying on the local population in order to satisfy the authoritarian regime.

To disrupt these races to the bottom, I offer two principles: *glocalization* counters the race to the deregulated bottom, while *do no evil* counters the race to the oppressive bottom. I consider the do no evil mandate in chapter 9 in connection with China. This chapter describes the glocalization principle and its limits.

Glocalization

Globalization, the worry goes, will sweep away local culture in favor of a mass commercialized, homogenized world. Indeed, the Internet is likely to increase this tendency, giving individuals ready access to media originating outside their countries.[11] Sociologists offer *glocalization* as an antidote—a way to embrace globalization without shedding local difference.[12] Glocalization, a portmanteau rooted in the seeming opposites "global" and "local," refers to "the simultaneity—the co-presence—of both universalizing and particularizing tendencies."[13] I use it here with reference to *law*. Globalization of services threatens to sweep aside local law through the use of offshore regulatory havens. Legal glocalization would require *the creation or distribution of products or services intended for a global market but customized to conform to local laws—within the bounds of international law.*[14]

Although the concept of insisting on local law may seem anodyne, the streets of Strasbourg and Berlin swelled to defend this principle when it was threatened.[15] As originally drafted, the European Union's proposed Services Directive would have mandated a "country of origin" rule within the union, under which a European could supply his or her services to any country within the

EU under the rules of the home, not host, country, at least in the absence of compelling public health or security rationales to the contrary.[16] Thus, a French service provider would be governed ordinarily by French law even while supplying services in Germany. This would apply equally to Polish plumbers and English e-commerce providers. The head of the European Trade Union Confederation charged that this directive would "fire the starting gun on a race to the bottom."[17] He worried that a country of origin rule would create "flags of convenience," as European corporations would reincorporate in states with relatively lax regulation. Such complaints had resonance: opposition to the country of origin principle helped derail the EU Constitution in 2005 and later led to that principle's retreat within the EU.[18]

Even before the Services Directive, the European Court of Justice had argued that requiring local certification of foreign suppliers would be unduly burdensome, as such suppliers would have to satisfy multiple authorities. The Court has repeatedly held that member states should accept the sufficiency of the services regulation of other member states but has generally allowed them nonetheless to derogate from this requirement based on public interest.[19] In electronic commerce, the EU has made plain its preference for home country regulation, requiring countries to defer to a foreign service provider's home regulation except where necessary and proportionate to protect the public interest.[20] Such country of origin rules might be easier to adopt in the EU, where supranational directives have laid the groundwork for widespread legal harmonization. GATS, however, eschews this interpretative approach, explicitly "*recognizing* the right of Members to regulate, and to introduce new regulations, on the supply of services within their territories in order to meet national policy objectives,"[21] and requiring nations to accept foreign credentials only voluntarily.[22]

Proponents of a country of origin principle often analogize the receipt of a crossborder net-worked service to travel to a foreign land. This raises a metaphysical question: *Where does an event in cyberspace occur?*[23] Is the *provider*, like a foreign sales representative, traveling (virtually) crossborder into the country of the *consumer*? Or is the *consumer*, like a tourist aboard a cruise ship, traveling (virtually) to the country of the *provider*?[24] If the metaphor of the virtual tourist holds, then that person should expect that service to be governed by the provider's home.[25] After all, states do not typically interfere with a person's consumption while abroad.[26] In the case of *United States—Gambling* (described in chapters 4 and 6), the WTO Appellate Body presumed without discussion that offering online gambling services is the equivalent of the provider traveling crossborder.[27] This seems wise: the alternate characterization, as consumption abroad, allows consumers to opt out of local mandatory law with the click of a mouse or the tap of a finger (rather than the more onerous boarding of a vessel) or, worse, subjects them to foreign law without the notice of entry into a foreign jurisdiction that would normally attend foreign travel. This traveling provider characterization also supports the argument for glocalization—requiring the foreign service provider to comply with local law—rather than requiring the consumer's home jurisdiction to relent in favor of the consumer's purported choice of (virtual) foreign travel.

Local law, after all, reflects local mores (however imprecisely, given defects in the political process). Allowing services to be provided according to the law of the home jurisdiction of the service provider would displace the local law of the service consumer, subjecting that consumer to a foreign rule. Of course, where a particular local rule is merely a default or optional rule, subject to change contractually, there is nothing offensive per se in the choice of a foreign rule. But with respect to mandatory law, democracy supports glocalization, at least until We the People elect to subject ourselves to foreign rules.[28]

In 2006, the European Parliament suggested that it would replace the "country of origin" principle in the draft Services Directive with the "freedom to receive services."[29] This is an appealing recharacterization of international trade in services, focusing attention on how liberalized trade empowers consumer choice. Indeed, management guru Kenichi Ohmae has characterized globalization as simply "consumer sovereignty."[30] But while globalization heightens consumer choice, it may at the same time make the consumer vulnerable to exploitation. This is because it is nation-states—their laws and their courts—not nongovernmental, supranational organizations, or even private associations, that serve as the principal protectors of consumers in today's world. To displace national sovereignty with consumer sovereignty would be to eliminate consumer protections in favor of "buyer beware." Some netizens would prefer the benevolence of technologists to national governments—but this is likely to result in either a technocracy—rule by system operators—or a plutocracy—rule by corporations.

The focus on consumers suggests that we may relax our concerns with respect to merchants, whom one presumes to have a greater degree of sophistication and economic interest with respect to contractual terms with foreign suppliers. Sometimes merchant-to-merchant agreements might implicate consumer protections, in which case they merit examination. As I describe below, the European Union regulates the onward transfer of personal data by European companies for processing outside the European Union, subjecting even these merchant-to-merchant agreements to stringent scrutiny.

Glocalization's assertion of municipal law in the face of global information flows thus stands in contrast to the world envisioned by cyberspace enthusiasts, who would deny the applicability of local law to a universal cyberspace.[31] Glocalization simultaneously confounds the desires of globe-trotting corporations, which seek to extend their markets without the troublesome impediments of local law.[32] The cosmopolitan, borderless world promised by both business strategists and cyberutopians seems yet remote—at least when such a world would defeat local law. The flat world of global business and the self-regulated world of cyberspace remain distant ideals.

Yet reasserting national sovereignty in the face of net-work need not stymie globalization. Indeed, it will strengthen globalization against a retrenching backlash.[33] If crossborder flows of information grossly undermine our privacy, security, or the standards of locally delivered services, they will not long be tolerated. Even the promise of more efficient production and its concomitant cost savings might not rebuff protectionist impulses bolstered by the emergence of well-publicized examples of crossborder net-work abuses. Some smaller states may well have conceded their own powerlessness in the face of cyberspace. Taiwan, for example, has apparently brought few (or perhaps even zero) cases against foreign corporations or individuals for activities (such as intellectual property infringement) in cyberspace. The principle of glocalization would perhaps strengthen the resolve of small states to assert their own law in cyberspace when necessary to protect important local concerns. Glocalization will also spur workers worldwide to train according to the requirements of the world's most demanding jurisdictions. This may spur human capital investment throughout the world and raise standards worldwide.

Whether a net-work provider will respond to glocalization efforts by offering a generalized service acceptable to all (a "one-size-fits-all" service) or a service tailored to each regulatory regime (a "bespoke" service) will depend largely on the economics of delivering variations of that service. In some cases, a net-work supplier will conclude that a bespoke service is warranted because a tailored service supplies profits in excess of the additional costs of tailoring. In other cases, a service provider may decide that it is not cost-effective to do so, and will thus prefer a one-size-fits-all service. For example, an American digital bookseller might remove the novel *Lady Chatterley's Lover* from its offerings worldwide rather than implement technology to block its transfer only to those few jurisdictions that label the book indecent. Such a result would indeed be unfortunate, though we might note that cyberspace is filled with those who would make less craven decisions, willing to risk the wrath of repressive regimes to disseminate information.[34] Indeed, efforts to block a classic book are exactly the kinds of activities that will likely prove futile and thus unlikely to succeed. The Pirate Bay, described above in chapter 4, is one such enterprise, gleefully snubbing authorities everywhere. WikiLeaks is another, disclosing information that authorities and corporations seek to suppress. Reporters once traced WikiLeaks through its Internet Protocol address to Sweden at the servers run by the founders of The Pirate Bay.

Return to the French orders to Yahoo! in California to desist from supplying Nazi material to French men and women, which we discussed in chapter 2. As California legal scholar Neal Netanel writes about a similar German law, "Germany's citizens, we may assume, have democratically chosen to prohibit the dissemination of neo-Nazi speech in their country. Indeed, German law combating neo-Nazism lies at the heart of Germany's postwar constitutionalism, born out of the trauma of that country's totalitarian past and designed to forge a 'militant democracy,' a liberal state capable of resisting those who would attack the constitutional order and foment ethnic hatred."[35] Yahoo! did not contest French (or German) authority to offer such a rule to regulate life in France (or Germany).

Rather, it told the French courts that they should not try to impose that rule on a global Internet corporation. Yahoo! argued that a French order would represent French efforts to impose its law on the world. Yahoo! worried that tolerating the French imposition would launch a parade of requests to remove material, whittling down the World Wide Web into a small, rump set of offerings acceptable to states ranging from China to France to Singapore to North Korea. The freest information medium in the world would rapidly become its most heavily regulated. The French court, however, satisfied itself that this was not inevitable; that technology would permit Yahoo! to offer a conforming service to French citizens yet simultaneously offer a nonconforming service to others, at least with 70 to 90 percent accuracy in identifying a user as French.[36] The French court relied on an expert panel including American Internet pioneer Vint Cerf to conclude that the Internet Protocol address of a user would likely give away his or her location. This technology of "geolocation" would permit a company to glocalize. Later in this chapter, I describe an international law rule that would allow France to rightfully insist on applying its hate speech regulations to Yahoo!'s US operations only where they pose a *substantial* harm in France.

If France has a right to insist on its anti-Nazi policy with respect to Yahoo!'s offerings in France, must US courts assist? After all, who has more enforcement authority than a service provider's home courts? For all the recent concern about US exceptionalism when it comes to foreign and international law, the United States has long followed a practice of recognizing and enforcing foreign judgments as long as they are not at odds with American public policy. In the classic 1895 case of *Hilton v. Guyot*, a French person sought to recover through US courts a French judgment against US parties arising out of a commercial dispute.[37] An Irish immigrant, Hilton had begun his business importing Irish lace and then moved to importing other items, including the French gloves that led to a French civil judgment against him.[38] The Supreme Court held that a US court could enforce the foreign money judgment as a matter of comity, which the Court described as "the recognition which one nation allows within its territory to the legislative, executive or judicial acts of another nation." Procedural differences between the two jurisdictions would not necessarily derail recognition, as long as the foreign court had subject-matter jurisdiction and offered an opportunity for a full and fair trial in an impartial process. But the Court found another stumbling block in French law: because French courts would refuse to honor a similar American judgment, comity did not require a US court to honor the French judgment at issue. Since *Hilton*, however, the reciprocity condition for recognition and enforcement has largely been forgotten in US jurisprudence.[39]

Before a US court, Yahoo! argued that the general rule favoring recognition was unavailable because of a constitutional constraint. Yahoo! argued that the First Amendment prevented a US court from enforcing the French order. The question presented was difficult: Does the First Amendment protect the speech of an American on American soil transmitted to a French citizen on French soil? A panel of eleven federal circuit court judges seemed uncertain and divided, and a majority cobbled together out of minority views dismissed the case as either lacking in personal jurisdiction or unripe. Judge William Fletcher wrote that defining the "extent of First Amendment protection of speech accessible solely by those outside the United States is a difficult and, to some degree, unresolved issue."[40] Judge Fletcher seemed to imagine a perfect geolocation-followed-by-glocalization regime, in which Yahoo! could, if it so chose, tolerate the offer of Nazi materials within the free-speech zone of the United States while barring it in France.

The scenario painted by Judge Fletcher is appealing: a US court would simply prevent a US provider from supplying to France speech barred in France while allowing the US provider to continue supplying that speech at home. But as the French court itself observed, geolocation is imperfect (though improving). For example, geolocation might mistakenly label a Frenchman as a Virginian if he uses Virginia-based AOL, a company with subscribers around the world. That mistake, of course, would not raise a First Amendment concern because it would simply allow more speech to hit French shores.

But geolocation technology might also mistake an American as a French man or woman, if he or she uses a service that uses IP addresses allocated to a French provider or perhaps if he or she communicates in French. A personal experience illustrates the problem. When I tried to access the video service Hulu to watch a favorite NBC comedy, the site reported, "Sorry, currently our video library can only be streamed from within the United States." This was a bit odd because I was sitting in a hotel in *Washington, DC*. Perhaps the error arose because the hotel was part of a Canadian chain and thus perhaps relies on a Canadian Internet service provider. The example shows that American enforcement of a foreign speech restriction can reduce speech in the United States. This is the *negative spillover effect* on speech.

The broader point is this: enforcing a foreign rule may cause it to spill over into the domestic arena. Thus, states should not lend a hand to enforce a foreign rule if that rule would violate public policy at home. More generally put, states should assist foreign states as a matter of comity or in the hope of inducing reciprocity in the future, but only where such assistance would not run afoul of local public policy.

As the *Yahoo!* case demonstrates, the one-size-fits-all approach might have a tendency to ratchet standards up, reducing what is available to everyone. Even glocalization by the United States does not stop this. The First Amendment after all does not require Yahoo! to convey Nazi material but merely permits it to do so. As a private corporation, Yahoo! is free (thankfully) to choose to divest itself of this material. This is true not only with respect to speech. Under pressure to follow strict European privacy rules, Yahoo! could decide to implement them throughout its global sites if it found that the costs of segregating information about Europeans from information about others could not be justified by the advantages of more lax privacy rules. As in the speech example, the US rules do not bar a company from treating private information with great care and processing and disclosing it only with permission. This parallels the regulatory spillover that arises in the goods context as well—the strict safety rules of one jurisdiction, say on the content of the paint used in consumer products, might lead global suppliers to apply those rules throughout their production for all markets. This is similar to what some have called the "California Effect" in areas such as automobile emissions.[41]

A web of states enforcing their own rules and enforcing each other's rules where consistent with local policy will reduce the jurisdictional evasion made possible by the Internet. The difficulty, as we have seen, is that enforcing a foreign rule on local Internet providers will likely have spillover effects in the local jurisdiction. In some cases, this may not be alarming, but in cases involving free speech, for example, this will be clearly deleterious.

Countries have been reluctant even to commit to enforcing a choice of court agreement, when two parties agree to settle any disputes in a particular court. The proposed Hague Convention on Choice of Court Agreements would enforce non-consumer contractual choices of one nation's courts to hear disputes arising out of the contract.[42] Despite the narrowness of the disputes covered by this treaty—after all it only applies to non-consumer crossborder contracts—to date only one state, Mexico, has adopted it. Perhaps this is because the Convention would only permit a state to disregard a foreign choice of court where the result would be "*manifestly* contrary to the public policy of the State."[43] By contrast, the widely subscribed United Nations Convention enforcing arbitral awards allows a state to refuse to enforce if "contrary to the public policy" of that state.[44] Leaving states clear escape valves from an international obligation to enforce a foreign law will enhance states' willingness to enter into the international obligation in the first place.

Harmonization

Glocalization raises a fistful of important concerns:

1. *Balkanization*—the creation of borders in cyberspace, thereby risking the advantages of global information and services sharing;
2. *Stalinization*—the imposition of the world's most repressive rules on cyberspace, in aggregated form;
3. *incursions upon sovereignty*, as efforts to regulate foreign service providers lead to extraterritorial assertions of prescriptive and adjudicative power;
4. *futility*—the difficulty of stamping out undesired information in cyberspace; and
5. the *costs* of compliance with multifarious and potentially conflicting local laws.

These are serious concerns, and they require ameliorative doctrines that I classify under the general heading of *harmonization*. I argue that the consequences of unrestrained glocalization require states to harmonize their laws and procedures wherever possible. The harmonization principle is just as important as the glocalization principle itself. While these concerns counsel very substantial limits on the glocalization principle, they do not undermine its central raison d'être: preserving the possibility of self-regulation in a net-worked world.

Both international law and US law establish significant metes and bounds for glocalization. Common perception notwithstanding, neither jurisprudence authorizes extraterritorial jurisdiction on the basis of effects alone. International law typically limits state exercise of prescriptive (the right to legislate) and adjudicative (the right to resolve disputes) authority over conduct outside its territory only where the effect on its own territory is "substantial."[45] As Yale legal scholar Michael Reisman describes, international law seeks "to resolve systematically" conflicts of laws "by allocating to particular states the competence to make or apply law to particular persons, things or events that are simultaneously" subject to "the control of two or more states."[46] The goal is not to eliminate overlapping jurisdictional authority but to manage it. In related fashion, the American Law Institute's principles for transnational intellectual property disputes permit courts faced with a ubiquitous alleged intellectual property infringement to choose the law of the state with the closest connections with the dispute.[47]

For its part, the due process clause of the US Constitution restrains judicial power, limiting a state's extraterritorial reach even in the face—quite literally—of an explosion on that state's soil. In the classic American case of *Worldwide Volkswagen v. Woodson*, involving a car that caught fire in Oklahoma, the Supreme Court denied an Oklahoma court jurisdiction over that car's New York distributor because that distributor lacked sufficient other ties to Oklahoma. Even though the distributor could have foreseen that the car might cause injury in Oklahoma (or anywhere in the continental United States), the Supreme Court declared the distributor off-limits to Oklahoma courts in the absence of more concerted ties to Oklahoma. The Court declared, "Every seller of chattels [does not] in effect appoint the chattel his agent for service of process."[48] We can recast this maxim for the digital age: every net-work provider does not appoint electrons as his or her agent for service of process. In recent cases involving the Internet, US circuit courts allow a state to assert jurisdiction over a foreign person only if there is "something more" than effects alone, typically some kind of known targeting of someone in that state.[49] A tragic motorcycle accident in California led the Court to revisit the *Worldwide Volkswagen* issue in the case of *Asahi Metal Industry Co., Ltd. v. Superior Court of California*, now in the context of a suit between a Taiwanese tire manufacturer and a Japanese tire valve manufacturer. The Supreme Court again repudiated the assertion of state court jurisdiction, this time because the California court failed, among other things, to "consider the procedural and substantive policies of other *nations*."[50] As we move from Worldwide Volkswagen to the World Wide Web, we may do well to remember the lessons learned from earlier globalizations.

It was technological change, and the changes that technology wrought on commerce, that led the United States to abandon strict territorial limits on the assertion of jurisdiction in the mid-twentieth century.[51] The Supreme Court has observed that technological progress has spurred interstate (and international) commerce, necessitating expansion of jurisdictional grounds: "As technological progress has increased the flow of commerce between the States, the need for jurisdiction over nonresidents has undergone a similar increase. At the same time, progress in communications and transportation has made the defense of a suit in a foreign tribunal less burdensome." Yet the Court has refused to abandon limits on personal jurisdiction entirely: "It is a mistake to assume that this trend heralds the eventual demise of all restrictions on the personal jurisdiction of state courts." The Court explained such restrictions as "more than a guarantee of immunity from inconvenient or distant litigation," but rather "a consequence of territorial limitations on the power of the respective States."[52] Limits on the assertion of jurisdiction are constitutional restraints on the power to impose one's law on others. Due process limits on personal jurisdiction function as limits not only on adjudication but on legislation as well. They constrain the domain of the local law.

Antitrust law has long grappled with the globalization of production. The early jurisprudential attitude was to confine US antitrust law only to acts occurring within the United States. When asked to hear a challenge to an effort to monopolize banana exports in Costa Rica, Justice Oliver Wendell Holmes wrote in the 1909 case of *American Banana Co. v. United Fruit Co.* that "it is surprising to hear it argued that" acts outside the jurisdiction of the United States "were governed by the act of Congress."[53] To apply US law, he continued, would be "contrary to the comity of nations."[54] But the courts and Congress came to recognize that refusing to apply American antitrust law abroad could dramatically undermine that law at home, as foreign anticompetitive practices would spill over into the United States. As Harvard professor Kingman Brewster pointed out in an influential book, antitrust law author Senator John Sherman himself worried about "jurisdiction-hopping and evasion," advising that such problems could be met by attaching the putative evader's property in the United States (a solution that is often unavailable with net-work).[55] In the 1976 *Timberlane Lumber Co. v. Bank of America*, a federal court of appeals famously offered a test that sought to balance the competing interests of various states in determining whether to assert both prescriptive and adjudicative jurisdiction over alleged foreign anticompetitive acts. The American lumber company Timberlane sued Bank of America and others for actions abroad that allegedly harmed Timberlane's efforts to export lumber from Honduras to the United States. Judge Herbert Choy articulated a "jurisdictional rule of reason" that required the court to consider seven factors before asserting extraterritorial jurisdiction:

1. "the degree of conflict with foreign law or policy";
2. "the nationality or allegiance of the parties and the locations or principal places of business of corporations";
3. "the extent to which enforcement by either state can be expected to achieve compliance";
4. "the relative significance of effects on the United States as compared with those elsewhere";
5. "the extent to which there is explicit purpose to harm or affect American commerce";
6. "the foreseeability of such effect"; and
7. "the relative importance to the violations charged of conduct within the United States as compared with conduct abroad."[56]

The American Law Institute largely adopted this flexible approach in its influential *Restatement (Third) on Foreign Relations Law* but added a crucial final factor:

8. "the importance of the regulation to the international political, legal, or economic system."[57]

As markets widened across the globe, it became necessary to extend US antitrust law overseas in order to protect Americans—but to do so in a way consistent with the needs and rights of the international community.

These cases show how the law has responded to the globalization of the production of goods. In the cases described above, covering the diverse range of goods subject to international trade—automobiles, motorcycles, bananas, lumber—the Supreme Court did not insist on local adjudication or local law, even where there was harm ultimately felt within the United States. In these cases, at least, the US courts have largely avoided provincialism, favoring instead due consideration of foreign and international interests.

This willingness to forbear in the interests of comity and the international order will prove essential with respect to services as well. The risks of Balkanization, the incursions on foreign sovereignty, and the costs of compliance with multifarious and potentially conflicting municipal laws all counsel restraint. An early US governmental study warned of the dangers of overregulation, worried that unnecessary content regulation of the Internet by states "could cripple the growth and diversity of the Internet."[58] We will need an extraterritoriality jurisprudence for Trade 2.0 modeled on *Timberlane* and its progeny. Of course, a multifactor standard such as the one in *Timberlane* does not promise the predictability of sharp rules. Yet such a common law approach may be the most suited to navigating the uncertain waters that trade in net-worked services will bring. As Judge Choy noted in *Timberlane*, "At some point the interests of the United States are too weak and the foreign harmony incentive for restraint too strong."[59] Common law courts seem far better suited to determine these points than legislatures demarcating sharp rules. A case-by-case analysis can more readily implement the international version of the golden rule applied to extraterritorial jurisdiction: a nation-state should assert jurisdiction only when such an assertion is universalizable, that is, when it would feel comfortable with other nation-states also asserting jurisdiction in similar cases.

I have assumed here that applying domestic law to foreign service providers supplying services via the Web to domestic consumers is an *extraterritorial* assertion of law. But should not efforts to regulate transmissions as they cross into this country be seen as an uncontroversial exercise of *intraterritorial* authority? The difficulty is that the persons who must modify their behavior are abroad; thus, the enforcement of a national rule against such persons will require an extraterritorial change of behavior. (This would not be the case if the regulation were effected only through domestic intermediaries such as ISPs or through targeting domestic users of the foreign service, and no liability was attached to the foreign provider—but censorship at the ISP level is likely to chill speech beyond even what is intended.) Given the direct demand to a foreign service provider, concerns about extraterritorial application of both US law and US judicial power appear appropriate. Cyberspace does not allow clean demarcations of political boundaries, with an American space here, a Brazilian space there, and so on. Requiring a foreign net-work provider to comply with local law entails a command to a party outside one's borders. In this sense, such regulation has an extraterritorial component.[60]

However, courts should not require a clear legislative statement of extraterritorial intent before applying a rule to net-work sourced from outside the country. Because most US law does not have an explicit extraterritorial application mandate, requiring clear legislative statement would simply serve to allow service providers (and perhaps consumers) to avoid the bulk of US law.

Just as US law should not be asserted carelessly against foreign service providers on behalf of domestic parties, US law should not be available to foreigners without a substantial US nexus. Again, here an antitrust case offers guidance. In *F. Hoffman-LaRoche Ltd. v. Empagran*, the Supreme Court said that efforts to extend US antitrust protections to foreigners smacked of "legal imperialism." "If America's antitrust policies could not win their own way in the international marketplace for such ideas," the Court reasoned, we should not impose these policies on foreign countries nonetheless. The Court accordingly refused to hear the claims of foreign plaintiffs where their foreign injuries are "independent of any adverse domestic effect."[61] Of course, if international law declares the defendant's actions illegal, then allowing a suit to proceed (for example through an Alien Torts Statute claim) would further the international order, not undermine it.

Choice of law also restrains excessive assertions of local law—and thus excessive parochialism. The *lex fori*—the law of the forum—need not have a stranglehold on the judicial imagination. Conflict of laws rules empower courts to select a foreign rule depending on the relative interests at stake of each jurisdiction.[62] The intensity of multijurisdictional transactions arising out of Trade 2.0 will require states to fortify such efforts rather than obstreperously insisting on the local rule. States must forgo an insistence on local law where the local interest is dwarfed by the foreign interest or is otherwise minimal.[63] Such forbearance will attract reciprocity from sister states. Moreover, it is necessary to alleviate the international conflicts that cyberspace trade will generate. As with the jurisdictional calculus, courts must be sensitive to the "needs of the interstate and international system,"[64] though judges should not embrace what they believe to be a "better" foreign law nor innovate a substantive set of new customs to govern Trade 2.0 disputes where a mandatory local law already exists.

Extravagant actions against foreigners have at times drawn legal responses from their home countries. Sufficiently noxious assertions of extraterritorial jurisdiction will be met with blocking statutes and other retaliatory measures by sister states.

Glocalization is unnecessary where (1) a state has agreed on an international standard (*harmonization*, in a strong sense); (2) a state has accepted a foreign regime as satisfactory for local purposes (*recognition*, which functions as a kind of middle level of harmonization because it sanctions certain alternative governing rules); or (3) a state determines that the relative interests do not justify enforcing its local rule (a weak, discretionary form of one-off harmonization).[65] Forbearance acts as a weak form of harmonization because, by not asserting jurisdiction, the locality is essentially yielding to a foreign law and in that sense is permitting that conduct to be governed by that law. Efforts to harmonize laws across nations and standards among professional associations will prove essential to preserve a global cyberspace in the face of national regulation.

Harmonization of services regulation is one of the goals of recent trade agreements. GATS permits members to "recognize the education or experience obtained, requirements met, or licenses or certifications granted in a particular country."[66] It goes further to mandate that states agree on disciplines to ensure that licensing and technical standards are not unduly "burdensome" and "based on objective and transparent criteria."[67] NAFTA similarly acknowledges the possibility that a party might recognize, "unilaterally or by agreement, education, experience, licenses or certifications obtained in the territory of another Party or of a non-Party."[68] ASEAN has recently adopted mutual recognition arrangements with respect to nursing and engineering, with the intention that a certification in one jurisdiction will be recognized in another.[69] Regional recognition arrangements might pave the way for recognition of the law or licensing of countries outside the region.[70] With respect to harmonization, NAFTA also encourages the parties to "develop mutually acceptable standards and criteria for licensing and certification of professional service providers."[71] The WTO's Technical Barriers to

Trade (TBT) Treaty makes broader demands still, requiring states to use international standards where consistent with regulatory aims, and requiring states to give "positive consideration to accepting as equivalent technical regulations of other Members, even if these regulations differ from their own, provided they are satisfied that these regulations adequately fulfill the objectives of their own regulations."[72] US recognition of foreign judgments' jurisprudence is similarly permissive, allowing recognition even where a foreign court's procedures differ from ours.[73] This recognition jurisprudence, of course, applies to foreign judicial judgments, not foreign certifications and standards. Moreover, the TBT Treaty, for its part, explicitly excludes services from its ambit.[74] WTO negotiators should seek to expand the TBT to cover services.

This will require harmonization projects, not only for the procedural aspects of transnational net-work described in chapter 7, but also in substantive areas. A dramatic example of a harmonization project shows the possibilities: the SEC recently permitted certain foreign issuers of securities in the US markets to use International Financial Reporting Standards (IFRS) accounting standards without reconciling them to the Generally Accepted Accounting Standards widely adopted in the United States.[75] The Securities and Exchange Commission has been considering allowing American companies to use IFRS as well domestically. If it does so, this would mean adopting international accounting standards even for American companies at home. This move to harmonize our rules seems a natural result of recognition because it would otherwise give a foreign company the option to choose between two standards (the American standard or the recognized foreign or international standard), leaving an American company in a disadvantageous position of having no option (being forced to use the American standard). States have incentives to harmonize standards because of the benefits of economies of scale and the possibilities of lower consumer prices, though, of course, regulatory capture by protectionist interests remains a significant concern.[76]

Moving toward international standards for certain services may involve deference to the results of technocratic legal processes. Some have critiqued such transnational processes as undemocratic, but I have argued elsewhere that the voluntary nature of national acquiescence to such processes makes them compatible with democracy.[77]

With glocalization and harmonization in reasonable relative measures, the Internet will offer the world's most important platform for regulatory competition. In the face of this competition, states may modify their own laws, finding that their laws are unnecessary, ineffective, or even inferior to foreign laws. Services regulations are especially likely to undergo rationalization, as they have never before faced foreign competition. Industry and consumer groups will establish sets of best practices and global standards in certain services, and governments may defer to such standards. Governments will find it in their own interests to seek international coordination because of the difficulty of finding national solutions to global problems.[78] Equally important, private parties are seeking to establish transnational rules and standards that will govern parts of Trade 2.0.[79] We are likely to witness the emergence, in certain domains, of a new *lex mercatoria*, a set of shared basic rules cobbled together through the common law, private coordination, statutory convergence, and treaty harmonization, thereby reducing Balkanization, incursions on sovereignty, and costs of global legal compliance. In yet other domains, there is likely to exist a preference for legal diversity, or at least disagreement on where to find legal harmony.

Jurisdictional evasion can demonstrate the injustice of laws, putting pressure on localities to justify their repression of an activity legal elsewhere. A famous 1967 United States constitutional case serves as an example. *Loving v. Virginia* involved an interracial Virginia couple who traveled to another jurisdiction to marry. When newlyweds Mildred and Richard Loving returned home, they were arrested, charged with leaving the state to evade the law with intent to cohabitate upon return. The Supreme Court sided with the Lovings, declaring the Virginia antimiscegenation rule unconstitutional, indeed "designed to maintain White Supremacy" by specifically forbidding whites to intermarry with others.[80] In *Loving*, it was a superior legal order that compelled Virginia to rewrite its repugnant law. The international legal order lacks a Supreme Court able to impose its views on national courts, but the World Trade Organization serves as a significant disciplinary mechanism. As set out in chapter 6, the WTO can sanction protectionist services regulation, though as the example of the United States vis-à-vis Antigua shows, some states might simply be content to suffer the sanction rather than change their law.

The European Union has sought to leverage control over domestic entities to control of information processing elsewhere. Recognizing that European privacy laws are often significantly more protective than those elsewhere and recognizing the usefulness of the outsourcing of data processing, the EU has sought to regulate the processing of data about Europeans by service providers *outside* Europe.[81] Under the EU's Data Protection Directive, data collectors within Europe may send data to foreign processors only if the outsourcer is in a country that the EU recognizes as providing sufficient privacy and security safeguards (currently, Andorra, Argentina, Australia, Canada, Faeroe Islands, Guernsey, Israel, Isle of Man, Jersey, and Switzerland, and, under a weak Safe Harbor, the United States)[82] or the outsourcer accepts a model contract protecting privacy. The model contract requires the outsourcer to permit third-party audits of its facilities and data, to submit to European law as governing its privacy practices with respect to the information, and to respect any related ruling of the courts of the data exporter's home jurisdiction.[83]

Regulatory theorists Daniel Esty and Damien Geradin suggest the following goal for countries facing international competition: "Regulatory systems should be set up with enough interjurisdictional cooperation (or harmonization) to ensure that transboundary externalities and other market failures are addressed, but with a sufficient degree of regulatory competition to prevent the resulting governmental structure from becoming an untamed, overreaching, or inefficient Leviathan."[84] The framework I have suggested here is driven not by market failure alone, but my ultimate counsel is similar.

Governments should respond to the net-work trade by rationalizing their laws wherever possible, engaging in international standards projects and recognizing the adequacy of certain foreign standards and enforcement, while not jettisoning efforts to ensure that net-work providers comport their service with local public policy. Even with such efforts, the imperfection of enforcement will always mean that there will remain some room for evasion and thus a potentially useful regulatory challenge.

Harmonize where possible, and glocalize where necessary. Such a maxim does not answer difficult questions of when to prefer one or the other, but it does establish a framework for understanding what is at stake.

The Silk Road originally established to carry precious goods ultimately carried Buddhism, transmitting it from its home in the Indian subcontinent to China, Japan, and Southeast Asia. In the next chapter I suggest that the Electronic Silk Road offers the world's best route for bringing political and cultural information to the peoples of totalitarian states. Perhaps like its Silk Road antecedent, the Electronic Silk Road will help China find enlightenment.

9

LAST STOP

Middle Kingdom

Alibaba, Baidu, Tencent, Renren, Sina, Tudou. China is full of innovative and successful Internet companies, many worth billions of dollars. Yet of these companies, only one, Alibaba, is a global trader—and then only to offer Chinese manufactures to the world. Most of these companies do not even bother to offer a version of their website in English or in any language other than Chinese. Even when listing their stock on the New York exchanges, they evince only an ambition to conquer China, not the world. Tencent describes itself as "a leading provider of Internet and mobile & telecommunications value-added services in China." Baidu tells us that it is "the leading Chinese language Internet search provider." Compare the prospectuses from Silicon Valley. Google describes itself as "a global technology leader . . . that improve[s] the lives of billions of people globally." Facebook declares its mission "to make the world more open and connected." Zynga reports that it is "the world's leading social game developer with 230 million average monthly active users . . . in 175 countries."

If Chinese companies seem content within China, China itself figures prominently in the business desires of many Silicon Valley enterprises. China now boasts the world's largest population of Internet users, with ever-increasing income. When American companies have raced into China, they have often been heavily criticized for assisting the Chinese government in suppressing information and in repressing political dissidents.

In this chapter I take up two puzzles involving the ancient heart of the Silk Road. First, why did not China, the champion of international trade in goods, not also become a champion of trade in services? Second, when Silicon Valley enterprises offer services in China, must they also become complicit in political repression?

Great Firewalls

Why has China not translated its success in the outsourcing of goods to the outsourcing of services? Even while Chinese factories have made that country the capital of outsourcing in manufacturing, China has greatly lagged India in the outsourcing of services. This may seem puzzling given three natural advantages, both of which China shared with India: (1) a large home market that should permit Chinese companies to develop economies of scale without braving an international market; (2) the existence of a large labor pool, including well-regarded institutions of higher learning; and (3) the existence of a diaspora concentrated especially along the

American West Coast, which should give Chinese companies crucial information about the American market and American companies crucial information about Chinese suppliers.

Yet Chinese entrepreneurs have been unable thus far to replicate their manufacturing success in services. In 2011, China exported $182 billion of commercial services while importing $236 billion, a deficit of $54 billion. We might offer three possible explanations for China's relatively weak international services trade. Most obviously, language barriers have made it difficult to recruit sufficient numbers of Chinese employees fluent in Western languages, especially English. Second, the government's fear of the open Internet has stymied information flows into and out of China. Uncertainty about information flows cannot be tolerated in a time-sensitive services environment. Furthermore, the services outsourcing often involves the transmission of sensitive personal or corporate information. Those outside China are likely to be less than keen to transfer personal data for processing to a country with few restraints on governmental snooping. It might prove difficult for companies to reveal to their customers that their personal data were being processed in China.

The fact that China has a better physical infrastructure than India has not proven as helpful as one might have expected. Indian companies have compensated for an inadequate municipal power supply by establishing their own power generation systems on their campuses. A neglected road infrastructure does not present a huge bottleneck for delivering services electronically. Of course, electronically mediated services require an excellent telecommunications infrastructure, but India has been able to build such an infrastructure. Because of its desire to control information flows, China was more reluctant in the 1990s to allow the free-for-all of private communications networks. Before undersea Internet cables tying India to the West became widely available, Indian IT companies relied on satellite links.[1]

Authoritarian countries eager to control information flow are far less willing to allow private companies to set up satellite links or other private and often encrypted channels of communication.

As the list of Internet companies at the beginning of this chapter indicates, the Chinese Internet itself is flourishing. Add to that list companies such as Youku, Netease, Shanda, Ctrip, Taobao, and Sohu, all wildly popular and highly profitable enterprises. The largest of the Chinese Internet firms, Tencent, is listed on Nasdaq, and boasts a market capitalization of $51 billion as of March 2012. Baidu has a market value close behind at $49 billion. Sina has a market value of $5 billion, RenRen $2 billion, DangDang $0.5 billion, Sohu $2 billion, YouKu $3 billion, and Tudou $1 billion (the last two have announced plans to merge). But these companies face an enormous roadblock, exemplified by market leaders Tencent and Baidu: Tencent's and Baidu's main websites exist only in Chinese. Indeed, this is true of most of these Chinese Internet companies. Ctrip, a travel portal, does offer services in English, but simply to serve foreign travelers to China. The popular Chinese social network kaixin001.com is available only in Chinese, as if the only people that one wishes to network with are Chinese-speaking. As this demonstrates, the ambitions of Chinese Internet enterprises are still limited to serving the Chinese market. That this market is growing has allowed them to become hugely profitable nonetheless, but it does limit their ultimate growth potential. They do not seek to go toe to toe with Silicon Valley companies outside China. This lack of a global presence might in the long run erode their success in China itself. As Chinese people themselves become increasingly globalized, they will increasingly turn to companies that can better connect them with the world at large, not just China.

Chinese Internet companies may have oddly benefited from censorship. China has banned some very popular services such as Facebook and Twitter, and Google's services are typically blocked. Such acts of political repression have the effect of eliminating the principal competition for local Chinese Internet entrepreneurs. But such protectionism, even if a by-product of another governmental policy, does not often build companies ready for the world, and it denies consumers access to some of the world's best enterprises.

One strategy for globalization is to purchase established Western Internet companies, using the money they earn in China to try to gain a foothold abroad. This seems a risky strategy. In 2011, Tencent purchased a majority interest in American online game company Riot Games for the princely sum of $231 million in cash. The risk of failing to meld corporate cultures seems quite high. Presumably, the American shareholders remained minority shareholders in the subsidiary to incentivize the American management in companies in which the major value is in human capital. However, as the controlling shareholder, the Chinese parent will bear significant fiduciary duties to the subsidiary's minority investors, raising risks of legal challenges. Whatever the merits of an acquisition strategy (and whatever the form it takes), it remains the case that most Chinese companies have thus far focused their energies on China itself.

In sum, China's political repression harms its global ambitions when it comes to cybertrade. The Great Firewall of China not only keeps American Internet companies out of China, it keeps Chinese Internet companies in.

Do No Evil

The Internet offers a global information platform that should increase what Martha Nussbaum and Amartya Sen call human capabilities, perhaps especially so for people in repressive societies.

Because foreign service providers lie beyond the easy reach of repressive governments, they can provide a crucial channel to gather and disseminate suppressed information. Where local television, radio, and newspapers must of necessity follow local diktats, foreign information providers can both distribute and supply information largely without jeopardizing either life or property.

Yet in the wrong hands, the Internet can bring the specter of a pernicious Big Brother closer than ever possible in George Orwell's time. Dissident pamphleteers who might have hid behind the anonymity of discreetly placed writings may find their tracks harder to hide in cyberspace. When allied with willing Internet service providers, websites, software providers, and financial intermediaries, a government can gain an omniscience heretofore unknown. Foreign service providers might yield to political and economic pressure from the government and, instead of providing channels for communicating suppressed information, assist the state in rooting out dissidents. As we saw above in chapter 2, China, for example, has relied in part on evidence gleaned from online activities to identify and jail political dissidents.

I have suggested that in the right circumstances, states should be able to insist that foreign Internet providers comply with local law. Does this mean that Google and Yahoo! should bend to the demands of repressive governments? No. I have justified glocalization on the right of the people to choose their own law through their duly elected national organs. Glocalization accordingly does not support a requirement to tailor one's service to the demands of an unelected, repressive state targeting dissidents.

This will require corporations to try to avoid becoming the surveillance arm of the repressive state. In some cases, this might mean keeping one's employees or assets out of that state, so there is no risk of effective local retaliation by the repressive government. In other cases, it might mean avoiding learning or keeping information that might jeopardize political dissidents. It would mean adopting the Safe Server Strategy described in chapter 2, wherein a net-work provider locates its computer servers in a jurisdiction that protects speech and privacy.

Some hope to establish Iceland as a haven for new media, with laws that protect journalists, bloggers, whistleblowers, and their sources. The Icelandic Modern Media Initiative would create a "Switzerland of bits," in which websites, their promoters, and their users could count on friendly source protection, communications protection, freedom of information laws, and libel protection.[2] The idea would be that if a repressive government or an annoyed private party sought to obtain information about, or to censor or sanction, a speaker, the law would generally prove speaker-friendly.

Should we then leave foreign corporations free to choose to ignore a government's demands because those corporations disagree with those laws? Consider, for example, French constraints on Nazi paraphernalia and Australian, Japanese, and Singaporean constraints on pornography. Should service providers located outside these jurisdictions be free to declare these rules repressive and flout them? The choice of which norms to follow should not be left entirely to a corporation's management—especially because management's judgment may well be colored by the color of money.

International law supports corporations that refuse to abet political repression. The United Nations Universal Declaration of Human Rights rejects incursions on freedom of speech unless they secure "morality, public order and the general welfare in a democratic society." The reference to "democratic society" suggests that "public order" concerns cannot be inconsistent with democracy itself. While the Universal Declaration does not constitute binding international law, it nonetheless offers "the primary source of global human rights standards."[3]

Respect for human rights could be translated, at least minimally, into the mandate *Do no evil.* Google has famously adopted a variant of this imperative as a corporate principle. We can understand do no evil as a kind of Pareto principle, whereby the corporation's presence does not, at the very least, make people worse off, in terms of human rights. Not doing evil is not the same as doing good and thus is not necessarily a sufficient criterion for corporate action. But it is the very least we can insist on for corporations.

Consider the actions of Google in China. In 2006, Google launched a Chinese-language version of its site that would, unlike its previous Chinese-language version, be hosted from servers in China itself. Access to Google's servers outside China had been uncertain and slow, due in part or entirely to Chinese blocking, and this move would allow Google to expand its presence in China. In moving its servers to China, Google abandoned its Safe Server Strategy in order to be able to provide its services to Chinese consumers with the least delay. With servers on Chinese soil, Google, however, would find it difficult to avoid Chinese governmental mandates for censoring results. Google, accordingly, took a number of steps to lessen the risk of doing evil: (1) it informed Chinese users of Google.cn when their search results were censored; (2) it continued to offer its uncensored services through the Google.com site; and (3) it did not offer services that allowed users to create content, such as blogs and email.[4] The last condition suggests that Google structured its direct Chinese presence to avoid learning information about dissident activity, information that it might, under Chinese law, be required to divulge to authorities. It thus tried to avoid falling into the trap into which Yahoo! fell and which subjected Yahoo! to a federal lawsuit it ultimately settled.

In 2010, Google retreated from mainland China. It denounced both Chinese censorship and the infiltration of the email accounts of Chinese human rights activists. No longer willing to abide Chinese government demands for censorship, it pulled its Chinese services to Hong Kong, where it is not required to engage in similar censorship. Google's services in China remain censored—but the censorship seems to be accomplished at the ISP level rather than through Google's services themselves.

In 2008, working with human rights organizations and other civil society groups, three new media companies—Google, Microsoft, and Yahoo!—established a set of voluntary principles to govern their response to government pressures that may infringe on the freedom of expression or privacy. Rather than requiring companies to withdraw from repressive states, the Global Network Initiative permits companies to remain as long as they have procedures in place to protect freedom of expression and privacy, including human rights impact assessments of their operations around the world. The initiative also commits its signatories to independent reviews of firm practices related to privacy. What the initiative requires in practice remains to be seen, though Google's challenge to Chinese repression at the beginning of 2010 was a watershed moment in honoring its initiative commitment. The initiative's principles declare it a work in progress, and experience will likely require change. Perhaps most important, it allows member companies to share intelligence and strategies, allowing them to better identify objectionable governmental requests and formulate responses.

Although the Initiative is a welcome effort at self-regulation, it is subject to at least four principal critiques.[5] First, because of its voluntary nature, a large number of companies remain outside its purview. Even those who did commit to the initiative could fall short of its obligations and would be subject only to the social sanction of "naming and shaming." Second, "I'm sorry, but I've signed on to a set of principles," is hardly an excuse likely to prove effective when a company is forced to defend against a repressive government order. Third, a voluntary arrangement will not stand against a legal requirement—even in the new media company's home country. Finally, the private initiative lacks the legal sanctions available to enforce a statutory obligation. But despite these concerns, the initiative is an important development for information service providers in a world sadly too marked by information repression.

The Intersection of Cybertrade and Human Rights

Proponents of human rights have often found themselves at odds with free traders. The desire to liberalize the flow of goods across borders in service of efficient production has at times been insufficiently attentive to the rights of workers and the health of the environment. Cyberspace, however, may offer a context in which the desire for free trade and the wish to promote political freedom go hand in hand. As the Chinese example shows, the bugaboos of repressive governments today are search engines, electronic bulletin boards, blogs, Facebook, YouTube, and microblogging services such as Twitter and Weibo. These technologies allow ordinary individuals to communicate outside the mainstream media channels that often prove subservient to governments. By liberalizing trade in cyberspace, international trade law can bolster the circulation of information that authoritarian regimes would repress. In this section, I want to sketch a few ways in which international trade law might help assist the cause of political freedom around the world. Unexpectedly, the General Agreement on Trade in Services might emerge as a human rights document.

Human rights law has typically sought to regulate the production of goods in order to avoid the exploitation of labor (or, relatedly, the environment). But with respect to trade in services delivered over the Internet, the nature of the work and the presence of an often highly educated workforce significantly reduce fears of worker exploitation. This does not mean that labor rights are no longer of concern with respect to trade in services, but those concerns are less with sweatshops, scandalously low wages, child labor, or perilous working conditions than with the right to organize, the right to speech, and the right to privacy. In China, young men are living and working in dormitories playing video games to earn in-game currency and goods that can then be exchanged for real-world currency through third-party markets.[6] But this practice, which does raise potential issues of sweatshop conditions, is thus far the exception rather than the rule. In trade mediated via cyberspace, human rights law comes to bear in a largely novel fashion: to further the right of individuals to share and receive information. Trade in services shifts the locus of human rights attention from the production process to its delivery and consumption.

Human rights norms require that nations provide their citizens not only with the right to free speech within their nation but also with the right to impart information "regardless of frontiers." This formulation is repeated in both the Universal Declaration of Human Rights and the International Covenant on Civil and Political Rights. The declaration describes the right to "impart information and ideas through any media regardless of frontiers," and the covenant subsequently reiterates the "freedom to seek, receive and impart information and ideas of all kinds, regardless of frontiers." Because of its nature as an international treaty, the covenant carries more binding force than the declaration. China has signed but not ratified the covenant. The covenant makes clear that a country's inhabitants have the right both to send and to receive information from another country and thus imposes obligations on both countries to allow the information exchange. Like the freedom of speech guaranteed by the US Constitution, the international free speech norm tolerates regulation within appropriate bounds. Indeed, the covenant explicitly contemplates it, permitting limitations set forth by law and necessary to support public order. As history's best medium for transmitting information worldwide, the Internet will test the limits of such regulation of crossborder information flows.

International trade law puts pressure on state repression of information through two principal mechanisms. First, the transparency obligations of GATS require what is often absent in authoritarian states—a set of public rules that governs both citizens and governmental authorities. GATS article III requires WTO member states to publish regulations governing services and establish inquiry points where foreign service providers can obtain information about such regulations. A publication requirement written for the benefit of foreigners may prove useful for local citizens, who will be given the opportunity to understand the rules that bind them—and the opportunity therefore to challenge those rules or their interpretation.

Second, the market access and national treatment commitments provide opportunities for foreign information service providers to disseminate information that local information service providers might eschew. Censorship by itself may not necessarily constitute either a market access or a national treatment violation. But consider three scenarios: What if a country (1) declared foreign blogging sites off-limits, or (2) required foreign information service providers to route their offerings through special traffic cops, or (3) required local Internet service providers to deny access to certain foreign services in toto? In cases like these, the censorship measures could run afoul of a country's market access and national treaty obligations. Of course, GATS permits derogation where "necessary to protect public morals or to maintain public order."[7] But as we saw in the Antigua case, any derogations must be "necessary" for the public morals or public order goal and there must be no "reasonably available alternative" to the trade restrictive measure. Furthermore, there is a substantial question as to whether the repression of political speech that promotes peaceful challenges to the existing government constitutes a cognizable public order or public morality goal under the World Trade Organization system.

If one considers the array of recent efforts to censor material mediated by the Internet, it seems clear that some of them would fall afoul of the "reasonably available alternative" requirement articulated in the *United States—Gambling* case (and described in chapter 6). That is, the stated public order or public morality goals could have been achieved at the desired level of protection by less trade-restrictive means. Consider, for example, the shuttering of Blogger because of one or two offending blogs or the disabling of YouTube because of one video some found objectionable or the shutting off of access to Wikipedia presumably because of a few politically charged (but truthful) entries.[8]

Could the United States bring a WTO claim against China for discriminating against Google? Once we understand Google as an exporter of services, such possibilities come into play. As it currently stands, the WTO seems to lack the power to order a local regulation dismantled because it runs afoul of human rights law.[9] However, a review of China's GATS accession schedule reveals a broad array of commitments to liberalize this type of crossborder trade, including in professional services. China promises both market access and national treatment for many services delivered cross-border. However, the schedule limits liberalization of "on-line information and database retrieval services" to joint ventures, with a maximum foreign participation of 30 percent. A note requires "all international telecommunications services . . . [to] go through gateways established with the approval of China's telecommunications authorities."[10] The requirement that such services must go through approved gateways cannot, however, camouflage discriminatory measures or even impediments to market access. Such gateways function like customs houses: insufficient staffing at a customs house could be grounds for a WTO claim. Because they rely on highly subjective and inconsistent judgments, Chinese actions regulating information might also run afoul of the GATS transparency obligation.[11] It is difficult to predict whether the United States would win a GATS claim against Chinese actions that interfered with crossborder supply of net-work by companies such as Google, but the very possibility of such claims has a disciplinary effect on potential regulations.[12]

The US complaint in *China—Audiovisual* against Chinese controls on the distribution of publications and audiovisual materials in that country stopped short of a direct effort to use trade law to improve freedom of expression. The United States did not question whether China's vast censorship apparatus could in fact restrict the importation of a wide variety of material. Joost Pauwelyn argues that rather than accepting censorship as advancing the cause of public morals, the WTO should ensure that any measure purportedly advancing public morals complies with "basic and universally accepted principles of free speech."[13] Panagiotis Delimatsis observes that the United States oddly pressed the possibility that government officers perform the censorship directly rather than delegate it to dispersed state-owned enterprises, a retrograde step for free speech.[14]

It is unlikely that GATS will help dismantle all restrictions of repressive regimes. For this reason, we must seek to nurture a corporate consciousness among information service providers of their role in liberation or oppression. Goods manufacturers have at times adopted corporate codes of responsibility, appointed corporate responsibility officers, and bonded themselves through independent monitors. Silicon Valley and Bangalore companies that seek to service the world need human rights lawyers, not just privacy officers and mergers and acquisitions counsel. At the very least, corporate counsel for Internet enterprises must include human rights in their bailiwick, if not to avoid doing evil, at least to avoid being subject to suit or public rebuke.

AFTERWORD

In the 1955 classic Indian film *Shri 420*, Raj Kapoor walks a dusty road from a rural village toward cosmopolitan Bombay, singing a song that would come to symbolize patriotism in the face of globalization:

> Mera joota hai Japani
> Yé patloon Inglistani
> Sar pé lal topi Rusi—
> Phir bhi dil hai Hindustani

(O, my shoes are Japanese
These trousers English, if you please
On my head, red Russian hat—
My heart's Indian for all that.)[1]

Salman Rushdie begins his *Satanic Verses* with the song, sung by Bollywood star Gibreel as he falls (magically safely) from an exploding airliner toward the English Channel. The philosopher Jeremy Waldron begins his discussion of minority cultures and cosmopolitanism by citing Rushdie's defense of *Satanic Verses*, which embraces the hybridity and mongrelization arising from cultural interaction. Waldron celebrates the cosmopolitan who feels no loss of identity "when he learns Spanish, eats Chinese, wears clothes made in Korea, listens to arias by Verdi sung by a Maori princess on Japanese equipment, follows Ukrainian politics, and practices Buddhist meditation techniques."[2] The human interaction made possible by crossborder net-work is far more intense than that made possible by Russian hats, English trousers, or Japanese shoes. The clothes after all do not make the man or woman.

Trade has made and remade the world for millennia. The addition of services to global trade flows will remake the world yet again. In an age when Indians tutor Koreans to speak English, Ghanaians process citations for quality-of-life offenses in New York City, and Chinese citizens use Silicon Valley search engines to learn about China, the effect on human lifestyles, livelihoods, and relationships is likely to be profound.[3] One Ghanaian who processes New York citations notes, "I am very used to the rules and regulations of New York now. . . . So I think I can live there."[4] While these developments hold much promise, human rights, cultural norms, privacy and security are all at risk in this net-worked world. Trade 2.0 will require us to grapple with the most difficult questions of human relationships—of opportunities, obligations, transgressions, and betrayals—crisscrossing borders. The *Economist* magazine declares, "The internet is as much a trade pact as an invention."[5] This trade pact can be undone, its commercial promise eroded by unnecessary or protectionist regulations. But a free trade zone should not be free of law. The trade made possible by the web must be as free as possible within a legal infrastructure to protect consumers.

Concluding her chronicle of the travels of a humble T-shirt in the global economy, Georgetown business professor Pietra Rivoli embraces the power of trade. She notes that some early Christians distrusted trade, with Augustine of Hippo declaring that "active traders . . . attain not the grace of God."[6] Augustine was hardly alone in his distrust of trade. At the turn the sixteenth century, after ruling the seas with four-hundred-foot treasure ships, the Chinese emperor declared it a crime to go to sea in a multi-masted ship.[7] In Japan, the *sakoku* policy limited trade from the seventeenth into the nineteenth century, yielding only to Commodore Matthew Perry's gunboats. In the twentieth century, developing countries such as India, when freed from imperial powers, retreated from trade as well, preferring a policy of "import substitution," in which foreign goods would be manufactured locally. All of these nations have since embraced trade in dramatic fashion, in each case to the great benefit of their peoples.

Trade creates a web of relationships that can enrich the lives (and finances) of both parties. Of course, trade can also be corrosive, exploiting people who have few opportunities, despoiling the environment, or undercutting local producers through unfair competition. Trade in services poses different risks than trade in goods, threats to privacy and security, and risks associated with the quality of a service. In this book, I have tried to find a middle ground between isolation and unregulated trade, embracing free trade and also its regulation.

As I worked on this manuscript over a winter holiday from teaching, two encounters brought the subject of the book close to home. At my California law school's annual holiday party, I ran across a retired colleague, a wonderful scholar who had chaired the committee that shepherded me toward tenure at the beginning of the millennium. I asked him, "What are you doing with your time?" He answered that he was writing an iPhone app to help people develop a training regimen for the triathlon. Visiting my parents a few days later, I asked the same question of my father, who had also recently retired, he from teaching English literature at a North Carolina university. My father—for whom I have long served via phone as a kind of outsourced IT help desk—told me he was teaching two English courses *online*.

These two men, in their sixties and seventies, respectively, were now well on their way to becoming Internet traders. Some budding triathletes would certainly lie beyond our shores and download my colleague's app via the iTunes global online store. And some students of my father's online courses might someday come from abroad, streaming and downloading lectures and readings, and uploading assignments and exams.

For the bulk of human history, geography was destiny. My own parents had both the inclination and resources to defy this destiny for increased opportunities in the West. They left their own parents behind to begin life again in a strange land. A Gallup world poll suggests that some 1.1 billion people would move abroad for temporary work. Some undoubtedly would move abroad for the adventure, but others for the economic opportunities not available at home. Many cannot move abroad, because of the lack of resources or visas, or because of family obligations at home.

Today, geography holds fewer limitations. Take a couple minutes away from the book. Type in www.MapCrunch.com. After reaching the site, click "Go." Using Google's amazing Street View service, the site "teleports" you instantly to a randomly selected street in the world. You can look around this new location, walking down the streets of São Paulo or Sydney. Often, one finds oneself gazing down a rural road—almost always it seems filmed on a glorious sunny day. To my eyes, the world looks both familiar and exotic, and also quite beautiful.

While I have focused on economic ramifications of Trade 2.0, a more fundamental change is afoot as well. Facebook relationships crisscross political borders, newspaper stories generate discussions involving a global audience, and, as this book's cover depicts, Twitter conversations span the world. Those with Internet access (and who live outside the Great Firewall of China and other totalitarian states) can search the storehouse of the world's information, accessing knowledge bases that far surpass the traditional encyclopedias available only to a small fraction of the world's population.

The nation-state plays a central role in this book, as the primary mechanism for consumer protection. Inevitably, however, the day-to-day engagement with the world made possible by cyberspace is hastening the day that our energies are directed beyond the confines of the nation-state. The increasing pressure on states to justify national deviations from international standards and the increasing difficulty of practically enforcing such differences will encourage the emergence of a set of global best practices. If we manage it well, the worldwide web of cyberspace will bind us more tightly together, increasing capabilities and understanding across the world.

The opportunity to participate in global trade makes our fate less circumscribed by the land into which we are born, without requiring the painful dislocations of migration. At the same time, the World Wide Web binds our fates more closely together, making possible both commerce and other interaction across humanity itself.

GLOSSARY

A Cheat Sheet for Global E-Commerce

BPO Business process outsourcing, the performance of a specified business process by a third-party service provider.

darknet A peer-to-peer file-sharing network designed to promote anonymous communications by, among other things, hiding the Internet Protocol address of users.

Data Protection Directive The European Union's 1995 directive, which imposes both strict privacy obligations on data collectors within the EU and obligations as well on the transfer of information to processors outside the EU.

dematerialization The replacement of physical in-person requirements with online substitutes wherever possible, such as for signatures, authentication, bureaucratic offices, education, testing, and even administrative and judicial hearings.

denial-of-service (DoS) or distributed denial-of-service (DDOS) attack A popular means of disabling access to a website by barraging a website with information requests, thus overloading it.

digital products Films, music, audiobooks, computer games, and software in electronic form.

DMCA The Digital Millennium Copyright Act of 1998, which outlaws the circulation of devices that might circumvent access and copy controls and also offers safe harbors for Internet intermediaries from copyright infringement claims.

DNS The domain name system, which allocates authority for matching a single alphanumeric string (in various languages) to a single computer.

GATS The General Agreement on Trade in Services, one of the principal WTO agreements, effective in 1995.

GATT The General Agreement on Trade and Tariffs, first effective in 1947 and then instituted as part of the WTO system in 1995.

geolocation Identifying where a web user is physically located through such clues as IP address, web browser language, log-in credentials, cookies, or mobile or wireless access information.

Global Network Initiative A nongovernmental organization founded in 2008 by Google, Microsoft, Yahoo!, civil society organizations, investors, and academics to promote freedom of expression and privacy on the Internet.

glocalization The creation or distribution of products or services intended for a global market but customized to conform to local laws—within the bounds of international law.

harmonization Concerted efforts by nations to agree on common standards, or where common standards are lacking, not imposing conflicting standards unless justified by substantial local policy grounds.

ICANN The Internet Corporation for Assigned Numbers and Names, based in Marina del Rey, California, established through a contract with the

US Department of Commerce in 1998 and with directors appointed by a loose group of regional Internet backbone companies and civil society organizations.

ICC The International Chamber of Commerce, an international business organization based in Paris, which includes task forces to promote international electronic commerce.

Incoterms Terms used to standardize commercial shipments of goods, promulgated by the ICC.

IP Internet Protocol, or intellectual property.

ISO The International Organization for Standardization, the international standards-setting body composed of representatives of national standards-setting bodies, based in Geneva.

ISP Internet service provider, typically used to refer to the company providing Internet access to a home or business.

IT Information technology.

ITU The International Telecommunications Union, a United Nations body composed of more than 190 countries and 700 industry and academic groups.

License Raj A private economy characterized by licenses and bureaucratic red tape in post-independence India until approximately 1990.

LPO Legal process outsourcing, the performance of law-related services by a third-party provider.

mode 1 Delivery of a service from the territory of one WTO Member into the territory of another Member (e.g., by the Internet).

mode 2 Delivery of a service in the territory of one WTO Member to the service consumer of another Member (e.g., by travel by the consumer).

mode 3 Delivery of a service within the territory of a country by a foreign service provider with a local commercial presence (e.g., by establishing a local office or subsidiary).

mode 4 Delivery of a service within the territory of a country by a foreign service provider who is physically present (e.g., by physical travel of the provider).

Nasscom New Delhi–based trade association representing the Indian software and services since 1988.

net-work Information services delivered remotely through electronic communications systems.

OECD The Organisation of Economic Co-operation and Development, based in Paris, consisting of 34 countries generally with advanced market economies, with a work program seeking to enhance the digital economy.

recognition Governmental action declaring that qualifying under a foreign law suffices for domestic law purposes. This can be done either unilaterally or mutually.

registrar One of the companies authorized by the top-level domain administrator (such as ICANN) to make changes to that top-level domain's registry.

registry The authoritative database matching mnemonic domain names to Internet Protocol addresses for a particular top-level domain, such as .com or .US.

root server The computer holding the authoritative database matching mnemonic domain names to Internet Protocol addresses for a particular top-level domain, such as .com, .edu, or .us. The contemporary architecture mirrors this database across multiple physical locations.

Safe Server Strategy Locating a computer server where one believes it will be beyond the reach of unfriendly governments.

Services Directive The EU's directive seeking to better achieve the goal of one market for the supply of services across Europe.

TBT The Agreement on Technical Barriers to Trade, one of the WTO agreements, effective in 1995. The TBT regulates technical standards for goods but does not extend to services.

technological neutrality The principle that the online service should be required to achieve regulatory goals at rates roughly equivalent to those achieved by offline versions of the service.

top-level domain (TLD) The term given to the last portion of the domain name, such as .com, .edu, and .US, with each domain name entry in a particular TLD subject to control of a single authority.

trade plus The broader legal environment through which trade occurs, including trade rules represented in the WTO and regional and bilateral agreements, as well as contracting and private-private dispute resolution and trade conventions such as Incoterms.

Trade 2.0 Electronically tradable services, also called "net-work."

TRIPs The Trade-Related Aspects of Intellectual Property Agreement, one of the principal WTO agreements, effective in 1995.

UNCITRAL The United Nations Commission on International Trade Law, which convenes alternately in New York and Vienna and which promulgates model codes and other legal material to promote international trade, including uniform rules on electronic signatures that have been embraced by jurisdictions such as the United States.

Web 2.0 Web-based services such as Facebook and YouTube that rely on individuals to contribute content.

WIPO The World Intellectual Property Organization, headquartered in Geneva.

World Trade Organization (WTO) A treaty-based body based in Geneva, established at the conclusion of the Uruguay Round of trade negotiations, and coming into being in 1995.

WTO Work Program on Electronic Commerce A work program, initiated at the WTO Ministerial in Geneva in 1998, that seeks to examine trade-related issues of global electronic commerce.

NOTES

Introduction

1. *Canada—Certain Measures Concerning Periodicals*, 17, WT/DS31/AB/R, June 30, 1997 ("A periodical is a good comprised of two components: editorial content and advertising content. Both components can be viewed as having services attributes, but they combine to form a physical product—the periodical itself").

2. *China—Measures Affecting Trading Rights and Distribution Services for Certain Publications and Audiovisual Entertainment Products*, ¶ 36, WT/DS363/AB/R, Dec. 21, 2009.

3. See Jagdish Bhagwati, "International Trade in Services and Its Relevance for Economic Development," in *The Emerging Services Economy*, ed. Orio Giarini (Oxford: Pergamon, 1987), 3; and Joseph Francois and

Bernard Hoekman, "Services Trade and Policy," *Journal of Economic Literature* 48 (2010): 642, 643.

4. Apple introduced the iTunes music store in April 2003. By April 2008, Apple was the biggest music retailer in the country. http://www.apple.com/pr/library/2003/04/28Apple-Launches-the-iTunes-Music-Store.html; http://www.apple.com/pr/library/2008/04/03iTunes-Store-Top-Music-Retailer-in-the-US.html.

5. Bobbie Johnson, "Google Urges UN to Set Global Internet Privacy Rules," *Guardian*, Sept. 14, 2007; Peter Fleischer, "The Need for Global Privacy Standards," Sept. 14, 2007, http://peterfleischer.blogspot.com/2007/09/need-for-global-privacy-standards.html.

6. These are the words of Grateful Dead lyricist turned Electronic Frontier Foundation–founder John Perry Barlow. See "A Declaration of Independence of Cyberspace," Feb. 8, 1996.

7. See, e.g., Niall Ferguson, "Sinking Globalization," *Foreign Affairs* 84:2 (2005) ("From around 1870 until World War I, the world economy thrived in ways that look familiar today. The mobility of commodities, capital, and labor reached record levels; the sea-lanes and telegraphs across the Atlantic had never been busier, as capital and migrants traveled west and raw materials and manufactures traveled east").

8. See Anupam Chander, "Next Stop, Kazaakhstan? The Legal Globe-Trotting of Kazaa, the Post-Napster File Sharing Company," *Findlaw.com*, Oct. 24, 2002, http://writ.news.findlaw.com/commentary/20021024_chander.html; Michael Tarm, "KaZaA! Youths from Cyber-Savvy Estonia Write the New Napster, Delivering a Blow to the Global Entertainment Industry," *City Paper—The Baltic States* (March–April 2003), http://www.citypaper.ee/kazaa.htm. Kazaa's founders would go on to create Skype following a similar model, incorporating their London-operated company in Luxembourg and relying on Estonians for programming. Ivar Ekman, "Skype Is 2nd Jackpot for Scandinavian Duo," *International Herald Tribune*, Sept. 13, 2005. Skype itself turns out to be a boon to net-work firms, which can now use it to engage in cheap international communications.

9. Nils Pratley, "The Porn Princess, the Indian Computer Whizz and the Poker Bet That Made $10bn," *Guardian*, June 3, 2005.

10. World Bank, *World Bank Atlas*, 36th ed. (Washington, DC: World Bank Publications, 2004) ("The services sector now accounts for two-thirds of global economic output").

11. World Trade Organization, *World Trade Report 2012* (2012), 19. It is likely that this figure undercounts cybertrade in services because national statistical accounts have yet to fully recognize the kind and volume of trade that is occurring.

12. Geza Feketekuty, *International Trade in Services: An Overview and Blueprint for Negotiations* (Cambridge, MA: Ballinger, 1988), 299–308.

13. General Agreement on Trade in Services, Apr. 15, 1994, Marrakesh Agreement Establishing the World Trade Organization, Annex, 1B, Legal Instruments—Results of the Uruguay Round, 1869 U.N.T.S. 183, 33 I.L.M. 1167 (1994) [hereinafter GATS].

14. Article 14 of the EC Treaty.

15. North American Free Trade Agreement, Ch. 12, U.S.–Can.–Mex., Dec. 17, 1992, 32 I.L.M. 289 (1993); Central America–Dominican Republic–United States Free Trade Agreement, U.S.–Cen. Am.–Dom. Rep., arts. 2.1, 3.1, 3.2, 7.2, 9.1(1)–(3), 11.1, 12.2, 12.3, 12.9(1), Aug. 5, 2004, 43 I.L.M. 514 (2004).

16. Jagdish Bhagwati et al., "The Muddles Over Outsourcing," *Journal of Economic Perspectives* 18:4 (2004): 93, 112 (concluding that outsourcing, defined as services traded internationally at arm's length, has "effects that are not qualitatively different from those of conventional trade in goods [and] . . . leads to gains from trade and increases in national income, with the caveats that are standard in this literature").

17. Paul Samuelson, "Where Ricardo and Mill Rebut and Confirm Arguments of Mainstream Economists Supporting Globalization," *Journal of Economic Perspectives* 18:3 (2004): 135 (arguing that changing terms of trade over the long term might result in real per capita income loss for a country like the United States); Alan S. Blinder, "Offshoring: The Next Industrial Revolution?" *Foreign Affairs* 85:2 (2006): 113. Challenged years ago to identify a social science proposition that was both true and nontrivial, Samuelson had famously selected the theory of comparative advantage. His concerns about comparative advantage for services thus merit serious inquiry, which Jagdish Bhagwati and Arvind Panagariya have undertaken. Arvind Panagariya, "Why the Recent Samuelson Article Is NOT About Offshore Outsourcing," http://www.columbia.edu/~ap2231/Policy%20Papers/Samuelson%20JEP%20(Summer%202004)_Not%20on%20Outsourcing.htm (arguing that Samuelson misapplies changing terms of trade model to outsourcing).

18. Google, Inc., Form 10-Q, July 24, 2012, 35; Facebook, Form 10-Q, July 27, 2012, 18.

19. David Wessel and Bob Davis, "Pain from Free Trade Spurs Second Thoughts," *Wall Street Journal*, Mar. 28, 2007.

20. In his classic study, Douglass North suggests that "the major role of institutions in a society is to reduce uncertainty." Douglass C. North, *Institutions, Institutional Change, and Economic Performance* (Cambridge: Cambridge University Press, 1990), 6.

1. The New Global Division of Labor

Epigraph: Writing at the end of World War I, Keynes describes this idyll, which comes crashing with the beginning of war. John Maynard Keynes, *The Economic Consequences of the Peace* (London: Macmillan, 1919).

1. Adam Smith, *An Inquiry into the Nature and Causes of the Wealth of Nations* [1776], ed. R. H. Campbell and A. S. Skinner (Oxford: Clarendon Press, 1976), 31.

2. Ibid., 32.

3. Ibid., 17–21.

4. Scholars have studied the implications of this new employment order for labor law. Katherine V. W. Stone, *From Widgets to Digits: Employment Regulation for the Changing Workplace* (Cambridge: Cambridge University Press, 2004); Miriam Cherry, "A Taxonomy of Virtual Work," *Georgia Law Review* 45 (2011): 951.

5. Folker Fröbel, Jürgen Heinrichs, and Otto Kreye, *The New International Division of Labour: Structural Unemployment in Industrialised Countries and Industrialisation in Developing Countries*, trans. Pete Burgess (Cambridge: Cambridge University Press, 1980).

6. Alfred D. Chandler Jr., *The Visible Hand: The Managerial Revolution in American Business* (Cambridge, MA: Belknap Press, 1977), 12 ("The visible hand of management replaced the invisible hand of market forces where and when new technology and expanded markets permitted a historically unprecedented high volume and speed of materials through the processes of production and distribution. Modern business enterprise was thus the institutional response to the rapid pace of technological innovation and increasing consumer demand in the United States during the second half of the nineteenth century").

7. Ibid., 368–69, 480.

8. Ibid., 369, citing the following books published in London: Fred A. McKenzie, *The American Invaders* (1901); and W. T. Stead, *The Americanization of the World* (1902).

9. "Facts About Microsoft," Microsoft.com, June 30, 2012, http://www.microsoft.com/presspass/inside_ms.mspx.

10. "Global Locations," Citigroup.com, http://www.citigroup.com/citi/global/.

11. Financial transactions often did require instantaneous interchange of information, and financial houses developed early global electronic networks such as SWIFT for such purposes.

12. See, e.g., Iris M. Reyes, "Special Feature," *BusinessWorld* (Philippines), July 29, 2002, available at 2002 WLNR 3220723 (reporting on the Internet's contribution to trade in architectural services).

13. Interview with Komal Shah, Mumbai, India, Jan. 2, 2005.

14. David Streitfeld, "Office of Tomorrow Has an Address in India," *Los Angeles Times*, Aug. 29, 2004.

15. Reyes, "Special Feature" ("because current engineering technology—be it CAD [computer-aided design] files or engineering computations—stores data electronically, off-shore engineering services are now an easy option for foreign companies").

16. Pete Engardio et al., "The New Global Job Shift," *Business Week*, Feb. 3, 2003, 50–51 ("Fluor Corp. . . . of Aliso Viejo, Calif., employs 1,200 engineers and draftsmen in the Philippines, Poland, and India to turn layouts of giant industrial facilities into detailed specs and blueprints").

17. Eric Bellman and Nathan Koppel, "More U.S. Legal Work Moves to India's Low-Cost Lawyers," *Wall Street Journal*, Sept. 28, 2005 ("increasingly, squads of experienced but inexpensive lawyers based in India are doing things ranging from patent applications to divorce papers to legal research for Western clients"); Daniel Brook, "Are Your Lawyers in New York or New Delhi?" *Legal Affairs* (May–June 2005).

18. Amol Sharma, "India Winning Higher-Status Jobs from US," *Christian Science Monitor*, June 18, 2003 (describing outsourcing of special effects production to Bangalore for movies such as *The Nutty Professor II* to *Independence Day*).

19. Ibid.

20. Ibid.

21. Kevin Voigt, "For 'Extreme Telecommuters,' Remote Work Means Really Remote—Enterprising Employees Swap Cubicles for Exotic Locales," *Wall Street Journal*, Jan. 31, 2001.

22. Ian Fisher, "A Quest for Carpets Reveals the Persian Past and the Soul," *New York Times*, Sept. 3, 2005.

23. Organisation for Economic Cooperation and Development, *GATS: The Case for Open Services Markets* (Paris: OECD, 2002), 18.

24. Ibid., 14.

25. Ronald Coase, "The Nature of the Firm," *Economica* 4 (1937): 386.

26. Bob Tedeschi, "Coase's Ideas Flourish in the Internet Economy," *New York Times*, Oct. 2, 2000.

27. See Coase, "Nature of the Firm," 397 ("It should be noted that most inventions will change both the costs of organising and the costs of using the price mechanism. In such cases, whether the invention tends to make firms larger or smaller will depend on the relative effect on these two sets of costs. For instance, if the telephone reduces the costs of using the price mechanism more than it reduces the costs of organizing, then it will have the effect of reducing the size of the firm").

28. See Larry Downes and Chunka Mui, *Unleashing the Killer App: Digital Strategies for Market Dominance* (Boston: Harvard Business School Press, 1998), 42; and Thomas W. Malone et al., "Electronic Markets and Electronic Hierarchies," *Communications of the ACM* 30 (1987): 484, 490 (suggesting information technology-led shift from intrafirm hierarchies to markets).

29. Jay Solomon and Kathryn Kranhold, "In India's Outsourcing Boom, GE Played a Starring Role," *Wall Street Journal*, Mar. 23, 2005 (quoting Nigel Andrews, a former top GE Capital executive who oversaw India).

30. Benjamin Klein et al., "Vertical Integration, Appropriable Rents, and the Competitive Contracting Process," *Journal of Law and Economics* 21 (1978): 297, 308.

31. Ibid., 303, 319.

32. Sathya Mithra Ashok, "Build or Buy," *Outsourcing World*, Dec. 6, 2005.

33. "Relocating the Back Office," *Economist*, Dec. 11, 2003 ("The business of shifting back-office functions offshore began in earnest in the early 1990s when companies such as American Express, British Airways, General Electric and Swissair set up their own 'captive' outsourcing operations in India. However, many of these captives are now finding that their costs are up to 50% higher than those of independent third parties.").

34. WNS (Holdings) Limited, Registration Statement (Form F–1), July 20, 2006, 71–72, http://www.sec.gov/Archives/edgar/data/1356570/000114554906001034/u92712bfv1za.htm.

35. Streitfeld, "Office of Tomorrow"; Sankar Mehta, "GE's Outsourcing Departure Sets a New Trend—Outsource Headaches Do Not Own It!" *India Daily*, Oct. 7, 2004 ("'GE can extract much more juice from the operation by opening it up to competitors who would feel too uncomfortable if it was still "captive,"' says one foreign executive").

36. British Airways sold its remaining minority stake as part of WNS's NYSE listing in July 2006. "BA Unloads Remaining Stake in Indian Outsourcer," July 27, 2006, http://dealbook.nytimes.com/2006/07/27/ba-unloads-remaining-stake-in-indian-outsourcer/.

37. Mark Gottfredson et al., "Strategic Sourcing: From Periphery to the Core," *Harvard Business Review* 83 (2005): 132.

38. Rajiv P. Patel and Ralph M. Pais, "Software Outsourcing Offshore—Business and Legal Issues Checklist" (2004), http://www.fenwick.com/FenwickDocuments/Outsourcing_Offshore.pdf.

39. Dylan Love, "Tim Cook Is Doing What Steve Jobs Never Did—Visiting China as Apple's CEO," *Business Insider*, Mar. 26, 2012.

40. Yochai Benkler, *The Wealth of Networks: How Social Production Transforms Markets and Freedom* (New Haven: Yale University Press, 2006), 59.

41. Yochai Benkler, "Coase's Penguin, or, Linux and the Nature of the Firm," *Yale Law Journal* 112 (2002): 369, 375 ("Commons-based peer production . . . relies on decentralized information gathering and exchange to reduce the uncertainty of participants").

42. Steven Weber, *The Success of Open Source* (Cambridge, MA: Harvard University Press, 2004), 71 (noting the "profoundly international nature" of the Linux open source community). Contributions to open source projects such as Linux and Gnome are not evenly distributed around the world, being largely the work of people who speak English and, increasingly, of Europeans. See David Lancashire, "Code, Culture and Cash: The Fading Altruism of Open Source Development," *First Monday*, Nov. 19, 2001 http://www.firstmonday.org/issues/issue6_12/lancashire/.

43. Ryan Paul, "Linux Kernel in 2011: 15 Million Total Lines of Code and Microsoft Is a Top Contributor," *ArsTechnica*, Apr. 4, 2012, http://arstechnica.com/business/2012/04/linux-kernel-in–2011–15-million-total-

lines-of-code-and-microsoft-is-a-top-contributor/; Steven J. Vaughan-Nichols, "Fast, Faster, Fastest: Linux Rules Supercomputing," *ZDNet*, June 19, 2012, http://www.zdnet.com/blog/open-source/fast-faster-fastest-linux-rules-supercomputing/11263.

44. Carliss Y. Baldwin and Kim B. Clark, *Design Rules* 1 (2000): 413 (describing emergence of modular design in computer systems).

45. Kevin Kelleher, "All Access Economy," *Wired*, July 2006, 140.

46. Tim Berners-Lee, *Weaving the Web: The Original Design and Ultimate Destiny of the World Wide Web by Its Inventor* (San Francisco: HarperSanFrancisco, 1999), 57.

47. See notes 31, 32, above, and accompanying text.

48. Samuel J. Palmisano, "The Globally Integrated Enterprise," *Foreign Affairs* 85:3 (2006): 127, 130.

49. Eben Moglen and Richard Stallman, "GPL Version 3: Background to Adoption," June 5, 2005, http://www.fsf.org/news/gpl3.html; Andrés Guadamuz González, "GNU General Public License v3: A Legal Analysis," *SCRIPT-ed* 3:2 (2006): 154, http://www.law.ed.ac.uk/ahrc/script-ed/vol3–2/guadamuz.asp.

50. "GNU General Public License," http://www.gnu.org/copyleft/gpl.html.

51. Moglen and Stallman, "GPL Version 3."

52. Of course, an increase in productivity does not, by itself, justify free trade. Societies may choose to protect domestic industry even at the price of productivity. Indeed, I have argued that a democratic society must retain the prerogative, however foolishly, to choose protectionism over trade. Anupam Chander, "Globalization and Distrust," *Yale Law Journal* 114 (2005): 1193, 1218.

2. Western Entrepôt

1. According to *Wikipedia*, the iTunes store operates in more than fifty countries. "Apple iTunes Store," *Wikipedia*. During its 2011 fiscal year (ending in September 24, 2011), Apple earned $66 billion in net sales revenues from hardware, software, and services sold outside the United States, accounting for 61 percent of its net sales worldwide. Apple Inc., Form 10-K, filed Oct. 26, 2011, 74 (accounting note 8). In the first quarter of 2012, Apple earned 54 percent of its net sales revenues worldwide from sales outside the United States.

2. "Global Presence," Ticketmaster, http://www.ticketmaster.com/international.

3. "About Paypal," Paypal, https://www.paypal-media.com/about.

4. "Send and Receive Payments Securely Worldwide," Paypal, https://www.paypal.com/worldwide; "Multiple Currencies," Paypal, https://www.paypal.com/cgi-bin/webscr?cmd=p/sell/mc/mc_intro-outside.

5. Josh Kun, "Mexico City's Indie Rock, Now Playing to the World," *New York Times*, May 13, 2007 ("Thanks mostly to the downloadable avalanche of globalization and the rise of MySpace the current independent rock scene is full of artists who may be from Mexico City but sound as if they could be from New York, Stockholm, or Paris").

6. Larry Page and Sergey Brin, "Founder's Letter," in Google Inc., *Annual Report 2007*, vi.

7. Google Inc., *Annual Report 2011* (Form 10-K), 8 ("We provide our products and services in more than 100 languages and in more than 50 countries, regions, and territories").

8. Yahoo! Inc., *Annual Report 2011* (Form 10-K), 3, 50.

9. John Markoff, "Software via the Internet: Microsoft in 'Cloud' Computing," *New York Times*, Sept. 3, 2007.

10. World Trade Organization, *World Trade Report 2012* (2012), 29; World Trade Organization, *World Trade Report 2011* (2011), 32; World Trade Organization, *World Trade Report 2010* (2010), 29.

11. "IBM in Big Push to Build Data Centers," *CIO Insight*, Nov. 15, 2007.

12. White House, *Remarks by the President in Announcement of Electronic Commerce Initiative*, July 1, 1997, http://clinton4.nara.gov/WH/New/Commerce/remarks.html.

13. Ibid.

14. World Trade Organization, "Declaration on Global Electronic Commerce," WT/MIN(98)/DEC/2, May 25, 1998; Sacha Wunsch-Vincent, *The WTO, the Internet and Trade in Digital Products: EC-US Perspectives* (Oxford: Hart, 2006), 37–43.

15. Tom Braithwaite and Tobias Bayer, "Bertelsmann Set to Be German Leader of Search Engine Project," *Financial Times*, Jan. 16, 2006. Germany has since left the French-German consortium, in favor of an alternative. Joel Hruska, "EU Approves $166 Million in Funding for Google Competitor," *ArsTechnica*, July 23, 2007, http://arstechnica.com/uncategorized/2007/07-eu-approves–166-million-in-funding-for-google-competitor.html.

16. Mariko Sanchanta and Richard Waters, "Japan to Fight Google Search Dominance," *Financial Times*, Sept. 4, 2007.

17. This is Judge Ferguson's translation of "la plus grande entreprise de banalisation du nazisme qui soit" in Judge Gomez's May 22, 2000, order. Yahoo! Inc. v. La Ligue Contre le Racisme, et L'Antisémitisme, 433 F.3d 1199, 1227 (Ferguson, J.); Ligue Internationale Contre le Racisme et l'Antisémitisme et Union des étudiants juifs de France v. Yahoo! Inc., Tribunal de grande instances [T.G.I.] [ordinary court of original jurisdiction] Paris, May 22, 2000, D. 2000, inf. rap. 172, Ordonnance de Refere (Fr.).

18. Before the French court, Yahoo's lawyer declared that any attempt of the French court to regulate the American enterprise's US-based .com website would amount to "French imperialism." Greg Wrenn, "Yahoo! v. Licra," *Commercial Law* 24 (Fall 2006): 5, 6.

19. 433 F.3d at 1234–35 (Fisher, J., concurring in part and dissenting in part).

20. "The display . . . of NAZI objects . . . constitutes an offense to the collective memory of the country profoundly damaged by the atrocities committed by and in the name of the Nazi criminal enterprise against French citizens and above all against citizens of the Jewish faith." Order of May 22, 2000, 4.

21. German laws criminalize insults against members of groups persecuted by Nazis or other totalitarian systems. Eric M. Barendt, *Freedom of Speech* (Oxford: Clarendon Press, 2005), 180.

22. Lyombe Eko, "New Medium, Old Free Speech Regimes: The Historical and Ideological Foundations of French and American Regulation of Bias-Motivated Speech and Symbolic Expression on the Internet," *Loyola of Los Angeles International and Comparative Law Review* 28 (2006): 69, 72.

23. Ligue Contre le Racisme et l'Antisémitisme & Union des Etudiants Juifs de France v. Yahoo! Inc. & Yahoo France, Tribunal de grande instance [T.G.I.] [ordinary court of original jurisdiction] Paris, Nov. 20, 2000 (Fr.), available in English at http://www.lapres.net/yahen11.html.

24. Ibid.

25. "Yahoo! Facing French Criminal Charges for Web Sites That Auction Nazi Memorabilia," *Electronic Commerce and Law Report*, Mar. 6, 2002, 221; "Yahoo Boss Cleared over Nazi Sales," *BBC News*, Feb. 11, 2003, http://

news.bbc.co.uk/2/hi/europe/2750573.stm; "French Court Ruling Ends Long-Term Saga over Nazi Memorabilia Auctions on Yahoo!" *Electronic Commerce and Law Report*, Feb. 19, 2003, 176.

26. "Ex-Yahoo Chief Acquitted over Nazi Sites," *CNN*, Feb. 11, 2003, http://www.cnn.com/2003/TECH/biztech/02/11/france.yahoo.reut/index.html. See Association L'Amicale des Deportes d'Auschwitz v. Société Yahoo! Inc., Tribunal de grande instance [T.G.I.] [ordinary court of original jurisdiction] Paris, Feb. 11, 2003 (Fr).

27. "French Court Exonerates Yahoo! Site and Ex-CEO in Auctions of Nazi Memorabilia," *Electronic Commerce and Law Report*, Apr. 13, 2005, 384.

28. Yahoo! Appellee Brief at 14–15.

29. Yahoo! v. La Ligue Contre le Racisme et L'Antisémitisme, 433 F.3d at 1218; Yahoo! Appellee Brief at 50, 52.

30. Yahoo! Inc. v. La Ligue Contre le Racisme et L'Antisémitisme, 145 F. Supp. 2d 1168, 1194 (N.D. Cal. 2001).

31. Yahoo! Inc. v. La Ligue Contre le Racisme et L'Antisémitisme, 379 F.3d 1120 (9th Cir. 2004), opinion vacated by en banc decision.

32. Yahoo! Inc. v. La Ligue Contre le Racisme et L'Antisémitisme, 433 F.3d at 1124 (9th Cir. 2006) (Fletcher, J.).

33. 433 F.3d at 1234.

34. Yahoo! Answering brief at 2.

35. 433 F.3d at 1235–36 (Fisher, J.)

36. Google Inc., *Annual Report* (Form 10-K), Mar. 16, 2006, vii, 19, 23, http://investor.google.com/pdf/2006_Google_AnnualReport.pdf.

37. Ação Civil Pública com Pedido de Antecipação de Tutela [Public Civil Action with Request for Protective Order] at 16, T.J.S.P.–17, Ap. Civ. No. 2006.61.00.018332–8, filed 22.8.2006 (Brazil), http://www.prsp.mpf.gov.br/prdc/area-de-atuacao/direitos-humanos/dhumint/ACP%20Google%20Brasil.pdf.

38. Andrew Downie, "Google and the Pedophiles," *Time*, Sept. 6, 2006. Brazil's prosecutors were not the only ones whose subpoenas Google initially resisted. A few months earlier, Google Inc. had refused to comply with demands for information from the US Justice Department, which sought information in connection with pornography. Arshad Mohammed, "Google Refuses Demand for Search Information," *Washington Post*, Jan. 20, 2006. The

Justice Department sought "every query typed into its search engine over the course of one week without providing identifying information about the people who conducted the searches," as well as "a random sample of 1 million Web pages that can be searched in the vast databases maintained by Google."

39. Richard Waters, "Brazil Lawyers Lean on Google," *Financial Times*, Aug. 24, 2006.

40. "Yahoo! Teams with Swatch to Deliver Live Video Webcast from the Great Wall of China," *Yahoo!*, Aug. 16, 2000, http://yhoo.client.shareholder.com/ReleaseDetail.cfm?ReleaseID=173723.

41. Hong Kong Privacy Commissioner, "The Disclosure of Email Subscriber's Personal Data by Email Service Provider to PRC Law Enforcement Agency," Case No. 200603619, Mar. 14, 2007, Report No. R07–3619, § 6.8.2, p. 16, http://www.pcpd.org.hk/english/publications/files/Yahoo_e.pdf.

42. Ibid., § 1.5, p. 2.

43. Ibid., § 5.1, p. 11, and § 8.14, p. 31.

44. Ibid. ("YHHK did not exercise control over the affairs of Yahoo! China").

45. Ibid. ("Such control was in fact exercised wholly by Yahoo! Inc.").

46. Luke O'Brien, "'Yahoo Betrayed My Husband,'" *Wired*, Mar. 15, 2007.

47. Ariana Eunjung Cha and Sam Diaz, "Advocates Sue Yahoo in Chinese Torture Cases," *Washington Post*, Apr. 19, 2007; Victoria Kwan, "Human Rights in China: Prisoner Profile: Wang Xiaoning," March 2006, http://hrichina.org/content/1208.

48. Kwan, "Human Rights." A *Wired News* report supports this summary. O'Brien, "Yahoo."

49. Miguel Helft, "Chinese Political Prisoner Sues in U.S. Court, Saying Yahoo Helped Identify Dissidents," *New York Times*, Apr. 19, 2007 (quoting Yahoo! spokesman Jim Cullinan).

50. O'Brien, "Yahoo."

51. Yahoo!, Yahoo! Inc. Reaches Settlement on Lawsuit[;] Works to Establish Human Rights Fund, November 13, 2007, http://investor.yahoo.net/releasedetail.cfm?ReleaseID=302980.

52. "Yahoo to Invest US$1 Billion in Chinese E-Commerce Site," *New York Times*, Aug. 11, 2005.

53. Human Rights Watch, *"Race to the Bottom": Corporate Complicity in Chinese Internet Censorship* 18:8(C) (August 2006).

54. Aaron Ricadela, "Computing Heads for the Clouds," *Business Week Online*, Nov. 19, 2007, http://www.businessweek.com/stories/2007-11-16/computing-heads-for-the-cloudsbusinessweek-business-news-stock-market-and-financial-advice.

55. "Google Sees Growth in 'Cloud Computing,'" *Albany (NY) Times Union*, Nov. 18, 2007.

56. https://www.google.com/intl/en/policies/privacy/.

57. Planned Parenthood of Columbia/Willamette, Inc. v. American Coalition of Life Activists, 290 F.3d 1058 (9th Cir. 2002).

3. Eastern Entrepôt

1. Anupreeta Das and Amanda Paulson, "Need a Tutor? Call India," *Christian Science Monitor*, May 23, 2005; Rachel Konrad, "Foreign Accountants Do U.S. Tax Returns," *USA Today*, Feb. 23, 2004; Raja Mishra, "Radiology Work Shifts to Overnight, Overseas: Mass. Clinics Rely on Outsourcing," *Boston Globe*, June 29, 2005; Keith Bradsher, "Own Original Chinese Copies of Real Western Art!" *New York Times*, July 15, 2005 (noting that "skilled painters in Xiamen . . . produce portraits of American families from photographs sent to them over the Internet").

2. Eric Bellman, "One More Cost of Sarbanes-Oxley: Outsourcing to India," *Wall Street Journal*, July 14, 2005; Sarbanes-Oxley Act of 2002 § 404(a), Pub. L. No. 107–204, 116 Stat. 745 (requiring management to assess effectiveness of company's internal controls over financial reporting); Saritha Rai, "As It Tries to Cut Costs, Wall Street Looks to India," *New York Times*, Oct. 8, 2003 (quoting business student Gayatri Srinivasan, "Imagine working directly for a Wall Street firm while continuing to live in India").

3. Hema Nair, "Outsourcing Prayers," *BeliefNet*, http://www.beliefnet.com/Faiths/2004/08/Outsourcing-Prayers.aspx; Saritha Rai, "Short on Priests, U.S. Catholics Outsource Prayers to Indian Clergy," *New York Times*, June 13, 2004 (quoting the Rev. Paul Thelakkat from Cochin saying, "The prayer is heartfelt, and every prayer is treated as the same whether it is paid for in dollars, euros or in rupees").

4. Beset with civil strife, Pakistan seems to have lost the opportunity to become its front office. S. Mitra Kalita, "Virtual Secretary Puts New Face on

Pakistan: Despite Area's Instability, More U.S. Firms Are Offshoring There," *Washington Post*, May 10, 2005 (describing a receptionist in Karachi, Pakistan, who greets visitors to a Washington, DC, firm via video monitor).

5. Elizabeth Barber, "Fashioned from Fiber," in *Along the Silk Road*, ed. Elizabeth ten Grotenhuis, *Asian Art and Culture*, vol. 6 (Washington, DC: Smithsonian Institution, 2002), 57, 59; Sally Hovey Wriggins, *The Silk Road Journey with Xuanzang* (Boulder, CO: Westview, 2004), 177.

6. "The Place to Be," *Economist*, Nov. 11, 2004.

7. One commentator satirically observes the potential benefits of outsourcing the chief executive officer position, not just back office positions: "The decision to outsource the CEO position to an equally competent former opium farmer living in Pakistan, a Mr. Mosul, was made as an alternative to moving plant operations to Mexico by a 76% vote of company shareholders over the last month."

"'It was one of the easiest decisions I've ever made,' commented Matilda Jenkins, a proud owner of 2,000 shares of CBI, 'Opium farmer for 80K a year or Mr. 1 million a year plus shares, options, bonuses, golden parachute plan and sexual harassment suits?'" This was originally posted on a website with the heading, "CEO Position Outsourced: Over 700 Jobs Saved," but the posting has since disappeared and is not available even through the Internet Archive's Wayback Machine.

8. William Underhill and Jason Overdorf, "Bottom to Best," *Newsweek International*, Sept. 9, 2007.

9. Nasscom, "Indian IT-BPO Industry," http://www.nasscom.org/indian-itbpo-industry.

10. Subramaniam Ramadorai, *The TCS Story . . . and Beyond* (New Delhi: Penguin Books India, 2011), 81–82.

11. Mark Kobayashi-Hillary, *Outsourcing to India: The Offshore Advantage* (Berlin: Springer, 2004), 80.

12. Thomas J. DeLong and Ashish Nanda, *Professional Services: Text and Cases* (New York: McGraw-Hill/Irwin, 2002), 467.

13. Ibid.

14. Thomas L. Friedman, *The World Is Flat: A Brief History of the Twenty-First Century*, 2nd ed. (New York: Farrar, Straus and Giroux, 2007), 5.

15. Kobayashi-Hillary, *Outsourcing*, 82; Was Rahman and Priya Kurien, *Blind Men and the Elephant: Demystifying the Global IT Services Industry* (New Delhi: Sage India, 2007).

16. Nasscom, "Indian IT-BPO Industry."

17. Tata Consultancy Services, *Annual Report, 2008–2009*, 75; Infosys, *Annual Report, 2009–10*, 30; Wipro, *Annual Report, 2008–2009*, 85.

18. Peter Fuhrman and Michael Schuman, "Now We Are Our Own Masters," *Forbes*, May 23, 1994.

19. Ramadorai, *TCS Story*, 77.

20. DeLong and Nanda, *Professional Services*, 468.

21. Fuhrman and Schuman, "Own Masters."

22. N. R. Narayana Murthy, *A Better India, a Better World* (New Delhi: Penguin Books India, 2009), 231.

23. N. R. Kleinfield, "I.B.M. to Leave India and Avoid Loss of Control," *New York Times*, Nov. 16, 1977.

24. Jay Solomon and Kathryn Kranhold, "In India's Outsourcing Boom, GE Played a Starring Role," *Wall Street Journal*, Mar. 23, 2005.

25. Ibid.

26. Eric W. Pfeiffer, "From India to America," *Forbes*, Aug. 23, 1999.

27. Murray E. Jennex, *Case Studies in Knowledge Management* (Hershey, PA: Idea Group, 2005), 292.

28. Kerry A. Dolan, "Offshoring the Offshorers," *Forbes*, Apr. 17, 2007 ("Tata Consultancy Services has opened offices in Budapest, Hungary and Hangzhou, China. Last year it acquired a 1,300-employee outsourcer in Chile, and it plans to add 1,500 to the 485 people at its Brazil arm").

29. Anand Giridharadas, "Outsourcing Works So Well, India Is Sending Jobs Abroad," *New York Times*, Sept. 24, 2007.

30. "The Ten Largest IT Servicing Deals in May 2010," http://www.globalservicesmedia.com/IT-Outsourcing/Market-Dynamics/The-Ten-Largest-IT-Services-Deals-in-May–2010/22/28/9716/GS10061118447.

31. Steve Lohr, "Global Strategy Stabilized I.B.M. During Downturn," *New York Times*, Apr. 19, 2010.

32. Steve Hamm, "IBM vs. Tata: Who's More American?" *Business Week*, Apr. 23, 2008.

33. Bruce Nussbaum, "Is Outsourcing Becoming Outmoded?" *Business Week*, Sept. 19, 2004; Arjun Sethi and Olivier Aries, "The End of Outsourcing (as We Know It)," *Business Week*, Aug. 10, 2010.

34. Julia Nielson and Daria Taglioni, *Services Trade Liberalisation: Identifying Opportunities and Gains*, OECD Trade Policy Working Paper no. 1 (Paris: OECD, 2004), 9.

35. Hal R. Varian, "Technology Levels the Business Playing Field," *New York Times*, Aug. 25, 2005.

36. Nielson and Taglioni, *Services Trade Liberalisation*, 9 (noting that "former colony/colonizer relationships" might prove important as facilitating both "capital and credibility for exporters from the latter").

37. Richard N. Pollack, *Contract Magazine*, June 1, 2005. See also John Tagliabue, "Eastern Europe Becomes a Center for Outsourcing," *New York Times*, Apr. 19, 2007 (describing Budapest outsourcing firm opened by a woman in Hungary, which her father had fled after the unsuccessful 1956 uprising); but cf. Eric Pfanner, "Co-Founder's Russian Roots Don't Translate for Google," *Houston Chronicle*, Dec. 31, 2006.

38. William Ouchi, "Markets, Bureaucracies, and Clans," *Administrative Science Quarterly* 25 (1980): 129–41; "Introduction," in Grahame Thompson et al., eds., *Markets, Hierarchies and Networks: The Coordination of Social Life* (Thousand Oaks, CA: Sage, 1991), 1.

39. Srilata Zaheer et al., "Cluster Capabilities or Ethnic Ties? Location Choice by Foreign and Domestic Entrants in the Services Offshoring Industry in India," *Journal of International Business Studies* 40 (2009): 944, 950; Anna-Lee Saxenian, *Regional Advantage: Culture and Competition in Silicon Valley and Route* (Cambridge, MA: Harvard University Press, 1994), 128.

40. Melanie Warner, "The Indians of Silicon Valley," *Fortune*, May 15, 2000.

41. Ibid.

42. Ibid.

43. J. H. Thrall, "Reinventing Radiology in the Digital Age: I. The All-Digital Department," *Radiology* 236 (2005): 382.

44. Emma Wilkinson, "X-Ray Technology in the 21st Century," *BBC News*, May 30, 2007, http://news.bbc.co.uk/2/hi/health/6700847.stm ("The radiology department at St Mary's which process around 250,000 X-rays a year have saved so much space on storage of films they are planning to install a new children's waiting room").

45. James Brice, "Globalization Comes to Radiology," *Diagnostic Imaging*, Nov. 1, 2003, 70.

46. NightHawk Radiology Services, *Annual Report, 2006*, 5 ("The advent of the Digital Imaging and Communications in Medicine, or DICOM, standard for transferring images and associated information, high-speed broadband internet connections, digitization and picture archival and

communication systems, or PACS, has contributed to increased utilization of diagnostic imaging technologies by permitting radiologists to practice remotely").

47. "International Teleradiology," *New England Journal of Medicine* 354 (2006): 662 (quoting Dr. Arjun Kalyanpur of Teleradiology Solutions).

48. Dawn Fallik, "The Doctor Is In—But Not in U.S.," *Philadelphia Inquirer*, Oct. 12, 2004.

49. Lindsey Tanner, "U.S. Doctors Turn to Outsourcing to Help Diagnose Ills," *AP*, Dec. 1, 2004.

50. Rob Stein, "Hospital Services Performed Overseas: Training, Licensing Questioned," *Washington Post*, Apr. 24, 2005.

51. See, e.g., Teleradiology Solutions, "Legal/Licensing," http://www.telradsol.com/legal.html ("All interpreting staff for US hospitals are [American Board of Radiology]-certified radiologists who are licensed to practice medicine within the United States"); and On Rad, Inc., http://www.onradinc.com/nighthawk-radiology-alternative/?gclid=CLSm1cCI6LECFUUZQgodwQsAEA ("100% of our radiologists are U.S.-based and certified by the American Board of Radiology").

52. Robert Steinbrook, "The Age of Teleradiology," *New England Journal of Medicine* 357 (2007): 5, 7 ("A teleradiologist will often have no information about the patient beyond that contained in the study requisition").

53. James Brice, "Globalization Comes to Radiology," *Diagnostic Imaging*, Nov. 1, 2003, 70.

54. Pathology is also being outsourced, but often from hospitals outside the United States to doctors within the United States: "The University of Pittsburgh Medical Center essentially manages a transplant hospital in Italy, performing some pathology from Pittsburgh. The Armed Forces Institute of Pathology in Washington, part of the Walter Reed Army Medical Center, provides second opinions on about 60,000 cases a year, for Americans and foreigners. Most of the time, slides and tissue samples are sent in by mail, but about 300 to 500 a year are analyzed by using telepathology." Andrew Pollack, "Who's Reading Your X-Ray?" *New York Times*, Nov. 16, 2003.

55. Ibid.

56. 42 U.S.C. § 1395y(a)(4) (preventing reimbursement for services that "are not provided within the United States").

57. CMS Publication 100–2, *Medicare Benefit Policy Manual*, chap. 16, sec. 60, Feb. 23, 2007.

58. Stein, "Hospital Services Performed Overseas."

59. Heather Timmons, "Due Diligence from Afar," *New York Times*, Aug. 5, 2010.

60. Ravi Shankar, *State of the Legal Outsourcing Sector*, Nov. 8, 2011, 2, http://jenner.com/system/assets/assets/6221/original/2011_20State_20of_20the_20Legal_20Outsourcing_20Sector.pdf?1329941149.

61. Mark L. Tuft, "Supervising Offshore Outsourcing of Legal Services in a Global Environment: Re-Examining Current Ethical Standards," *Akron Law Review* 43 (2011): 825.

62. Ibid., 837.

63. San Diego County Bar Association, "Ethics Opinon 2007–1," http://www.sdcba.org/index.cfm?Pg=ethicsopinion07–1.

64. "Website Disclaimer," Clutch Group, http://www.clutchgroup.com/home/website-disclaimer/.

65. Dilip Ratha, Sanket Mohapatra, and Ani Silwal, *Migration and Remittances Factbook*, 2nd ed. (Washington, DC: World Bank, 2011), 13.

66. Aidan Jones, "World's Leading Location for Call Centers? It's Not India," *Christian Science Monitor*, Apr. 19, 2011.

67. Reuters, "Move Over India, Philippines Eyes Broader Outsourcing Role," *Times of India*, Mar. 10, 2012.

68. Vikas Bajaj, "A New Capital of Call Centers," *New York Times*, Nov. 26, 2011.

69. Antonio Regalado, "Soccer, Samba and Outsourcing?" *Wall Street Journal*, Jan. 25, 2007.

70. Nasscom, "Indian IT-BPO Industry."

71. Scott DeCarlo, "The World's Leading Companies: Forbes Global 2000," *Forbes*, Apr. 18, 2012.

72. Infosys, *Annual Report, 2011–2012* (reporting 149,994 employees as of Mar. 31, 2012, of which approximately 141,790 are technology professionals, including trainees); Tata Consultancy Services, *Annual Report, 2011–2012*, 25–26 (reporting over 238,583 employees, including 17,329 non-Indians); Wipro, *Annual Report, 2011–2012*, 16 (reporting 135,920 employees in its IT Services and Products Business segments).

73. R. Gopalakrishnan, "India and Tata: National Development and the Corporation," *Innovations* (Fall 2008): 13 ("65.8 percent of the shares of Tata Sons, the holding company of the group, are controlled by trusts").

74. Murthy, *A Better India*, x, 13. Nehru attributed this quote to Gandhi in his "Tryst with Destiny" speech. "The Tale of Two Gandhiji Quotes," *Financial Express*, July 7, 2004.

75. Anita Raghavan, "Azim Premji, India's Bill Gates," *Forbes*, Apr. 30, 2010.

76. Frances Wood, *The Silk Road: Two Thousand Years in the Heart of Asia* (Berkeley: University of California Press, 2002), 66.

77. Nasscom, "Indian IT-BPO Industry."

78. UNESCO, *Reaching the Marginalized: Education for All Global Monitoring Report, 2010* (2010).

79. Alejandro Lazo, "D.C. Firm Charts New Territory on Visas," *Washington Post*, May 5, 2008.

80. Rafiq Dossani and Martin Kenney, "Service Provision for the Global Economy: The Evolving Indian Experience," *Review of Policy Research* 26:1–2 (2009): 77, 83.

81. "India: The Economy," *BBC News*, Dec. 3, 1998, http://news.bbc.co.uk/2/hi/south_asia/55427.stm.

82. Celia W. Dugger, "India's High-Tech, and Sheepish, Capitalism," *New York Times*, Dec. 16, 1999.

83. Rafiq Dossani, "Entrepreneurship: The True Story Behind Indian IT," in *Making IT: The Rise of Asia in High Tech*, ed. Henry S. Rowen et al. (Palo Alto, CA: Stanford University Press, 2007), 221, 231 (reporting that "from 1986 to 1987, 58 percent of IIT [Indian Institute of Technology] graduates in computer sciences and engineering left India").

84. Jonathan Karp, "The IT Guys: New Corporate Gurus Tap India's Brainpower to Galvanize Economy," *Wall Street Journal*, Sept. 27, 1999.

4. Pirates of Cyberspace

1. David R. Johnson and David Post, "Law and Borders—The Rise of Law in Cyberspace," *Stanford Law Review* 48 (1996): 1367, 1372.

2. Don Yaeger, "Bucking the Odds," *Sports Illustrated*, Jan. 8, 2001.

3. Wayne Coffey, "An Offshore Thing," *New York Daily News*, Mar. 26, 2000.

4. Yaeger, "Bucking the Odds" ("an estimated 80% of all gaming URLs on the Web can be traced back to servers on the 108-square-mile island").

5. John Greenwood, "Billion$ and Billion$ Served," *Financial Post Business*, Oct. 1, 2005.

6. Nils Pratley, "The Porn Princess, the Indian Computer Whizz and the Poker Bet That Made $10bn," *Guardian*, June 3, 2005.

7. Kurt Eichenwald, "At PartyGaming, Everything's Wild," *New York Times*, June 26, 2005; Eric Pfanner, "Is Party Over for Online Gambling?" *International Herald Tribune*, July 3, 2006.

8. Paul Blustein, "Against All Odds," *Washington Post*, Aug. 4, 2006.

9. "Any Given Sunday," *CBS News*, Sept. 7, 2003, http://www.cbsnews.com/stories/2003/09/04/60minutes/main571621.shtml.

10. United States v. Cohen, 260 F.3d 68, 78 (2d Cir. 2001) (affirming conviction of Cohen for violating Wire Act by facilitating sports betting over the Internet).

11. "Life Online Means Being on the Lam," *New York Daily News*, Mar. 26, 2000.

12. "Any Given Sunday."

13. Decision by the Arbitrator, *United States—Measures Affecting the Cross-Border Supply of Gambling and Betting Services*, ¶¶ 4.118–4.119, WT/DS285/ARB (Dec. 21, 2007). See also Gary Rivlin, "Gambling Dispute with a Tiny Country Puts U.S. in a Bind," *New York Times*, Aug. 23, 2007. Antigua sought a far greater amount as a sanction—equaling the lost revenues from the entire online gambling sector, not just the small fraction of it devoted to horse racing. Indeed, it remains unclear whether the United States could have complied with the WTO appellate body decision by simply inviting Antiguan companies to supply online horse-race gambling services. One would think that that remedy would have been insufficient unless the United States could have shown that online gambling with respect to horse racing was somehow far less prone to the vulnerabilities allegedly afflicting other forms of online gambling. Without such a demonstration, the United States defense that online gambling was a threat to morals and public order was called into question by the United States' own law permitting online gambling.

14. See Anupam Chander, "Next Stop, Kazaakhstan? The Legal Globe-Trotting of Kazaa, the Post-Napster Filing Sharing Company," *Findlaw*, Oct. 24, 2002, http://writ.news.findlaw.com/commentary/20021024_chander.html; Michael Tarm, "KaZaA! Youths from Cyber-Savvy Estonia Write the New Napster, Delivering a Blow to the Global Entertainment Industry," *City Paper—The Baltic States* (March–April 2003), http://www.citypaper.ee/kazaa.htm.

15. John Borland, "Ruling Bolsters File-Traders' Prospects," *CNET*, Mar. 28, 2002, http://news.cnet.com/Ruling-bolsters-file-traders-prospects/2100–1023_3–870396.html.

16. Joris Evers, "Dutch Supreme Court Rules Kazaa Legal," IDG News Service, Dec. 19, 2003, http://www.pcworld.com/article/id,113968-page,1/article.html.

17. Metro-Goldwyn-Mayer Studios Inc. v. Grokster, Ltd., 243 F. Supp.2d 1073, 1087–88 (2003).

18. "KazaA Site Becomes Legal Service," *BBC News*, July 27, 2006, http://news.bbc.co.uk/2/hi/5220406.stm.

19. Kalika N. Doloswala and Ann Dadich, "The Accidental Criminal: Using Policy to Curb Illegal Downloading," *First Monday*, June 6, 2011, http://www.firstmonday.org/htbin/cgiwrap/bin/ojs/index.php/fm/article/viewArticle/3412/2984.

20. Adrian Chen, "The Underground Website Where You Can Buy Any Drug Imaginable," *Gawker*, June 1, 2011, http://gawker.com/5805928/the-underground-website-where-you-can-buy-any-drug-imaginable.

21. Ivar Ekman, "Skype Is 2nd Jackpot for Scandinavian Duo," *International Herald Tribune*, Sept. 13, 2005.

22. Thomas Crampton, "Russian Download Site Is Popular and Possibly Illegal," *New York Times*, June 1, 2006; Frank Ahrens, "Music Store Cold War," *Washington Post*, Oct. 26, 2006 ("Beck's most recent album, 'The Information,' costs $11.99 on iTunes. On [AllOfMp3.com], it costs $2.62").

23. Doug Aamoth, "Former AllOfMp3.com Owner Faces Jail Time," *CrunchGear*, July 25, 2007, http://crunchgear.com/2007/07/25/former-AllOfMp3com-owner-faces-jail-time/.

24. "Legal Info," AllofMP3, http://www.AllofMP3.com.

25. Thomas Crampton, "MP3 Web Site in Russia Goes from Cheap to Free Amid Legal Battles," *International Herald Tribune*, Oct. 18, 2006.

26. Mark Savage, "'Illegal' MP3 Site Defends Itself," *BBC News*, June 9, 2006, http://news.bbc.co.uk/2/hi/entertainment/5061610.stm; Alex Nicholson, "Russian Music Site Down, Sister Site Up," *USA Today*, July 3, 2007.

27. Sabra Ayres, "Russian Site Sells Music for a Song," *Arizona Republic*, Oct. 29, 2006.

28. Richard Menta, "AllofMP3.com Hits Web Top 1000," *MP3Newswire*, July 21, 2006, http://www.mp3newswire.net/stories/6002/AllofMP3.com_itunes.html.

29. http://img.allofmp3.ru/img/allofmp3_faq.pdf.

30. Crampton, *MP3* ("Domain-name ownership records kept by Verisign . . . show that Ivan Fedorov of Media Services in Moscow is the owner" of the domain name AllofMP3.com).

31. Tom Corelis, "RIAA Drops $1.65T AllOfMP3 Lawsuit, Claims Victory," *Daily Tech*, May 28, 2008, http://www.dailytech.com/RIAA+Drops+165T+AllOfMP3+Lawsuit+Claims+Victory/article11882.htm.

32. Lucie Guibault et al., *Study on the Implementation and Effect in Member States' Laws of Directive 2001/29/EC on the Harmonisation of Certain Aspects of Copyright and Related Rights in the Information Society* (2007), 38, http://www.ivir.nl/publications/guibault/Infosoc_report_2007.pdf.

33. Kelly Fiveash, "AllTunes.com Claims Win in Russian Copyright Claim," *Register*, July 16, 2007.

34. "U.S. Pushes Russia in WTO Talks to Close MP3 Site," *Reuters*, Oct. 5, 2006, http://www.wto.ru/en/news.asp?msg_id=17913.

35. "Cheap Russian MP3s Raise a Ruckus," *Wired*, June 2, 2006, http://www.wired.com/techbiz/media/news/2006/06/71076.

36. "AllOfMP3 Owner Last Word," *Cnews*, Aug. 1, 2007, http://eng.cnews.ru/news/top/indexEn.shtml?2007/08/01/261106.

37. "Allofmp3.Com Shut Down, But More Russian Music Websites Opened," July 18, 2007, http://www.edri.org/edrigram/number5.14/russian-music-websites. The proprietors seem to have moved their site to other locations such as MP3Sparks and AllTunes.com, but these sites are no longer active.

38. Zack Whittaker, "U.K.'s Largest ISP Blocks the Pirate Bay, But to No Avail," *CNET*, June 20, 2012, http://news.cnet.com/8301–1023_3–57457001–93/u.k.s-largest-isp-blocks-the-pirate-bay-but-to-no-avail/.

39. "Ruling to Shut Down Leak Site Called Censorship," *National Public Radio*, Feb. 23, 2008 (Westlaw 2008 WLNR 3629478).

40. http://mirror.WikiLeaks.info/.

41. http://WikiLeaks.ch/.

42. Adam Liptak and Brad Stone, "U.S. Judge Orders WikiLeaks Web Site Shut Down," *New York Times*, Feb. 20, 2008; Declan McCullagh, "Wiki Leaks Domain Name Yanked in Spat over Leaked Documents," *CNET*, Feb. 19, 2008, http://news.cnet.com/8301–13578_3–9874167–38.html.

43. David F. Gallagher, "WikiLeaks Site Has a Friend in Sweden," *New York Times Bits Blog*, Feb. 20, 2008, http://bits.blogs.nytimes.com/2008/02/20/WikiLeaks-site-has-a-friend-in-sweden/.

44. Bank Julius Baer & Co. v. WikiLeaks, 535 F.Supp.2d 980 (N.D. Cal. 2008).

45. Chris Amico, "WikiLeaks Stays Visible, But Is Net Closing In?" *PBS Newshour Rundown blog*, Dec. 3, 2010, http://www.pbs.org/newshour/rundown/2010/12/the-cat-and-mouse-game-between-wikileaks.html.

46. http://aws.amazon.com/message/65348/.

47. Alexia Tsotsis, "PayPal VP on Blocking WikiLeaks: 'State Department Told Us It Was Illegal,'" *TechCrunch*, Dec. 8, 2010, http://techcrunch.com/2010/12/08/paypal-wikileaks/.

48. "WikiLeaks Dodges Obstacles to Stay Online," *National Public Radio*, Dec. 8, 2010 (Westlaw 2010 WLNR 24326485); http://www.youtube.com/user/keanucange.

49. Charles Arthur and Josh Halliday, "WikiLeaks Fights to Stay Online After US Company Withdraws Domain Name," *Guardian*, Dec. 3, 2010.

50. Seth F. Kreimer, "Censorship by Proxy: The First Amendment, Internet Intermediaries, and the Problem of the Weakest Link," *University of Pennsylvania Law Review* 155 (2006): 11.

51. Ronald J. Mann and Seth R. Belzley, "The Promise of Internet Intermediary Liability," *William and Mary Law Review* 47 (2005): 239, 247.

52. Ibid.

53. "YouTube Tries to Resolve Thai Ban," *BBC News*, Apr. 7, 2007, http://news.bbc.co.uk/2/hi/asia-pacific/6535509.stm.

54. Noah Shachtman, "Army Squeezes Soldier Blogs, Maybe to Death," *Wired*, May 2, 2007, http://www.wired.com/politics/onlinerights/news/2007/05/army_bloggers.

55. Jatin Gandhi and Jairaj Singh, "Orkut Site Creates More Controversy," *Hindustan Times*, Oct. 20, 2006.

56. "The remedy to be applied [to expose falsehood and fallacies] is more speech, not enforced silence." Whitney v. California, 274 U.S. 357, 377 (1927) (Brandeis, J., concurring).

57. "Google's Social Networking Site in Trouble," *Times of India*, Oct. 10, 2006.

58. "Orkut Faces Ban as HC Takes Up Plea," *Press Trust of India*, Nov. 23, 2006.

59. "Orkut in Trouble Again," *Times of India*, Nov. 18, 2006.

60. Shivam Vij, "Are Internet Service Providers Blocking Blogs?" *Rediff*, July 17, 2007, http://in.rediff.com/news/2006/jul/17blog.htm.

61. OpenNetInitiative, *India* (undated), http://opennet.net/research/profiles/india.

62. This is the result of a WHOIS search conducted on March 27, 2012, at http://www.pir.org.

63. "Proxy Server," *Wikipedia*, http://en.wikipedia.org/wiki/Proxy_bypass.

64. "Kproxy Terms of Use," http://www.kproxy.com/termsofuse.jsp.

65. Universal City Studios v. Reimerdes, 273 F.3d 429 (2d Cir. 2001); "Gallery of CSS Descramblers," http://www.cs.cmu.edu/~dst/DeCSS/Gallery/.

66. Anupam Chander, "Whose Republic?" *University of Chicago Law Review* 69 (2003): 1479, 1490.

67. Anupam Chander, "The New, New Property," *Texas Law Review* 81 (2003): 715, 791–93.

68. Ibid., 758.

5. Facebookistan

1. Mike Swift, "Facebook to Assemble Global Team of 'Diplomats,'" *San Jose Mercury News*, May 22, 2011; Cyrus Farivar, "Mr. Ambassador, Meet President Zuckerberg," *Slate*, May 27, 2011, http://www.slate.com/id/2295700/.

2. Rebecca Mackinnon, "Life in Facebookistan," *On the Media*, Feb. 3, 2012, http://www.onthemedia.org/2012/feb/03/life-facebookistan/.

3. East Coast Code is "the 'code' that Congress enacts (as in the tax code or 'the U.S. Code') . . . that say[s] *in words* how to behave." West Coast Code is "code that code writers 'enact'–the instructions imbedded in the software and hardware that make cyberspace work." Lawrence Lessig, *Code and Other Laws of Cyberspace* (New York: Basic Books, 1999), 53.

4. See David R. Johnson and David Post, "Law and Borders—The Rise of Law in Cyberspace," *Stanford Law Review* 48 (1996): 1367, 1372 (arguing that "efforts to control the flow of electronic information across physical borders . . . are likely to prove futile").

5. Alfred C. Yen, "Western Frontier or Feudal Society? Metaphors and Perceptions of Cyberspace," *Berkeley Technology Law Journal* 17 (2002): 1207, 1234 (characterizing cyberspace as consisting of fiefdoms, where "political authority" is "an incident of private property").

6. Somini Sengupta, "Zuckerberg's Unspoken Law: Sharing and More Sharing," *New York Times*, Sept. 23, 2011.

7. Lori Andrews, *I Know Who You Are and I Saw What You Did: Social Networks and the Death of Privacy* (New York: Simon and Schuster, 2011), 1.

8. Julian Lee, "Facebook's Power Should Worry Us All," *Sydney Morning Herald*, Oct. 10, 2011, http://www.smh.com.au/opinion/society-and-culture/facebooks-power-should-worry-us-all–20111009–1lfu0.html.

9. Brad Fitzpatrick, "Thoughts on the Social Graph," Aug. 17, 2007, http://bradfitz.com/social-graph-problem/. Fitzpatrick now works at Google, which also offers its own social graph API (application processing interface) for the social web.

10. "Statement of Rights and Responsibilities," *Facebook*, last modified Apr. 26, 2011, https://www.facebook.com/legal/terms ("You will not post content that: is hateful, threatening, or pornographic; incites violence; or contains nudity or graphic or gratuitous violence"). What appear to be Facebook's guidelines to its content moderators have been leaked and posted online. http://gawker.com/5885714/inside-facebooks-outsourced-anti+porn-and-gore-brigade-where-camel-toes-are-more-offensive-than-crushed-heads.

11. Kim Pemberton, "Breastfeeding Mom Takes on Facebook Nudity Policy," *Vancouver Sun*, Jan. 11, 2012.

12. https://www.facebook.com/fbsitegovernance.

13. James Grimmelmann, "Saving Facebook," *Iowa Law Review* 94 (2009): 1137, 1149.

14. "David and Goliath," *Economist*, Apr. 10, 2010, 56.

15. See, e.g., Therese Poletti, "Facebook Gets Wrist Slapped by the FTC," *MarketWatch*, Nov. 29, 2011, http://www.marketwatch.com/story/facebook-gets-wrist-slapped-by-the-ftc–2011–11–29.

16. Missouri State Teachers Ass'n v. Missouri, No. 11AC-CC00553, 2011 WL 4425537 (Mo. Cir. Ct. Aug. 26, 2011).

17. Jason Hancock, "Nixon Signs Revised 'Facebook Law,' MOSIRA," *St. Louis Post Dispatch*, Oct. 21, 2011.

18. Riva Richmond, "As 'Like' Buttons Spread, So Do Facebook's Tentacles," *New York Times*, Sept. 27, 2011.

19. Melissa Eddy, "German Privacy Watchdog Dislikes Facebook's 'Like,'" *USA Today*, Aug. 19, 2011.

20. Stuart Tiffen, "Facebook's 'Like' a Hot Button Issue in Germany," *Deutsche Welle*, Sept. 9, 2011.

21. "Data Use Policy," *Facebook*, last updated June 8, 2012, https://www.facebook.com/full_data_use_policy.

22. Press Release, Unabhängiges Landeszentrum für Datenschutz Schleswig-Holstein [the Independent Center for Data Protection for Schleswig-Holstein ("ULD")], "ULD to Website Owners: 'Deactivate Facebook Web Analytics,'" Aug. 19, 2011, https://www.datenschutzzentrum.de/presse/20110819-facebook-en.htm.

23. Tiffen, "Facebook's 'Like.'"

24. "German Minister Advises Colleagues to Shun Facebook," *Agence France-Presse*, Sept. 11, 2011, http://www.google.com/hostednews/afp/article/ALeqM5hyxHKd75Jl–0hl_RfeclhEvMPZ8w?docId=CNG.ee29706d29744c955731a90381f66cc5.831.

25. Article 12 of the Data Protection Directive requires each EU member state to provide citizens a "right of access" to the information stored and processed about them.

26. Kashmir Hill, "Max Schrems, the Austrian Thorn in Facebook's Side," *Forbes*, Feb. 7, 2012, http://www.forbes.com/sites/kashmirhill/2012/02/07/the-austrian-thorn-in-facebooks-side/.

27. Data Protection Commissioner, *Facebook Ireland Ltd.: Report of Audit*, Dec. 21, 2011, 4.

28. Ibid., 21 ("The position of the Data Protection Commissioner should not however be interpreted as asserting sole jurisdiction over the activities of Facebook in the EU").

29. See Rick Mitchell, "French Court Fines Facebook for Page with Photo of Bishop, 'Insulting' Caption," *Electronic Commerce and Law Report (BNA)* 15, Apr. 28, 2010, 662.

30. Hervé G. v. Facebook France, Paris Court of First Instance, Apr. 13, 2010.

31. See Joséphine Bataille, "Condamné pour outrage à un évêque, Facebook gagne en appel," *La Vie*, Nov. 1, 2011 (providing an image of the Facebook page).

32. Mitchell, "French Court."

33. See Elizabeth Denham, Office of the Privacy Commissioner of Canada, *Report of Findings into the Complaint Filed by the Canadian Internet Policy and Public Interest Clinic (CIPPIC) Against Facebook Inc. Under the Personal Information Protection and Electronic Documents Act* (2009), http://publications.gc.ca/collections/collection_2010/privcom/IP54–31–2009-eng.pdf.

34. Ibid.

35. 2011 QCCS 1506 (2011).

36. 2007 SCC 34; [2007] 2 S.C.R. 801.

37. 2011 QCCS at ¶ 54.

38. "Twitter and Facebook Force End to Canada's Election Night Internet Gag," *National Post*, Jan. 13, 2012.

39. R. v. Bryan, 2007 SCC 12, [2007] 1 S.C.R. 527, 564.

40. Reshma Patil, "Chinese Think-Tank Finds Facebook a Political Threat," *Hindustan Times*, July 10, 2010.

41. "Syria Blocks Facebook After Golan Israel Recognition," *Globes* (Israel), Sept. 15, 2009.

42. Ibid. Maps are, of course highly political. See, e.g., Kwame Opam, "Google Legitimizes Libya's New Government on Google Maps," *Gizmodo*, Aug. 22, 2011, http://gizmodo.com/5833297/google-legitimizes-libyas-new-government-on-google-maps.

43. Alexis Madrigal, "The Inside Story of How Facebook Responded to Tunisian Hacks," *Atlantic*, Jan. 24, 2011.

44. Georgina Prodhan, "Egypt Shows How Easily Internet Can Be Silenced," *Reuters*, Jan. 28, 2011, http://af.reuters.com/article/egyptNews/idAFLDE70R09P20110128.

45. Madrigal, "Inside Story."

46. Ryan Singel, "Facebook Enables HTTPS So You Can Share Without Being Hijacked," *Wired*, Jan. 26, 2011, http://www.wired.com/threatlevel/2011/01/facebook-https/.

47. Yasmine Ryan, "How Tunisia's Revolution Began," *Al Jazeera*, Jan. 26, 2011, http://www.aljazeera.com/indepth/features/2011/01/2011126121815985483.html ("Facebook, unlike most video sharing sites, was not included in Tunisia's online censorship").

48. Madrigal, "Inside Story."

49. Ryan, "Tunisia's Revolution."

50. Prodhan, "Egypt Shows."

51. Catharine Smith, "Egypt's Facebook Revolution: Wael Ghonim Thanks the Social Network," *Huffington Post*, Feb. 11, 2011, http://www.huffingtonpost.com/2011/02/11/egypt-facebook-revolution-wael-ghonim_n_822078.html.

52. See Richard T. Ford, "Law's Territory (a History of Jurisdiction)," *Michigan Law Review* 97 (1999): 843, 855–56.

53. Press Release, "ULD to Website."

54. Sean Sinico, "German Minister Talks to Facebook, Google on US Tech Tour," *Deutsche Welle*, Sept. 21, 2011, http://www.dw.de/german-minister-talks-to-facebook-google-on-us-tech-tour/a-15404365-1.

55. Council Regulation 44/2001, O.J. (L 012), art. 5(3), sec. 2 ("A person domiciled in a Member State may, in another Member State, be sued: . . . 3. in matters relating to tort, *delict* or *quasi-delict*, in the courts for the place where the harmful event occurred or may occur"). Ralf Michaels observes that "the main objective of the Regulation is 'to allocate jurisdiction to the most appropriate Member State, regardless of sovereignty interests of the Member States.'" Ralf Michaels, "Two Paradigms of Jurisdiction," *Michigan Journal of International Law* 27 (2006): 1003, 1042.

56. Council Directive 2000/31/EC, On Certain Legal Aspects of Information Society Services, in Particular Electronic Commerce, in the Internal Market 2000, O.J. (L 178), 1, recital 22.

57. Mitchell, "French Court."

58. Press Release, "ULD to Website."

59. Deloitte, *Measuring Facebook's Economic Impact in Europe*, January 2012.

60. Samuel Bovard, "Germans Take on Facebook over Data Privacy," *Washington Times*, July 7, 2010 (emphasis added).

61. Ilse Aigner, German Federation Minister of Consumer Protection, to Mark Zuckerberg, CEO, Facebook, Apr. 5, 2010, http://www.spiegel.de/international/germany/german-government-minister-s-letter-to-facebook-dear-mr-zuckerberg-a–687285.html.

62. Christopher Kuner, "Data Protection Law and International Jurisdiction on the Internet (Part I)," *International Journal of Law and Information Technology* 18 (2010): 176, 190.

63. See Facebook, "Statement of Rights and Responsibilities" ("Certain specific terms that apply only for German users are available here").

64. For a discussion of why Facebook users might be able to influence Facebook, see generally Grimmelmann, "Saving Facebook."

65. Albert O. Hirschman, *Exit, Voice, and Loyalty: Responses to Decline in Firms, Organizations, and States* (Cambridge, MA: Harvard University Press, 1970).

66. Rebecca MacKinnon, *Consent of the Networked: The Worldwide Struggle for Internet Freedom* (New York: Basic Books, 2012), 149.

67. Facebook, "Statement of Rights and Responsibilities" ("You will resolve any claim, cause of action or dispute [claim] you have with us arising out of or relating to this Statement or Facebook exclusively in a state or federal court located in Santa Clara County. The laws of the State of California will govern this Statement, as well as any claim that might arise between you and us, without regard to conflict of law provisions. You agree to submit to the personal jurisdiction of the courts located in Santa Clara County, California for the purpose of litigating all such claims").

68. See Doe 1 v. AOL LLC, 552 F.3d 1077 (9th Cir. 2009); America Online, Inc. v. Super. Ct. of Alameda Cnty. (Mendoza), 90 Cal.App.4th 1, 108 Cal.Rptr.2d 699 (2001).

69. Bovard, "Germans Take on Facebook."

6. Freeing Trade in Cyberspace

1. For alternative characterizations of the differences between trade in goods and trade in services, see Drusilla K. Brown et al., "Modelling Multilateral Trade Liberalization in Services," July 6, 1995, http://www.fordschool.umich.edu/rsie/workingpapers/Papers376–400/r378.pdf (Drusilla Brown and her coauthors identify the following potential differences between trade in services and trade in goods: "The movement of factors internationally to permit onsite production of services, the perishability of services, the distinctive nature and size of transport costs in services, the role of traditional comparative advantage in determining patterns of services trade, and the embodiment and disembodiment of services into and out of goods"). See also Jagdish N. Bhagwati, "Splintering and Disembodiment of Services and Developing Nations," *World Economy* 7 (1984): 133 (outlining economic differences between two categories); Miroslav N. Jovanović, *The Economics of European Integration: Limits and Prospects* (Cheltenham, UK: Edward Elgar, 2005), 410–11 (describing technical and social differences, including the fact that women make up a higher percentage of the European workforce in services than in manufacturing).

2. See Ravi Aron and Jitendra V. Singh, "Getting Offshoring Right," *Harvard Business Review* (December 2005): 135, 139 (describing typology of services by availability of metric for such service).

3. United Nations Conference on Trade and Development, *World Investment Report, 2004: The Shift Towards Services* (New York: United Nations, 2004), xxv.

4. Kalypso Nicolaïdis and Susanne K. Schmidt, "Mutual Recognition 'on Trial': The Long Road to Services Liberalization," *Journal of European Public Policy* 14 (2007): 717, 719 ("for services almost all regulations have to do with processes").

5. Cf. Organisation for Economic Cooperation and Development, *Barriers to Trade in Services in South Eastern European (SEE) Countries—How Much Do They Matter?* OECD Doc. CCNM/TD/SEE(2003)4/FINAL (Oct. 29, 2003), 5 (identifying nontariff barriers often imposed on services as including "quantitative restrictions, price based instruments, licensing or certification requirements, discriminatory access to distribution, and communication systems").

6. General Agreement on Tariffs and Trade, art. III.1, Oct. 30, 1947, 61 Stat. A–11, 55 U.N.T.S. 194 ("contracting parties recognize that internal . . . regulations . . . should not be applied to imported or domestic products so as to afford protection to domestic production") [hereinafter GATT].

7. GATS, art. XVI (market access obligations for scheduled services only); ibid., art. XVII(1) (national treatment obligation for scheduled services only).

8. See, e.g., United States–Colombia Trade Promotion Agreement, U.S.–Colom., arts. 2.1–2.2, 3.3(1), 7.2, 9.1(1)–(5), 10.8, 11.1–11.3, 11.6, 12.2–12.3, 12.9, 16.1(8)–(10), 16.13, 19.6, Nov. 22, 2006, http://www.ustr.gov/trade-agreements/free-trade-agreements/colombia-fta/final-text; Free Trade Agreement Between the United States of America and the Republic of Korea, arts. 12, 15, June 30, 2007, http://www.ustr.gov/trade-agreements/free-trade-agreements/korus-fta/final-text.

9. Agreement Between the Government of the United States of America and the Government of the Sultanate of Oman on the Establishment of a Free Trade Area, U.S.-Oman, arts. 2.1–2.3(2), 3.2(1), 4.1, 9.1(1)–(4), 11.1, Jan. 19, 2006, 120 Stat. 1191, http://www.ustr.gov/Trade_Agreements/Bilateral/Oman_FTA/Final_Text/Section_Index.html; Agreement Between the Government of the United States of America and the Government of the Kingdom of Bahrain on the Establishment of a Free Trade Area, U.S.-Bahr., arts. 1.3, 2.1–2.2, 3.2(1), 7.1, 9.1(1)–(3), 10.1, 12.1, 17.6, Sept. 14, 2004, 119 Stat. 3581, http://www.ustr.gov/Trade_Agreements/Bilateral/Bahrain_FTA/final_texts/Section_Index.html; United States–Morocco Free Trade Agreement, U.S.–Morocco, arts. 2.1–2.2, 7.1, 9.1, 10.3–10.4, 10.7, 10.12, 11.1, 11.6, 20.2, June 15, 2004, 118 Stat. 1103, http://www.ustr.gov/Trade_

Agreements/Bilateral/Morocco_FTA/Final_Text/Section_Index.html; United States–Australia Free Trade Agreement, U.S.–Austl., arts. 2.1–2.2, 8.1, 10.1, 17.9(1)–(3), 21.2, May 18, 2004, 118 Stat. 919, http://www.ustr.gov/Trade_Agreements/Bilateral/Australia_FTA/Final_Text/Section_Index.html; United States–Singapore Free Trade Agreement, U.S.–Sing., arts. 8.2, 8.7, 9.1(1)–(2), 11.2, 13.2 (1)–(3), May 6, 2003, 117 Stat. 948, http://www.ustr.gov/Trade_Agreements/Bilateral/Singapore_FTA/Final_Texts/Section_Index.html; United States–Chile Free Trade Agreement, U.S.–Chile, arts. 3.1–3.2, 3.20(1), 7.1, 9.1(1)–(2), 11.1, 11.6, July 6, 2003, http://www.ustr.gov/trade-agreements/free-trade-agreements/chile-fta/final-text; United States–Peru Trade Promotion Agreement, U.S.–Peru, arts. 2.1–2.2, 2.3(2), 3.3, 7.2, 9.1(1)–(6), 9.2(1)–(2), 9.2(6), 10.8, 11.1, 16.1(11), Apr. 12, 2005, 121 Stat. 1455, http://www.ustr.gov/Trade_Agreements/Bilateral/Peru_TPA/Final_Texts/Section_Index.html.

10. Earlier cases—*Canada—Periodicals, EC—Bananas*, and *Canada—Automobile Industry*—had raised GATS issues, but as supplements to GATT claims related to goods. See Mitsuo Matsushita, "Appellate Body Jurisprudence on the GATS and TRIPS Agreements," in *The WTO Dispute Settlement System, 1995–2003*, ed. Federico Ortino and Ernst-Ulrich Petersmann (The Hague: Kluwer Law International, 2004), 455. A US claim against Mexico considered services more directly but required the interpretation of a special telecommunications side-agreement rather than basic GATS obligations. Appellate Body Report, *Mexico—Measures Affecting Telecommunications Services*, WT/DS204/R (Apr. 2, 2004).

11. Executive Summary of the Second Written Submission of the United States, *United States—Measures Affecting the Cross-Border Supply of Gambling and Betting Services*, ¶ 26, WT/DS285, Jan. 16, 2004, http://www.antiguawto.com/wto/22_US_Exec_sum_2nd_Written_Sub_16Jan04.pdf ("Antigua has not offered evidence of any restriction that would stop its suppliers from supplying their services by the same non-remote means available to domestic suppliers. Hence there is no national treatment violation").

12. "These laws represent domestic regulation limiting the characteristics of supply of gambling services, not the quantity of services or suppliers." Executive Summary, United States Appellant Submission, *United States—Measures Affecting the Cross-Border Supply of Gambling and Betting Services* (AB–2005–1), ¶ 21.

13. GATS, art. XIV(a) (making exception for measures "necessary to protect public morals or to maintain public order"); GATS, art. XIV(b) (making exception for measures "necessary to protect human, animal or plant life or health"). On the public morals exception, see Mark Wu, "Free Trade and the Protection of Public Morals: An Analysis of the Newly Emerging Public Morals Clause Doctrine," *Yale Journal of International Law* 33 (2008): 215.

14. See Appellate Body Report, *United States—Measures Affecting the Cross-Border Supply of Gambling and Betting Services*, WT/DS285/AB/R, adopted Apr. 20, 2005 (*US—Gambling*), ¶¶ 283, 323, 347.

15. Gary Rivlin, "Gambling Dispute with a Tiny Country Puts U.S. in a Bind," *New York Times*, Aug. 23, 2007. Antigua relies on a precedent: When the EU refused to comply with a WTO ruling on Ecuadorian banana exports, Ecuador sought and received the right to sanction the EU by infringing their intellectual property rights, a practical means for a small party to pressure a larger party to comply and one that would not harm Ecuadorians more than Europeans. *European Communities—Regime for the Importation, Sale and Distribution of Bananas*, WT/DS27/ARB/ECU, ¶ 173(d), Mar. 24, 2000 (arbitral ruling).

16. The appellate body upheld the panel's finding that concerns underlying the US statutes barring remote gambling fell within the scope of the "public morals" and/or "public order" exception. See *US—Gambling*, ¶¶ 373(D)(iii).

17. GATS, art. XIV (requiring that "measures are not applied in a manner which would constitute a means of arbitrary or unjustifiable discrimination between countries where like conditions prevail, or a disguised restriction on trade in services").

18. *US—Gambling*, ¶ 308.

19. See Financial Action Task Force, *Handbook for Countries and Assessors* (2007), http://www.menafatf.org/images/UploadFiles/Handbook%2007%20%28En%29.pdf.

20. In the GATT context, the WTO has examined whether a trade restrictive measure was necessary to protect against fraud. See Appellate Body Report, *Korea—Measures Affecting Imports of Fresh, Chilled and Frozen Beef*, ¶¶ 177–80, WT/DS161/AB/R (Dec. 11, 2000).

21. "Party Poker: Responsible Gaming," http://www.partypoker.com/responsible_gaming/ (offering self-imposed deposit limits and "the self-exclusion

tool," which gives the customer the ability to bar him- or herself from the website for specified period).

22. Granholm v. Heald, 544 U.S. 460 (2005).

23. Brief for Private Respondents at 11, Swedenburg v. Kelly, 543 U.S. 954 (2004) (No. 03–1274).

24. 544 U.S. at 490.

25. See *US—Gambling*, ¶ 308.

26. Appellate Body Report, *United States—Import Prohibition of Certain Shrimp and Shrimp Products*, ¶ 177, WT/DS58/AB/R (Oct. 12, 1998).

27. John Borland, "Napster Blasts Court's Technical Meddling," CNET, Aug. 9, 2001, http://news.cnet.com/2100–1023–271351.html.

28. GATS, art. XVII.

29. *China—Measures Affecting Trading Rights and Distribution Services for Certain Publications and Audiovisual Entertainment Products*, ¶ 340, WT/DS363/AB/R, Dec. 21, 2009.

30. Ibid., ¶ 377.

31. Ibid., ¶ 397.

7. Handshakes Across the World

1. United Nations Convention on Contracts for the International Sale of Goods, Preamble, Apr. 10, 1980, 19 I.L.M. 668.

2. Certain other aspects of the legal infrastructure for goods, such as letters of credit, arbitration, and anticorruption laws, can be extended to network.

3. Model Law on Electronic Commerce, UN G.A. Doc. A/RES/51/162, Jan. 30, 1997, with additional art. 5 bis adopted by UNCITRAL, June 1998; Electronic Signatures in Global and National Commerce Act (E-Sign), 15 U.S.C. §§ 7001–31 (2000). In 2005, UNCITRAL promulgated a treaty to promote crossborder electronic contracting, with ratifications thus far by the Dominican Republic, Hondura and Singapore. Convention on the Use of Electronic Communications in International Contracts, annexed to UN G.A. Doc. A/RES/60/21, Nov. 23, 2005.

4. GATS, art. III.3.

5. GATS, art. III.4.

6. Canada's Department of International Trade provides the portal at www.dfait-maeci.gc.ca/tna-nac/TS/contact-point-en.asp, an unnecessarily cumbersome web address.

7. World Trade Organization, http://www.wto.org/english/tratop_e/tbt_e/tbt_enquiry_points_e.htm (listing the inquiry points, including email addresses, for the Technical Barriers to Trade Treaty).

8. Council Directive 2006/123/EC, Services in the Internal Market, art. 7(3), 2006, O.J. (L 376), 53 (EC), http://eur-lex.europa.eu/LexUriServ/LexUriServ.do?uri=OJ:L:2006:376:0036:0068:en:PDF.

9. Ibid., art. 8(1).

10. See http://www.youtube.com/watch?v=ZUNAhzwZkdU.

11. Concord Law School, "Passing the California Bar Examination," http://info.concordlawschool.edu/pages/bar_exam.aspx. Given that the Concord Law School requires four years of study and forty thousand dollars in tuition alone over those years, this seems a highly risky investment.

12. Graeme B. Dinwoodie and Laurence R. Helfer, "Designing Non-National Systems: The Case of the Uniform Domain Name Dispute Resolution Policy," *William and Mary Law Review* 43 (2001): 141.

13. Information Technology Act at § 58 (India).

14. Cyber Appellate Tribunal, "Procedure for Filing Applications," http://www.catindia.gov.in/Procedure.aspx.

15. Cyber Appellate Tribunal, "E-Filing," http://www.catindia.gov.in/E_Filing.aspx.

16. See Margaret Jane Radin, "Boilerplate Today: The Rise of Modularity and the Waning of Consent," *Michigan Law Review* 104 (2006): 1223; Margaret Jane Radin, "Regime Change in Intellectual Property Law: Superseding the Law of the State with the 'Law' of the Firm," *University of Ottawa Law and Technology Journal* 1 (2003–4): 173.

17. But cf. James E. Byrne and Dan Taylor, *ICC Guide to the EUCP: Understanding the Electronic Supplement to the UCP 500*, ICC Publication vol. 639 (2002), 14–15 (observing the possibility of automated compliance checking for electronic letters of credit).

8. Glocalization and Harmonization

1. See Ted J. Janger, "The Public Choice of Choice of Law in Software Transactions: Jurisdictional Competition and the Dim Prospects for Uniformity," *Brooklyn Journal of International Law* 26 (2000): 187, 196 (arguing that allowing

software providers to be governed by the law of their location, rather than the law of their licensees, may lead to a race to the bottom).

2. Simson Garfinkel, "Welcome to Sealand. Now Bugger Off," *Wired*, July 2000 (cover story).

3. Even HavenCo has its limits, prohibiting "spamming, obscenity, and child pornography" and activities "against international law, linked with terrorism, or contrary to international custom and practice." Declan McCullagh, "HavenCo: Come to Data," *Wired*, June 5, 2000, http://www.wired.com/politics/law/news/2000/06/36756; Declan McCullagh, "Has 'Haven' for Questionable Sites Sunk?" *CNET*, Aug. 4, 2003, http://news.cnet.com/2100–1028_3–5059676.html.

4. Sealand's web-hosting ultimately foundered, and HavenCo has gone offline. Jan Libbenga, "Offshore Hosting Firm HavenCo Lost at Sea," *Register*, Nov. 25, 2008, http://www.theregister.co.uk/2008/11/25/havenco/.

5. Charles Tiebout, "A Pure Theory of Local Expenditure," *Journal of Political Economy* 64 (1956): 416 (arguing that jurisdictional competition to attract residents on the basis of differing tax and benefits would produce a Pareto-superior outcome).

6. Mahmood Bagheri and Chizu Nakajima, "Optimal Level of Financial Regulation Under the GATS: A Regulatory Competition and Cooperation Framework for Capital Adequacy and Disclosure of Information," *Journal of International Economic Law* 5 (2002): 507, 521 (citing J. D. Cox, "Regulatory Competition in Securities Markets: An Approach Reconciling Japanese and United States Disclosure Philosophies," *Hastings International and Comparative Law Review* 16 [1993]: 149, 157).

7. Esty and Geradin identify a set of variables that affect whether regulatory competition is likely to prove virtuous or malign; the variables include: "the scope of uninternalized externalities; whether the information base of the particular 'market' is sufficient for competition . . .; the capacity of citizens and companies to obtain and to understand information that is relevant to their choices." Daniel C. Esty and Damien Geradin, "Introduction," in *Regulatory Competition and Economic Integration*, ed. Esty and Girardin (New York: Oxford University Press, 2001), xix, xxv.

8. Ralph K. Winter Jr., "Shareholder Protection, and the Theory of the Corporation," *Journal of Legal Studies* 6 (1977): 251; Roberta Romano, *The Genius of American Corporate Law* (Washington, DC: AEI Press, 1993);

Ralph K. Winter Jr., "The 'Race for the Top' Revisited," *Columbia Law Review* 89 (1989): 1526.

9. Edward J. Janger and Paul M. Schwartz, "The Gramm-Leach-Bliley Act, Information Privacy and the Limits of Default Rules," *Minnesota Law Review* 86 (2002): 1219, 1240–42 (discussing lemons equilibrium in the privacy market); Paul M. Schwartz, "Property, Privacy, and Personal Data," *Harvard Law Review* 117 (2004): 2055, 2076–84.

10. Writing of interstate pollution, Richard Revesz suggests that transactions costs of such bargaining might be high, eliminating the likelihood of Coasian bargaining. Richard L. Revesz, "Federalism and Interstate Environmental Externalities," *University of Pennsylvania Law Review* 144 (1996): 2341, 2375; Robert P. Inman and Daniel L. Rubinfeld, "Making Sense of the Antitrust State-Action Doctrine: Balancing Political Participation and Economic Efficiency in Regulatory Federalism," *Texas Law Review* 75 (1997): 1203, 1222–25 (expressing skepticism that bargaining between governments will easily satisfy the conditions for Coasian bargaining).

11. Mira Burri observes that new media put stress on efforts to preserve cultural diversity. Mira Burri, "Cultural Protectionism 2.0: Updating Cultural Policy Tools for the Digital Age," in *Transnational Culture in the Internet Age*, ed. Sean Pager and Adam Candeub (Cheltenham, UK: Edward Elgar, 2012).

12. Roland Robertson, "Comments on the 'Global Triad' and 'Glocalization,'" in *Globalization and Indigenous Culture*, ed. Inoue Nobutaka (Tokyo: Institute for Japanese Culture and Classics, Kokugakuin University, 2001), http://www2.kokugakuin.ac.jp/ijcc/wp/global/15robertson.html.

13. Ibid.

14. Thomas Friedman also uses the term *glocalization* but describes it somewhat differently as "the ability of a culture, when it encounters other strong cultures, to absorb influences that naturally fit into and can enrich that culture, to resist those things that are truly alien and to compartmentalize those things that, while different, can nevertheless be enjoyed and celebrated as different." Thomas L. Friedman, *The Lexus and the Olive Tree: Understanding Globalization* (New York: Farrar, Straus and Giroux, 1999), 295; see also Thomas L. Friedman, *The World Is Flat: A Brief History of the Twenty-First Century* (New York: Farrar, Straus and Giroux, 2005), 325 ("The more you have a culture that naturally glocalizes—that is, the more your own culture easily absorbs foreign ideas and best practices and melds those with its own traditions—the greater advantage you will have in a flat world").

15. Graham Bowley, "EU Lowers Barriers to Moves by Companies but Amendments Weaken Services Law, Setting Off Protests," *International Herald Tribune*, Feb. 17, 2006. The previous year had also seen massive demonstrations in Brussels. "Demonstrators March Against EU Labor Reforms," *Deutsche Welle*, Mar. 20, 2005.

16. "Commission Proposal for a Directive of the European Parliament and of the Council on Services in the Internal Market" (Mar. 5, 2004); Kalypso Nicolaïdis and Susanne K. Schmidt, "Mutual Recognition 'on Trial': The Long Road to Services Liberalization," *Journal of European Public Policy* (2007): 717, 722–23 (characterizing draft proposal as "bold" and "sweeping").

17. "'Frankenstein' Directive Resurrects EU Divisions," *Finance Week*, Apr. 13, 2005, 16. Another union official opined, "The idea somehow there's a license for companies not to observe the laws of the country in which they are trading, that's a step too far and I think it's anti-democratic." "MEPs Debate New Law on Services," *BBC News*, Feb. 15, 2006, http://news.bbc.co.uk/2/hi/europe/4711086.stm.

18. The EU ultimately adopted a services directive that did not require states to accept the validity of foreign regulation in lieu of their own. They permitted European member states to require a foreign service provider to be licensed before providing a service, but only as long as that licensing requirement was "justified by an overriding reason related to the public interest" and "proportionate to that public interest objective." Council Directive 2006/123/EC, Services in the Internal Market, art. 10, 2006, O.J. (L 376), 53 (EC), http://eur-lex.europa.eu/LexUriServ/LexUriServ.do?uri=OJ:L:2006:376:0036:0068:en:PDF.

19. Case C–384/94, Alpine Invs. BV v. Minister van Financien, 1995 E.C.R. I–1141 (Dutch ban on cold-calling violated the freedom to provide services but might be justified by "imperative reasons of public interest"); Case C–243/01, Tribunale di Ascoli Piceno (Italy) v. Gambelli, 2003 E.C.R. I–13031 (Italian prosecution of English company for providing gambling service via Internet to Italians without an Italian license violated freedom of services but might be justified by imperative reasons of public interest); Case C–76–90, Sager v. Dennemeyer & Co. Ltd., 1991 E.C.R. I–4221 (striking down German requirements that only German registered patent agent can provide patent renewal services because such services are of a "straightforward nature and do not call for specific professional aptitudes" and thus

German registration is unnecessary to protect persons against bad advice); see generally Editorial Comments, "The Services Directive Proposal: Striking a Balance Between the Promotion of the Internal Market and Preserving the European Social Model," *Common Market Law Review* 43:2 (2006): 307, 309 ("the case law of the Court of Justice takes the country of origin principle as its starting point when assessing the application of the justification for restrictions on the free movement").

20. Council Directive 2000/31/EC, On Certain Legal Aspects of Information Society Services, in Particular Electronic Commerce, in the Internal Market 2000, O.J. (L 178) 1, art. 3.

21. GATS, preamble.

22. Ibid., art. VII.

23. Compare the "metaphysical" question of where an intangible such as a debt is sited or whether it is sited anywhere at all. Arthur Taylor von Mehren, "Adjudicatory Jurisdiction: General Theories Compared and Evaluated," *Boston University Law Review* 63 (1983): 279, 297.

24. This question of crossborder delivery versus virtual tourism corresponds to a typology for characterizing services introduced in GATS: if a service provider delivers a service from one country into another country, the service is classified as mode 1; if the recipient travels to consume the service abroad, it is mode 2.

25. See David Johnson and David Post, "Law and Borders: The Rise of Law in Cyberspace," *Stanford Law Review* 48 (1996): 1367, 1370–71.

26. In certain narrow domains, such as sex tourism, countries have sought to limit consumption abroad by their citizens. See, e.g., End Demand for Sex Trafficking Act of 2005, H.R. 2012, 109th Cong. (2005) (declaring goal of barring sex tourism).

27. See Appellate Body Report, *United States—Measures Affecting the Cross-Border Supply of Gambling and Betting Services*, ¶¶ 251–52, WT/DS285/AB/R (Apr. 7, 2005) (holding that barring the supply of services crossborder amounts to a "zero quota" in violation of the United States' mode 1 trade commitments).

28. Jack Goldsmith and Tim Wu also argue in favor of national regulation of cyberspace, but they do so principally because they believe that the state holds the monopoly on legitimate physical coercion. They preface their book by arguing that "even for the most revolutionary global communication technologies, geography and governmental coercion retain fundamental

importance." Jack Goldsmith and Tim Wu, *Who Controls the Internet? Illusions of a Borderless World* (New York: Oxford University Press, 2006), viii. Their final chapter, titled "Globalization Meets Governmental Coercion," concludes that "physical coercion by government . . . remains far more important than anyone expected. . . . Yet at a fundamental level, it's the most important thing missing from most predictions of where globalization will lead, and the most significant gap in predictions about the future shape of the Internet" (180). But as Lessig taught us, the West Coast Code of computer programmers can be as cogent a regulator as the East Coast Code of legislators. Lawrence Lessig, *Code and Other Laws of Cyberspace* (New York: Basic Books, 1999), 221. Indeed, Microsoft, Facebook, and Google might well have more power than many medium-sized countries to effect a norm in cyberspace. The question is not who can most effectively enforce a regulation but who can most *legitimately* do so. To wit: the issue is not whether France *can* regulate Nazi glorification but whether it has a *right* to do so within the existing international legal order. I bottom my claim for glocalization not on the need for coercive authority to achieve desired regulatory goals but on the need to sustain democracy in a net-worked world.

29. European Parliament, "Free Movement of Services: MEPs Take a Big Step Forward," Feb. 16, 2006, http://www.europarl.europa.eu/sides/getDoc.do?type=IM-PRESS&reference=20060213IPR05194&language=BG.

30. Kenichi Ohmae, *The Borderless World: Power and Strategy in the Interlinked World Economy* (New York: Harper Business, 1990).

31. John Perry Barlow, "Declaration of Independence for Cyberspace," Feb. 8, 1996, http://homes.eff.org/~barlow/Declaration-Final.html ("Governments of the Industrial World, you weary giants of flesh and steel, I come from Cyberspace, the new home of Mind. . . . You are not welcome among us. You have no sovereignty where we gather"); Johnson and Post, "Law and Borders," 1371; David G. Post, "Against 'Against Cyberanarchy,'" *Berkeley Technology Law Journal* 17 (2002): 1365, 1384–86. The classic response is Jack Goldsmith, "Against Cyberanarchy," *University of Chicago Law Review* 65 (1998): 1199.

32. Kenichi Ohmae, *The Next Global Stage: The Challenges and Opportunities in Our Borderless World* (Upper Saddle River, NJ: Pearson Education, 2005).

33. Aaditya Mattoo and Sacha Wunsch-Vincent, "Pre-Empting Protectionism in Services: The GATS and Outsourcing," *Journal of International*

Economic Law 7 (2004): 765, 772 (describing "political opposition in importing countries and pressure for trade barriers" against crossborder outsourcing of services).

34. Bank Julius Baer & Co. Ltd. v. WikiLeaks, 2008 WL 554721 (N.D. Cal., February 29, 2008) (dismissing for lack of subject matter jurisdiction Swiss bank suit against foreign website dedicated to disclosing "leaks").

35. Neil W. Netanel, "Cyberspace Self-Governance: A Skeptical View from Liberal Democratic Theory," *California Law Review* 88 (2000): 395, 492.

36. Ligue Internationale Contre le Racisme et l'Antisémitisme et Union des étudiants juifs de France v. Yahoo! Inc., Tribunal de grande instances [T.G.I.] [ordinary court of original jurisdiction] Paris, May 22, 2000, D. 2000, inf. rap. 172, Ordonnance de Refere (Fr.).

37. Hilton v. Guyot, 159 U.S. 113 (1895); Anupam Chander, "Homeward Bound," *New York University Law Review* 81 (2006): 60, 87–88.

38. Louise Ellen Teitz, "The Story of *Hilton:* From Gloves to Globalization," in *Civil Procedure Stories*, ed. Kevin Clermont, 2nd ed. (New York: Foundation Press, 2004), 445, 449.

39. Ibid., 465–66; Jagdeep S. Bhandari and Alan O. Sykes, *Economic Dimensions in International Law: Comparative and Empirical Perspectives* (Cambridge: Cambridge University Press, 1997), 600.

40. Yahoo! Inc. v. La Ligue Contre le Racisme et l'Antisémitisme, 433 F.3d 1199, 1217 (9th Cir. 2006) (Fletcher, J.).

41. David Vogel, *Trading Up: Consumer and Environmental Regulation in a Global Economy* (Cambridge, MA: Harvard University Press, 1995), 259.

42. Convention on Choice of Court Agreements, Jun. 30, 2005, http://www.hcch.net/index_en.php?act=conventions.text&cid=98.

43. Convention on Choice of Court Agreements, art. VI.

44. Convention on the Recognition and Enforcement of Foreign Arbitral Awards, art. V(2)(b), June 10, 1958.

45. Restatement (Third) of Foreign Relations §§ 18, 403 (1987). US courts have adopted this approach in interpreting US statutes. See, e.g., Hartford Fire Ins. Co. v. California, 509 U.S. 764, 796 (1993) (applying Sherman Act to foreign conduct "that was meant to produce and did in fact produce some substantial effect in the United States"); F. Hoffman-LaRoche, Ltd. v. Empagran, 542 U.S. 155, 159 (2004) (limiting applications of Sherman Act

abroad to cases where there is "direct, substantial, and reasonably foreseeable effect" on domestic commerce); Atlantic Richfield Co. v. Arco Globus Intern., 150 F.3d 189, 194 (2d Cir. 1998) (refusing to apply US trademark law against foreign activity in absence of "substantial effect" on US commerce).

46. W. Michael Reisman, "Introduction," in *Jurisdiction in International Law*, ed. Reisman (New York: Oxford University Press, 1999).

47. American Law Institute, "Intellectual Property: Principles Governing Jurisdiction, Choice of Law, and Judgments in Transnational Disputes, Proposed Final Draft," § 321 (2008).

48. World-Wide Volkswagen Corp. v. Woodson, 444 U.S. 286, 288 (1980).

49. Bancroft & Masters, Inc. v. Augusta National, Inc., 223 F.3d 1082, 1087 (9th Cir. 2000); Young v. New Haven Advocate, 315 F.3d 256 (4th Cir. 2002) (noting that jurisdiction requires "something more than posting and accessibility" and stating that jurisdiction appropriate only where defendants "manifest an intent to target and focus on" state residents); Revell v. Lidov, 317 F.3d 467, 475 (5th Cir. 2002) (requiring defendant to have "knowledge of the forum at which his conduct is directed" before assertion of personal jurisdiction); ALS Scan, Inc. v. Digital Service, 293 F.3d 707, 712 (4th Cir. 2002) (noting that "because the Internet is omnipresent," jurisdiction based on access to information placed on the Web would eliminate geographic limits on judicial power); Yahoo! Inc. v. La Ligue Contre le Racisme et l'Antisémitisme, 433 F.3d 1199, 1206 (9th Cir. 2006) (en banc) (Fletcher, J.) (permitting jurisdiction only where defendant "expressly aimed at the forum state" and knew that harm "is likely to be suffered" in that state).

50. Asahi Metal Indus. v. Superior Ct., 480 U.S. 102, 115 (1987).

51. This shift can be seen in the move from Pennoyer v. Neff, 95 U.S. 714 (1878), to International Shoe v. Washington, 326 U.S. 310 (1945).

52. Hanson v. Denckla, 357 U.S. 235, 250–51 (1958).

53. American Banana Co. v. United Fruit Co., 213 U.S. 347, 355 (1909).

54. Ibid., 356.

55. Kingman Brewster Jr., *Antitrust and American Business Abroad* (New York: McGraw-Hill, 1958), 20–22.

56. Timberlane Lumber Co. v. Bank of America, N.T. and S.A., 549 F.2d 597, 614 (9th Cir. 1976).

57. Restatement (Third) of Foreign Relations Law, § 403(2)(e) (1987).

58. White House, *A Framework for Global Electronic Commerce* (Washington, DC: White House Office, 1997), 18.

59. 549 F.2d at 609.

60. As Dean Kramer writes, the term *extraterritorial* has been "used in different ways at different times and in different contexts." Larry D. Kramer, "Vestiges of Beale: Extraterritorial Application of American Law," *Supreme Court Review* (1991): 179, 181 n.9.

61. F. Hoffman-LaRoche Ltd. v. Empagran, 542 U.S. 155, 169 (2004).

62. Restatement (Second) of Conflict of Laws § 6(2)(b)–(c) (1971).

63. Cf. Friedrich Juenger, "Choice of Law in Interstate Torts," *University of Pennsylvania Law Review* 118 (1969): 200, 206–7.

64. Restatement (Second) of Conflicts of Laws § 6(2)(a). Cf. Brainerd Currie, *Selected Essays on the Conflict of Laws* (Durham, NC: Duke University Press, 1963), 616; Paul Schiff Berman, "Towards a Cosmopolitan Vision of Conflict of Laws: Redefining Governmental Interests in a Global Era," *University of Pennsylvania Law Review* 153 (2005): 1819.

65. Reisman observes that the international community can "transcend" the challenge of multi-jurisdictional competence by (1) "creating vastly expanded sectors of substantive international law"; (2) "establishing networks of international tribunals" with exclusive competence; and (3) "establishing private international law conventions that would allocate competences on the basis of a specific code." Reisman, "Introduction," xix.

66. GATS, art. VII(1); see generally Kalypso Nicolaïdis and Gregory Shaffer, "Transnational Mutual Recognition Regimes: Governance Without Global Government," *Law and Contemporary Problems* 68 (2005): 263.

67. GATS, art. VI(4).

68. NAFTA, art. 1210(2).

69. See Association of Southeast Asian Nations, "Agreements and Declarations," http://www.aseansec.org/19087.htm.

70. However, one major recognition scheme, the Multijurisdictional Jurisdiction Disclosure System between Canada and the United States, introduced in 1991, has been an experiment that the US Securities and Exchange Commission has not yet extended to other countries, not even the United Kingdom. Hal S. Scott, "Internationalization of Primary Public Securities Markets," *Law and Contemporary Problems* 63 (Summer 2000): 71, 80–86.

71. NAFTA Annex 1210.5, Professional Services, § A.2.

72. Technical Barriers to Trade Treaty, art. 2.4 (hereinafter TBT).

73. Hilton v. Guyot, 159 U.S. 113 (1895); Society of Lloyd's v. Ashenden, 233 F.3d 473 (7th Cir. 2000) (procedures need only be fair in a broad international sense).

74. TBT, Annex 1.

75. Deloitte Touche Tomatsu offers a list of countries adopting IFRS. See http://www.iasplus.com/country/useias.htm.

76. For a discussion with respect to standards for goods, see Vogel, "Trading Up"; and Alan O. Sykes, *Product Standards for Internationally Integrated Goods Markets* (Washington, DC: Brookings Institution Press, 1995).

77. Cf. Paul B. Stephan, "The Futility of Unification and Harmonization in International Commercial Law," *Virginia Journal of International Law* 39 (1999): 743, with Anupam Chander, "Globalization and Distrust," *Yale Law Journal* 114 (2005): 1193, 1196 (rebutting claims that there exists a "democratic deficit at the international level").

78. Cf. Jonathan R. Macey, "Regulatory Globalization as a Response to Regulatory Competition," *Emory Law Journal* 52 (2003): 1353, 1357 ("as capital markets and currency markets have become more globalized, the ability of regulators in a particular country to regulate domestic firms has declined significantly").

79. Alec Stone Sweet, "The New Lex Mercatoria and Transnational Governance," *Journal of European Public Policy* 13:5 (2006): 627.

80. 388 U.S. 1 (1967).

81. Directive 95/46/EC of Oct. 24, 1995, on the protection of individuals with regard to the processing of personal data and on the free movement of such data, art. 25(6).

82. European Commission, "Commission Decisions on the Adequacy of the Protection of Personal Data in Third Countries," http://ec.europa.eu/justice/data-protection/document/international-transfers/adequacy/index_en.htm.

83. European Commission, "Decision Amending Decision 2001/497/EC as Regards the Introduction of an Alternative Set of Standard Contractual Clauses for the Transfer of Personal Data to Third Countries," Dec. 27, 2004, 2004/915/EC, II(g), IV, V(c).

84. Esty and Geradin, "Regulatory Competition," xxv.

9. Last Stop

1. Abhishek Pandey et al., "India's Transformation to Knowledge-Based Economy—Evolving Role of the Indian Diaspora," *Evalueserve*, July 21, 2004 ("In 1985, Texas Instruments [TI] setup an office in Bangalore with a direct satellite link to the US and, in 1989, an Indian Government Telecom Company [VSNL] commissioned a direct 64-kbps satellite link to the US").

2. Jonathan Stray, "Iceland Aims to Become Offshore Haven for Journalists and Leakers," *Nieman Journalism Lab*, Feb. 11, 2010, http://www.niemanlab.org/2010/02/iceland-aims-to-become-an-offshore-haven-for-journalists-and-leakers.

3. Hurst Hannum, "The Status of the Universal Declaration of Human Rights in National and International Law," *Georgia Journal International and Comparative Law* 25 (1995/96): 287, 290.

4. David P. Baron, "Google in China," Nov. 15, 2006, http://harvardbusinessonline.hbsp.harvard.edu/b01/en/common/item_detail.jhtml;jsessionid=SA0OZLEL2BHWSAKRGWCB5VQBKE0YOISW?id=P54&_requestid=32332; Frank Dai, "Google's China Problem," *Global Voices*, June 10, 2006, http://www.globalvoicesonline.org/2006/06/10/china-googles-china-problem/.

5. For additional critiques, see Colin Maclay, "Can the Global Network Initiative Embrace the Character of the Net?" in *Access Controlled: The Shaping of Power, Rights, and Ruse in Cyberspace*, ed. Ronald Deibert et al. (Cambridge, MA: MIT Press, 2010), 87, 101–2 (noting arguments that the initiative does not require companies to develop technologies of dissent, that it does not cover sufficient ground, and that it permits too much room for interpretation).

6. Julian Dibbell, "The Life of the Chinese Gold Farmer," *New York Times Magazine*, June 17, 2007 (describing Chinese workers who earn a livelihood by gathering gold in a virtual world). The video of the workplace and dormitory space accompanying the *New York Times Magazine* story is especially revealing.

7. GATS, art. XIV(a).

8. Somini Sengupta, "You Won't Read It Here First: India Curtails Access to Blogs," *New York Times*, July 19, 2006; Brad Stone, "Pakistan Cuts Access to YouTube Worldwide," *New York Times*, Feb. 26, 2008; "Wikipedia Blocking of Wikipedia in Mainland China," http://en.wikipedia.org/wiki/Blocking_of_Wikipedia_in_mainland_China. Pakistan's rerouting of

requests for YouTube to an Internet black hole because of a video it disliked was perhaps the most dramatic, causing temporary outage of YouTube for many across the world.

9. Joost Pauwelyn, "Human Rights in WTO Dispute Settlement," in *Human Rights and International Trade*, ed. Thomas Cottier, Joost Pauwelyn, and Elisabeth Bürgi (New York: Oxford University Press, 2005), 205, 206 ("It is . . . out of the question that within the present system a WTO panel would examine, say, a claim of violation under the UN Covenant on Civil and Political Rights").

10. China, "Schedule of Specific Commitments on Services," WT/ACC/CHN/49/Add.2 (Oct. 1, 2001).

11. "Report of the Working Party on the Accession of China," WT/ACC/CHN/49, at 62–63 (Oct. 1, 2001).

12. For the view that a GATS challenge against China on behalf of Google would likely fail, see Henry S. Gao, "Google's China Problem: A Case Study on Trade, Technology and Human Rights Under the GATS," *Asian Journal of WTO and International Health Law and Policy* 6 (2011): 347–85.

13. Joost Pauwelyn, "Squaring Free Trade in Culture with Chinese Censorship: The WTO Appellate Body Report on 'China—Audiovisuals,'" *Melbourne Journal of International Law* 9 (2010): 9.

14. Panagiotis Delimatsis, "Protecting Public Morals in a Digital Age: Revisiting the WTO Rulings on *US—Gambling* and *China—Publications and Audiovisual Products*," *Journal of International Economic Law* 14:2 (2011): 293.

Afterword

1. Salman Rushdie, *The Satanic Verses* (New York: Viking, 1988), 5. The translation is Rushdie's. Salman Rushdie, "Imaginary Homelands" [1982], reprinted in Rushdie, *Imaginary Homelands: Essays in Criticism, 1981–1991* (New York: Penguin, 1991), 11.

2. Jeremy Waldron, "Minority Cultures and the Cosmopolitan Alternative," *University of Michigan Journal of Law Reform* 25 (1992): 751, 754.

3. Cho Jin-Seo, "Indians to Teach English via Internet," *Korea Times*, Aug. 3, 2007; Robert F. Worth, "In New York Tickets, Ghana Sees Orderly City," *New York Times*, July 22, 2002.

4. Worth, "New York Tickets."

5. "The Internet: The Web's New Walls," *Economist*, Sept. 2, 2010.

6. Pietra Rivoli, *The Travels of a T-Shirt in the Global Economy: An Economist Examines the Markets, Power, and Politics of World Trade* (Hoboken, NJ: Wiley and Sons, 2007), 257; see also Douglas A. Irwin, *Against the Tide: An Intellectual History of Fair Trade* (Princeton, NJ: Princeton University Press, 1996), 17.

7. Joseph Needham, Ling Wang, and Lu Gwei-Djen, *Science and Civilisation in China*, vol. 4: *Physics and Physical Technology*, part 3: *Civil Engineering and Nautics* (Cambridge: Cambridge University Press, 1971), 526.

INDEX